Exploring Digital Communication

Routledge Introductions to Applied Linguistics is a series of introductory level textbooks covering the core topics in Applied Linguistics, primarily designed for those beginning postgraduate studies or taking an introductory MA course, as well as advanced undergraduates. Titles in the series are also ideal for language professionals returning to academic study.

The books take an innovative 'practice to theory' approach, with a 'back-to-front' structure. This leads the reader from real-world problems and issues, through a discussion of intervention and how to engage with these concerns, before finally relating these practical issues to theoretical foundations.

Exploring Digital Communication aims to discuss real-world issues pertaining to digital communication, and to explore how linguistic research addresses these challenges. The text is divided into three sections (Problems and practices; Interventions; and Theory), each of which is further divided into two subsections which reflect linguistic issues relating to digital communication.

The author seeks to demystify any perceived divide between online and offline communication, arguing that issues raised in relation to digital communication throw light on language use and practices in general, and thus linguistic interventions in this area have implications not only for users of digital communication but for linguists' general understanding of language and society.

Including relevant research examples, tasks and a glossary, this textbook is an invaluable resource for postgraduate and upper undergraduate students taking New Media or Communication Studies modules within Applied Linguistics and English Language courses.

Caroline Tagg is lecturer in the Department of English Language and Applied Linguistics, University of Birmingham. Her publications include *The Language of Social Media: identity and community on the internet* (edited with Philip Seargeant, 2014, Palgrave) and *The Discourse of Text Messaging* (2012, Continuum).

A range of further resources for this book are available on the Companion Website: www.routledge.com/cw/rial

'The innovative approach devised by the series editors will make this series very attractive to students, teacher educators, and even to a general readership, wanting to explore and understand the field of applied linguistics. The volumes in this series take as their starting point the everyday professional problems and issues that applied linguists seek to illuminate. The volumes are authoritatively written, using an engaging 'back-to-front' structure that moves from practical interests to the conceptual bases and theories that underpin applications of practice.'

Anne Burns, *Aston University, UK,*
University of New South Wales, Australia

'This book provides an insightful and wide-ranging examination of the nature of digital communication, and makes a cogent argument for why a focus on language can be particularly productive for understanding the impact that internet-based communications technologies are having on society.'

Philip Seargeant, *The Open University, UK*

Routledge Introductions to Applied Linguistics

Series editors:
Ronald Carter, *Professor of Modern English Language*
University of Nottingham, UK
Guy Cook, *Professor of Language and Education*
Open University, UK

Routledge Introductions to Applied Linguistics is a series of introductory level textbooks covering the core topics in Applied Linguistics, primarily designed for those entering postgraduate studies and language professionals returning to academic study. The books take an innovative 'practice to theory' approach, with a 'back-to-front' structure. This leads the reader from real-world problems and issues, through a discussion of intervention and how to engage with these concerns, before finally relating these practical issues to theoretical foundations. Additional features include tasks with commentaries, a glossary of key terms and an annotated further reading section.

Exploring English Language Teaching
Language in action
Graham Hall

Exploring Classroom Discourse
Language in action
Steve Walsh

Exploring Corpus Linguistics
Language in action
Winnie Cheng

Exploring World Englishes
Philip Seargeant

Exploring Health Communication
Kevin Harvey, Nelya Koteyko

Exploring Professional Communication
Stephanie Schnurr

Exploring Vocabulary
Dee Gardner

Exploring Language Pedagogy through Second Language Acquisition Research
Rod Ellis, Natsuko Shintani

Exploring Intercultural Communication
Zhu Hua

Exploring Language Assessment and Testing
Anthony Green

Exploring Digital Communication

Language in action

Caroline Tagg

Routledge
Taylor & Francis Group

LONDON AND NEW YORK

First published 2015
by Routledge
2 Park Square, Milton Park, Abingdon, Oxon OX14 4RN

and by Routledge
711 Third Avenue, New York, NY 10017

Routledge is an imprint of the Taylor & Francis Group, an informa business

British Library Cataloguing-in-Publication Data
A catalogue record for this book is available from the British Library

Library of Congress Cataloging-in-Publication Data
A catalog record for this book has been requested

ISBN: 978-0-415-52491-9 (hbk)
ISBN: 978-0-415-52493-3 (pbk)
ISBN: 978-1-315-72716-5 (ebk)

Typeset in Sabon
by Saxon Graphics Ltd, Derby

Printed and bound in Great Britain by
TJ International Ltd, Padstow, Cornwall

Contents

Introduction
Digital communication and applied linguistics

This book addresses concerns that are frequently voiced about the internet, and it does so by focusing specifically on language. Thus the book immediately raises two important questions. Firstly, why look specifically at internet-mediated communications, as if setting them apart from other interactions? Secondly, why focus, given the range of problems associated with the internet – including privacy, harassment and social isolation – specifically on language? How can language help us tackle such complex and important issues? These questions are central to an understanding of what this book is trying to do. In this introductory chapter, I look at the importance of digital communication across contemporary societies, and the fears that people have about it, whilst making the point that new technologies throughout history have always shaped what people can do and in the process engendered concern and distrust (as well as optimism). Bearing in mind the continuities between older technologies and the internet, I then highlight what is distinctive about the interactions that modern digital technology facilitates, and the extent to which digital communications must be understood in the context of our wider interactions. Finally, I look at the centrality of language in our internet interactions. We shall see that, although language-focused research cannot single-handedly resolve social problems, it can play an important role in understanding and addressing them, and thus language-related research has much to contribute to contemporary debates about the internet.

Why focus on digital communication?

The importance of digital communication to contemporary society is strikingly evident in terms of its scale and visibility. The internet is increasingly prevalent in more people's lives and there has been a rapid proliferation of new media through which to communicate. New media options have expanded from chat forums and email in the 1990s to encompass Google and other search engines, blogs and wikis, including Wikipedia; social network sites (such as Facebook); the microblogging site Twitter; media-sharing sites such as YouTube and Instagram; shopping websites such as eBay and Amazon (and online shopping in general) and user-review sites like TripAdvisor; as well as private channels of communication such as WhatsApp, Skype and Snapchat (and so on). With the proliferation in media has come a growth in users, so that the virtual world is no longer dominated by geeks, academics, scientists and governments, but is visited by people from all walks of life: for example, having access to mobile phones has transformed the lives of African farmers, enabling them to obtain information about agricultural markets and farming practices (e.g. Furuholt and Matotay, 2011). This is not the same as saying that everyone has equal access to digital technology, and statistics even from well-resourced countries like the UK point to a 'digital divide' between 'digital-haves' and 'digital-have-nots' (Royal Geographical Society, 2014). However, it is increasingly assumed that people across the globe have access to technology and those that do not are thus excluded from various resources, from medical information to bargains and best prices. In this sense, the internet is no longer something novel but a mundane part of life. This argument is made by Susan Herring, who predicted in 2004 that the internet was 'slouching toward the ordinary'.

Nonetheless, the internet is still often treated as an exotic beast – set apart from ordinary life and watched fearfully – particularly by adults. Linguists have described internet-related fears as a generational issue, arguing that adults are framing young people's everyday online behaviour as 'unprecedented' or 'transformational' (Herring, 2008a; and see Thurlow, 2005, 2006). To younger generations, the internet is normal, at least to those who have never known life without it. Adults' concerns are not so much about the technology, but what young people are doing with it. Adults have always worried about what their children are up to, and they likely always will (a point I return to in Chapter 1).

Bound up as they are with concerns about young people and social change, fears about technology are nothing new. The advent of past communication technologies, from the telegram and the typewriter in the 1830s to the phonogram and (landline) telephone in the 1870s, engendered a similar distrust as we see today with digital technologies. The telephone, for example, threatened nineteenth-century expectations about privacy and social order. One problem was that of not knowing how to talk to someone whom you couldn't see to determine their position in society. Half a century later, in 1928, science fiction writer H.G. Wells wrote of his despair over the radio, the quality of its scheduling, and its suitability for the things it broadcast. Wells held up older technologies such as the gramophone and printed matter as far superior to the radio. He wondered:

> what in particular the broadcasting was giving us that we could not get far better in some other fashion ... Music one can have at home

now, very perfectly and beautifully rendered by the gramophone ... The much discussed 'talks' and debates and so on are, we discover, merely spoken magazine matter; they can be far more effectively studied in the magazine itself, where diagrams and illustrations can be used in conjunction with them.

(Wells, 1928, pp. 172–3)

Interestingly, on its invention, the gramophone was berated for discouraging people from gathering together to sing; and in its early days print itself was seen as less aesthetically pleasing than handwritten work (the scribe, incidentally, was only killed off in the nineteenth century by the typewriter). The postcard, in its turn, was considered 'little short of an insult to the recipient, inasmuch as if the communication was not worth a penny it was not worth sending at all' (*The Times*, 1 November 1899, cited by Gillen and Hall, 2009, p. 7); it was 'utterly destructive of style, and gave absolutely no play to the emotions' (George Sims, 1902, cited by Gillen and Hall, 2009, p. 7). These concerns – the demise of one technology at the hands of another, the impact of a new technology on the linguistic and social status quo – are echoed in modern-day complaints about the internet (Baron, 2000).

Evident in people's responses to the landline, radio and internet alike is the assumption that technology can be blamed for social change or problems. The tendency to hold technology responsible for human actions – to credit machines with agency – is known as 'technological determinism'. Raymond Williams argues that the interplay between a technology and society is more complex than a simple cause and effect relationship. Their mutual influence is evident in his account of the popularisation of photography in the 1800s:

The photograph is in one sense a popular extension of the portrait, for recognition and for record. But in a period of great mobility, with new separations of families and with internal and external migrations, it became more centrally necessary as a form of maintaining, over distance and through time, certain personal connections. Moreover, in altering relations to the physical world, the photograph as an object became ... a means of observing and analysing motion itself, in new ways.

(Williams, 1974, pp. 15–16)

This argument can be used to challenge assertions about the impact of digital media. The point is that digital technology is not itself a driver of social change but that it emerges from what is already going on in wider society to address existing needs and fulfil existing goals; and because of this can quickly become seen as indispensable (Miller and Horst, 2012). For example, it is interesting to note that the ethos of the internet – open access, sharing, collaboration – was never inevitable, but shaped by the beliefs of the people behind its development. When Tim Berners-Lee invented the World Wide Web in the 1990s, he did so in order to fulfil his vision of a world where information could be freely shared. Berners-Lee describes how 'People have sometimes asked me whether I am upset that I have not made a lot of money from the Web. In fact, I made some quite conscious decisions about which way to take my life' (Berners-Lee and Fischetti, 1999, p. 116). The idea that people should have free access to the web is now widely assumed (witness the outrage when Google agreed to abide by Chinese censorship laws in 2006 [Jennings, 2010]).

The technical development of online sites has similarly been driven by what its users have chosen to do with it. Twitter, for example, was set up by Evan Williams only after his attempt to initiate audioblogging failed – unlike Twitter, it wasn't what people wanted (Jones and Hafner, 2012, pp. 72–3). The prompt on Twitter was initially 'What are you doing?' but this was changed in 2009 to 'What is happening?' after people started using the site for a wider range of purposes than envisaged, such as sharing and commenting on topical events. The conventionalisation of the hashtag (#) as a way of signalling the topic of a 'Tweet', and the @ sign as a way of addressing (or mentioning) another Twitter user, similarly followed popular usage. People converged on particular ways of using the site, and thus drove its development in a particular way (albeit in ways they may never have previously predicted). These examples highlight that it is not the technologies that create a certain outcome, but the way in which people use them (and how technology developers respond to this).

To the extent that it is up to people to decide what use to make of a technology, its features are best described as affordances (Gibson, 1986; Lee, 2007). Affordances are possibilities which people perceive to be provided by a technology, which may or may not be exploited by individuals, depending on their technical competence, their past experiences of using similar technologies and their communicative purposes. The point is that nothing inherent to the technology determines how it is used. For example, as Miller and Sinanan (2014) point out, there is 'no technical reason' for someone to use Skype and MSN Messenger to address two distinct types of audience, as one person in their study claimed:

> [on] MSN I have two hundred and something [contacts] I think, and on Skype, I think about thirty-something. ... on MSN it just have people who might see me on Facebook and just add me, but on Skype I only have people who I casually know, like actual real friends and family.
>
> (Miller and Sinanan, 2014, p. 140)

In this case, the differences are explained through this individual's history of using the two media: MSN being an older technology through which she gradually accumulated too many contacts. This is not surprising if we consider how social conventions and patterns of interactions grow up around a technology. People become used to doing something in a particular way, using familiar tools. This is a process which Rodney Jones calls 'technologization of practice' (Jones, 2002; Jones and Hafner, 2012, p. 100), whereby a social practice or behaviour becomes dominated by – or inextricably entwined with – a particular technology. You do not have to use MSN in a more public way than Skype (and many people do not), but you can become accustomed to perceiving MSN as public through the way you or others use it.

In terms of addressing concerns related to new media (the aim of the book), the above discussion helps us to focus on human agency in issues like bullying or social isolation. The internet is not an external force acting on an unsuspecting society; it is a tool designed by people and shaped by people, which in many cases allows us to do what we were already doing (or wanting to do), but in new and potentially transformative ways.

What sets digital communication apart?

So far, I've emphasised the fact that contemporary technology-mediated communications are not radically different from what has gone before; earlier technologies similarly extended what was possible and engendered similar fears and concerns about what a new technology means for language and society. In this section, I define what is meant by communication via digital technologies and their principal affordances: user-generated content, interactivity, networked resources and convergence.

No term perfectly captures the complexity of contemporary technology-mediated interactions. Use of the term 'digital communication' in this book can be criticised for placing too much emphasis on the role of technology in shaping online interactions; at the same time, the focus captures what to many people is the defining characteristic of online interactions (the technology). Specifically, the term refers to interactions between people that are mediated by digital communications technology (tools which transmit information in digital form). In practice, this means communication over the internet or GSM (Global System for Mobile Communications, through which SMS text messages are sent), via a range of devices, including desktop computers, laptops, notebooks, tablets and smartphones; and on various media (Facebook, Twitter, Wikipedia). Digital communications can be asynchronous (as on websites where people may comment on posts written days or weeks earlier), as well as synchronous (such as when people conduct fast-paced interactions through online chat) but, as we shall see, they have the potential for interactivity, however delayed the responses.

Digital communication is most usefully defined not by technology but by practices – that is, by how people choose to exploit the affordances that they perceive a technology to have and what they subsequently do with the technology. The importance of practices can be seen in popular and academic debate when digital communications are contrasted with older forms of communication, such as the television and radio. These traditionally analogue devices are being digitalised and so it is becoming increasingly difficult to distinguish them from desktop computers solely in terms of the underlying technology. Instead, televisions (for example) differ from computers in terms of the interactions associated with them. The television allows primarily (if not solely) for one-way transmission of information from the broadcasting company to the consumer. Given the increasingly diverse ways of accessing content originally made for television, users may now have more say in what is broadcast and how they access it but ultimately people are positioned as audiences with little opportunity to participate. In many internet-mediated interactions conducted via computers, the model is that of decentralised participation in which the 'people formally known as the audience' (Rosen, 2012) shape and create the content they access. On the one hand, users can search for content online and filter what they are not interested in (they 'pull' the information rather than having it 'pushed' on to them); while hyperlinks enable them to make their own path through online content, choosing whether to read a text from start to finish, or to follow links to other sites. On the other hand, people not only access information in new ways but actively contribute to its creation, by commenting on websites and by posting on social network sites, media-sharing sites and blogs. This element of digital communication is captured by terms such as 'peer production' (Benkler, 2006) and 'participatory media' which focus on the collaborative process of creating user-generated content rather than the finished product and which highlight, in different ways, the potentially democratic nature of the internet (Mandiberg, 2012). As discussed previously, we must not see this shift as inevitable, but shaped by the way in which people use the internet and develop its functionalities, together with the priorities of site developers and other interested parties.

Ongoing developments to the internet mediascape have shifted attention from content generation on to the interactions, networks and relationships which people establish and nurture online. The potential interactivity of the internet is best captured by the term social media. As Tagg and Seargeant (forthcoming) point out, social media is perhaps epitomised by social network sites such as Facebook or LinkedIn, whose raison d'être is to facilitate user networks and the sharing of personal information (boyd and Ellison, 2007), as well as media-sharing sites such as Instagram, Tumblr and Flickr, which facilitate network-building. Used broadly, however, the term social media can be applied to a wide range of online sites (Leppänen et al., 2014; Mandiberg, 2012), including websites which encourage interaction through commenting functionalities, wikis, blogs, online gaming and virtual worlds, and instant messaging apps (application software) such as WhatsApp and Snapchat. The social nature of the internet means that information is not only collaboratively created but is also filtered through people's networks of online contacts (Jones and Hafner, 2012), so that in some situations online readers will access information not directly from professional news outlets but through the repostings and recommendations appearing on their Facebook page or Twitter feed. Rather than new, this is somewhat reminiscent of older forms of communication (think of gossip spreading through a medieval town), transformed in terms of speed of dissemination and global reach.

Digital communication can also be distinguished from other forms of communication because it takes place 'in the network'; that is, it is 'embedded in the global digital mediascape of the web' (Androutsopoulos, forthcoming). This means that, as well as forging connections with a web of individuals online, people can also search for and link to networked resources: 'all the semiotic resources the global computer network has to offer' (Androutsopoulos, forthcoming). For example, in designing a website, I might use a translation tool; copy and paste a quotation from another website; insert a hyperlink to a YouTube video; and embed a live Twitter feed. Central to 'networked media' are the observations made by Microsoft researcher danah boyd[1] that digital communication is *persistent* (information online persists indefinitely), *searchable* (it can be retrieved across different contexts) and *replicable* (it can be copied, linked to or reposted into new contexts) (e.g. boyd and Marwick, 2011). These qualities enable people to take advantage of networked resources. This exploitation of resources has implications for how we communicate and how we manage information: on the one hand, it means online posts have the potential for great visibility or *scalability* (the fourth of boyd's affordances) and that people cannot be sure who will access their posts (Tagg and Seargeant, 2014); on the other, we can make complex, multiple links between different data points, rather than filing information in separate folders (Jones and Hafner, 2012). Practices are transformed through people's exploitation of technological affordances.

The networked nature of digital communications (and specifically the interconnections between different services) also means that it is increasingly difficult to distinguish or isolate different media. For example, from many newspaper websites, readers are given the option to 'Share' the story on Facebook, the entertainment and news site Reddit, or the professional social network site LinkedIn; to 'Tweet' it (on Twitter), or 'Pin' it on the photo-sharing site Pinterest. This complex interrelationship between online media is known as 'convergence'. Henry Jenkins' discussion of convergence culture (Jenkins, 2006, 2012) focuses on the way that traditional media converge online, sometimes uneasily, with grassroots movements within a reconfigured media ecology. Consider, for example, the complex relationship between traditional media institutions and Twitter in the early twenty-first century: not only is Twitter used by traditional media as a source of responses and sound bites from public figures, but Twitter users are often able to shape the news agenda. And yet the media still play a role in disseminating news broken on Twitter and bringing it to public consciousness. The convergence that characterises networked media can also be seen in the way that individual media comprise various elements (facilitated in part by networked resources). Androutsopoulos (2010) identifies what he calls *integration* ('the co-existence of various communication modes on a single platform' such as status updating, private messaging and instant messaging on Facebook), *embedding* ('the ability to place digital content, especially videos, on a web page', as on YouTube) and *modularity* ('the way in which web pages are composed of a number of different elements – different in terms of origin, authorship, affordances, conditions of production and so on', including adverts) (Androutsopoulos, 2010, p. 208). So, convergence is present at all levels, from the mediascape as a whole to individual websites, as well as in users' ability to access various media through one device (usually their smartphone).

Ordinary internet users are thus faced with an array of increasingly complex and overlapping choices regarding which platform or service they can use for any one interaction. Miller and Madianou (2012) use the term 'polymedia' to describe 'the particular configuration of different media that an individual deploys' (Miller and Sinanan, 2014, p. 136). As they suggest, it might be more accurate to talk in terms of a configuration of affordances, rather than media. Their argument is that users no longer see their choices in terms of different media, but as one 'integrated environment' with various functionalities and possibilities. I've already used the terms 'mediascape' and 'media ecology' (Ito et al., 2010; Gillen, 2014; McLuhan, 1964), which similarly focus on the internet as a system of interrelated and complex relationships (complex in the sense that they cannot be broken down and individual media cannot be understood in isolation). An implication of polymedia is that any one media must be understood in relation to its place amongst other technologies within a particular context. For example, Miller and Sinanan (2014, pp. 145–9) explain how the use of Skype by Trinidadians around 2011–12 can only be understood with reference to their older, established use of Blackberry Messenger (BBM) as a way of maintaining constant contact with friends and family; in contrast to BBM, using webcam showed individuals that they were being given special attention. In this case, given the fact that the choice between these free, widely available services is not determined by cost or access, people's media selections are shaped by their past experiences with earlier technologies and the practices that grow up around them.

The fact that individuals make choices between media according to social and personal motivations opens up these decisions to evaluation by others (Miller and Madianou, 2012). In other words, decisions about technology are seen as indicating something about the individuals who make them, which in turn feeds into others' judgements and responses. For example, when I am invited to a party through Facebook I feel less obliged to respond and am probably less likely to attend than if the invitation had been sent by email. My judgement here is based less on any technology-related factors (people around me do not respond in the same way) than on my preconceptions as to what each technology means – email as private, Facebook as a forum for somewhat one-sided general announcements – and my expectations as to how social acts such as sending invitations should be carried out. Polymedia can also be extended to include non-digital forms of communication, such as when someone decides to talk to their interlocutor face-to-face rather than continuing with an online conversation – another source of social evaluation which shapes behaviour, such that I may know which of my colleagues respond better to a face-to-face discussion than an email and act accordingly (whilst making wider judgements about my colleagues as more or less tech-comfy). Understanding choices between forms of communication like this allows us to look beyond a divide between what happens online and what happens offline, to explore digital communications within the wider context of an individual's or community's social practices, interactions and values (Jurgenson, 2012). Although the focus of this book is on people's 'digital communication' – their participation across the social, networked media discussed above – many of the issues explored extend across online and offline contexts, and people's online participation must be seen only as part of their social lives. The question is not 'how do people use language online?' but 'how do digitally mediated communications extend and transform what people are already doing with language?'

Why look at language when exploring digital communication?

As mentioned above, this book seeks to understand digital communication by looking primarily at the language used online. Defining what is meant by 'language' is not as straightforward as one might think. One distinction is that between 'language in general' and 'a language in particular' (Crystal, 2003, p. 265). However, the existence of particular languages is a social as well as a linguistic construct – that is, the boundaries distinguishing one set of linguistic features from another are determined by people for social and political reasons: this is why the languages spoken within China are designated as dialects, although they are mutually unintelligible; whilst Hindi and Urdu are classified as different languages despite their close resemblance. Their classification in each case is bound up with issues of national identity, religion and political expediency. The implications of this challenge to 'a language' as a straightforward linguistic category are explored in Chapter 18 on 'translanguaging'. For the purposes of this chapter, it is sufficient to note that what we recognise as 'a language' is to some extent imagined, codified and enforced by those in power, and does not map onto any one user's actual practices. People are usually aware of national standards and community norms and are likely to adhere to them; but they also routinely diverge from them and actively subvert or exploit them. Many linguists describe individuals not as using one language or another, but as selecting from a set of resources which are acquired and deployed in particular contexts. The set of language resources which any one individual has access to is emergent (resources are built up through exposure and interactions with different communities and in varying contexts) and shifting (an individual's repertoire will change during their lifetime).

It is increasingly recognised that language cannot be looked at in isolation from other resources available for meaning-making. These resources or modes include the paralinguistic features which accompany speech: intonation, tone of voice, facial expression, eye contact, gestures, physical positioning, movement (and so on). For written text, the resources include orthography, typography, font, layout and image. Online text also facilitates the inclusion of video, music and links to other sites. In this book, these modes are considered alongside language or, in some cases, as facilitating communication where no 'language' is apparent. For example, Japanese users of the social network and instant messaging app Line hold whole conversations using stickers, or emojis (Lee, 2014); while Snapchat users communicate through photos and videos, set to delete after the 'Snap' is viewed. In their study of webcam, Miller and Sinanan (2014, pp. 160–1) describe the communicative function of the green light on

Skype, indicating that someone is online and available to talk. For some participants in their Trinidad-based study, the green light was enough to reassure them that the other person was there for them, without their having to disturb them. Similarly, Donner (2007) describes a widespread practice, particularly across African countries, of 'beeping', whereby missed calls are used to signal a request for a return call or deliver a pre-determined message (such as 'I'm ready; come and pick me up'). It makes little sense to ignore such instances of communication by narrowing the focus to language alone. Of course, in many online texts, language combines with other modes to form multimodal texts (such as a video with a voiceover, caption and user comments), in which the different modes can sit in various relationships with each other – of complementarity or contrast (Unsworth, 2006) – and where the full meaning cannot be retrieved from the language alone. So, 'communication' in the book's title is not meant to indicate language alone.

Nor is 'communication' meant to refer simply to the transmission of information from one person to another. Instead, it refers to the rich, varied and complex social encounters that people engage in with each other for various reasons, including the bolstering of social relationships. By focusing in this way on what we can *do* with digital communications technology, this book takes a practices approach to the study of language. Language practices are defined as social activities where language is a means to an end: 'A language practices approach focuses on how language is part of our daily routines and how it functions to help us get things done, establish and maintain relationships, and express creativity and playfulness' (Mayor and Allington, 2012, p. 6). Within this perspective, language can be seen not only, as it tends to be portrayed, as a victim of technology (shaped and changed by its use in new online contexts) but also as a particularly important tool – alongside other visual modes – for getting things done in largely 'disembodied' environments (that is, where physical cues ranging from a person's gender to their body language are often unavailable).

This leads us to the question as to why a focus on language is important in exploring digital communication. There are two answers to this question, depending on the type of issue under consideration. Firstly, in Section A, Part I of this book, 'Digital language and literacy', the focus of concern is on language itself, including the effect of digital communications on spelling and grammar, its impact on reading practices, and on the way in which people write. We also look at fears about the dominance of English on the web, which both reflects and perpetuates wider power relations. In these cases, language is central to the concerns being expressed, and applied linguistics research is essential if we are to tackle these issues. For example, applied linguistics research reveals the extent to which phonetic spelling in digital communication relies on awareness of orthographic principles, which may explain a correlation between children's use of phonetically spelt variants and good literacy skills (see Chapter 9). Literacy is a key focus of these chapters, and it is used in varying ways. To the general public and in studies of children's online spelling, literacy tends to refer to the mechanical skills needed to read and write, and this understanding of literacy is evident in Chapter 9. Within recent literacy research (and in this book), literacy is seen as a social practice, so that 'being literate' also involves understanding social and cultural assumptions, values and goals (see Chapter 17).

In Section B, Part II, 'Social issues and social media', language is not the focus of concern. In this part, I look at online identity, which poses the two seemingly contradictory problems of anonymity and exhibitionism; as well as online privacy (whether people appropriately recognise the difference between what 'should' be private and what 'can' be made public). I also look at fears about the breakdown of society, and at cyberbullying. In these cases, language plays an indirect, but no less crucial, role. One interpretation held by language researchers is that language constructs context; that social phenomena are brought into being through discourse and do not have a meaning beyond what is said about them through language (e.g. Fairclough, 1992). This is not particularly a view taken in this book. Nonetheless, through a practices approach to language it is evident that context and language interact in complex ways, so that language reflects existing relations and inequalities and can reinforce or challenge them. It is in part through language that we present ourselves, reach out to other people, collaborate to get things done and seek to make sense of the world. And it may be that language is particularly significant in many online contexts, where (as previously mentioned) there is often less access to other social resources such as physical appearance and bodily contact. danah boyd talks about 'writing oneself into being' online (boyd, 2001, p. 119); that is, in digital communication, much of what we are and what we do is constructed through writing. More accurately, as discussed above, we should see digital communication goals being fulfilled by various modes: the written word alongside font, layout, image, colour and sound, all of which form a part of what 'communication' involves. In Chapter 14, for example, I explore the way people can manage their privacy through language choices ranging from vague expressions to multilingual code-switching (Tagg and Seargeant, 2014). In Chapter 16 on cyberbullying I look at applied linguistics research which explores the linguistic strategies that bullies use to intimidate their victims and the way that victims also use language to defend themselves (Herring, 2002).

The research discussed in this book is situated in the well-established discipline of applied linguistics, a field of language-related study that involves 'theoretical and empirical investigation of real-world problems in which language is a central issue' (Brumfit, 1995) and is thus a discipline grounded in its desire to tackle social issues (see Cook, 2003). Empirical applied linguistics research in the past has transformed how dictionaries are compiled, how foreign languages are taught, how texts are translated and even how criminals are caught (forensic linguistics). Furthermore, applied linguistics theories are in the process of transforming how we conceptualise language itself and thus how different languages, speakers and practices are evaluated (for example, as discussed above, the reconceptualisation of language as a process in which people engage rather than a product that exists separately from the people who speak it).

Aims and approach

This book does not claim to offer solutions to problems perceived to be caused by digital technology and nor will it necessarily calm all readers' worries. What it aims to do is provide insights from applied linguistics that enable readers to make informed judgements about the digital communication practices in which they and those around them are engaging.

In keeping with the ethos and aims of the Routledge Applied Linguistics series, the book takes the novel approach of starting with the *Problems and practices* commonly associated with digital media. These include its implications for language and literacy; and its effects on how we portray ourselves, manage our privacy and connect with others. The book then goes on to look at *Interventions* from within applied linguistics; that is, the ways in which applied linguists have sought to look beyond popular portrayals of these problems to understand through empirical investigation what people are actually doing when they communicate digitally. Finally, the book steps back to consider the *Theories* that drive and justify the interventions that applied linguistics has made.

Further reading

The following at the time of writing provide some of the best overviews of digital communication.

Baron, N. (2008) *Always On: language in an online and mobile world.* Oxford: Oxford University Press.
Crystal, D. (2011) *Internet Linguistics.* London: Routledge.

Herring, S.C., D. Stein and T. Virtanen, eds (2013) *Handbook of Pragmatics of Computer-Mediated Communication*. Berlin: Mouton de Gruyter.

Jones, R.H. and C.A. Hafner (2012) *Understanding Digital Literacies: a practical introduction*. Abingdon: Routledge.

Seargeant, P. and C. Tagg, eds (2014) *The Language of Social Media: identity and community online*. London: Palgrave.

Thurlow, C. and K. Mroczek, eds (2012) *Digital Discourse: language in the New Media*. Oxford: Oxford University Press.

Note

1   danah boyd spells her name in lower case.

Section A

Problems and practices

I

Digital language and literacy

1 Is digital communication ruining language?

Introduction

Concerns about the effects of digital communication on language can be traced back to (as least as far as) the use of email and SMS text messaging at the turn of the twenty-first century. In 2001, for example, a heated debate sprang up in the Greek media when a group of intellectuals and writers known as the Academy of Athens launched a campaign against the rise of 'Greeklish' – the writing of Greek using Roman characters which is associated with digital communication (Koutsogiannis and Mitsikopoulou, 2003). At the time, the BBC captured the flavour of the debate as follows:

> The manifesto argues that use of computers is responsible for bastardising the language of Aristotle and Homer ...
>
> However, the industry's defenders point out that computers are sold with Greek language software ... The Greeks are themselves to blame, they say.
>
> (BBC, 2001)

A decade later and the technology had moved on – from email to social network sites and from chatrooms and SMS to instant messaging (IM) platforms such as WhatsApp and Line – but the language-related issues had not. In 2013, similar concerns were being expressed in the Arab world about the effect of the English language on Arabic, resulting in the emergence of 'Arabizi' (Arabic written using a mix of Roman letters and Arabic numerals). As one journalist writing from Jeddah, Saudi Arabia, explains,

> Most Arab Internet users find this way easier than typing in Arabic. Teachers fear that this will weaken their Arabic ability or even replace the language in the future. Arabic professional professors ... consider it a war against the Arabic language to make it disappear in the long run.
>
> (Ghanem, 2011)

Meanwhile, in East Asia, the rapid rise of digital technologies is seen by some as a threat to the ancient tradition of handwriting. On phones and computers, people use a 'syllabery' of the Roman alphabet to type the pronunciation of the kanji they want, and then choose the appropriate character from the options suggested by the device. The fear is not simply that young people will be physically unable to form the complex characters but that they will forget their shape entirely, thus losing forever a significant element of Asian culture. For an article which described 'ancient writing collid[ing] with the digital age', Japanese journalist Miwa Suzuki spoke to a graduate student working part-time in an electronics shop:

> Matsumara said his reliance on devices leaves him adrift when faced with filling in forms for repairs at the electronics shop ... 'I sometimes can't recall kanji on the spot while a customer is watching me,' he said. 'I remember their rough shapes but I can't remember exact strokes'.
>
> (Suzuki, 2013)

Despite differences between the three contexts (Greece, Saudi Arabia, Japan), evident in each case are strikingly similar concerns. On the one hand, all writers see the conventions of digital communication – the use of Greeklish or Arabizi (what we might call forms of 'digitalese'), and the autotype function – as having a profound and worrying effect on the languages themselves and on young people's literacy skills. This may be a commonly held belief: an unscientific online poll held by Edutopia (http://www.edutopia.org) in 2012 asked respondents 'Does text messaging harm students' writing skills?' At the time of writing, the poll was ongoing but 53 per cent of the 3,246 respondents had selected the answer, 'Yes. I believe students are carrying over the writing habits they pick up through text messaging into school assignments' and only 25 per cent chose 'No. I believe students can write one way to their friends and another way in class. They can keep the methods separate.' In the UK, this fear reached its zenith in 2003 when a 13-year-old girl's school essay hit the headlines. The UK newspaper, *The Telegraph* (Cramb, 2003), reproduced the start of the essay, translating it for the benefit of its readers:

> My smmr hols wr CWOT. B4, we usd 2go2 NY 2C my bro, his GF & thr 3 :- kds FTF. ILNY.
> ('My summer holidays were a complete waste of time. Before, we used to go to New York to see my brother, his girlfriend and their three screaming kids face to face. I love New York.')

Looking at these different contexts reveals the various forms that digitalese can take – not only an unconventional mix of scripts and languages (so that Greek, Arabic and Chinese are written not in their traditional scripts but using the Roman alphabet), but also the unconventional spelling – what linguists call 'respelling' – particularly associated with digital communication. Both practices are seen as spreading from digital contexts to affect wider language use.

On the other hand, the concerns expressed in Greece, Saudi Arabia, Japan and the UK seem to be about more than simply language. Instead, this linguistic problem may thinly mask unease about wider and more complex issues related to historical tradition, a reluctance to change and the perception of a threat, to a script or an orthography inextricably bound up with the history of each culture. In a more immediate fashion, there is also a suggestion that (young) people are adopting habits associated with digital communication because it is easier – implying lack of effort or laziness – than the traditional way of doing things: as the East Asian article explains, for example, Matsumura once 'spent hundreds of hours learning the intricate Chinese characters' only to have his digital devices now 'remember them for him'. In other words, the concerns expressed about language can also be seen as statements about social decline and changes in (young) people's behaviour. This anxiety is often fuelled by adults' ignorance of what young people are up to. In the UK school essay case, one concern expressed was that the adults involved could not understand what had been written. *The Telegraph* reported the way in which the girl's teacher described the essay: 'The page was riddled with hieroglyphs, many of which I simply could not translate.' This practical problem was exploited in 2012 by developers of a smartphone app called TextGenie designed to translate abbreviations and slang 'into plain English for confused parents'.[1]

In the rest of the chapter, I want to expand on this last point, and argue that concerns about the effects of digital communication on language can in most cases be construed as misconceptions, based around the concerns that adults have about young people and the impact of change on society.

Task 1.1

What kind of language do you use online, and does your language differ across media?

Do you feel that the effects of digital communication on language are seen as a problem by people you know and is it something you read about in the papers? How do *you* feel about the kind of unconventional language on the digital platforms with which you are familiar? To what extent do you feel that the fears mentioned above are real – that they equate to real linguistic, educational or social problems – and to what extent do you think the fears are overblown?

Focus on: Twitter

Although concerns about 'digitalese' initially focused on SMS text messaging, other newer forms of digital communication have since taken the limelight. One cause for concern has been the microblogging site, Twitter. The language used on Twitter has no doubt come to public attention because of the prominent and often controversial part the site has played in breaking stories, setting the media agenda and facilitating public demonstrations, rallies and riots. Twitter is also implicated in issues of privacy (see Chapter 6) in cases where its users appear to be treating the site as they would a private dinner party; and in cyberbullying (see Chapter 7), as celebrities and other individuals are targeted by a bombardment of threatening and abusive tweets. It is not surprising that language should also be an issue, given that the stringent character restraint (140 characters) can encourage users to vary their spelling in order to compact their message. A study in March 2013 by the social media monitoring company Brandwatch, for example, analysed one million English language interactions across Twitter, Facebook and Google+, and concluded that Twitter users were the worst spellers, misspelling one in every 150 words (compared to 323 on Facebook and 238 on Google+) (O'Mahoney, 2013).

Twitter has also seen the birth of a number of new and still evolving language conventions, including the @ sign used before a person's name to address a tweet to them, or to talk about them; and the hashtag (#) used to tag a tweet with a topic and so include it in a wider discussion and, increasingly, to mark a sarcastic aside, as in:

Woken up feeling terrible. #likeIdidn'tseethatcoming

In this sense, the hashtag may be fulfilling a function previously carried out by asterisks, as in these 2010 World Cup tweets:

RT @SocialGround: Japanese World Cup Tweeters Help Break Twitter Record http://bit.ly/cBjzUG *like that's a surprise*

anywhoo ... the same way ALLLLLL Africans should be backing Ghana for the world cup ... I'm supporting Brazil *shrugs*

It is chiefly this use that has spread from Twitter to other forms of digital communication (and to spoken language), in ways that are not to everyone's liking. In an online article entitled 'How the hashtag is ruining the English Language', blogger Sam Biddle complains of its invasion of sites such as Facebook and Foursquare (a location-based social network site, through which users check in at different venues), explaining:

> Hashtags at their best stand in as what linguists call 'paralanguage', like shoulder shrugs and intonations. That's fine. But at their most annoying, the colloquial hashtag has burst out of its use as a sorting tool and become a linguistic tumor – a tic more irritating than any banal link or lazy image meme.
>
> (Biddle, 2011)
>
> The argument against hashtags is also reminiscent of earlier concerns about the overuse of LOL ('laughing out loud') and other acronyms in digital and spoken communication.
>
> #somethingsneverchange

Nothing more than moral panic?

Deborah Cameron (1995/2012) claims that language can often be found at the centre of media-generated 'moral panics'. A moral panic is said to occur when widespread fears of a somewhat abstract and vague threat to the social order are expressed in reactions against something more specific and concrete – drug use, vicious dogs, teachers' perceived inadequacies, digitalese – where the specific case in fact represents wider social issues (Cohen, 1973; McLuhan, 1964). In her discussion of the ongoing debates about the teaching of grammar in UK schools, Cameron shows how attempts to reinstate traditional methods are mixed up with the desire to instigate order among social groups deemed to be spiralling out of control (Cameron, 1995/2012; and see Kramer-Dahl, 2003, for a discussion of similar beliefs in Singapore). We might argue that, at the beginning of the twenty-first century, digitalese similarly stood in for wider concerns about breakdowns in parental and teacher authority and hence social order itself. This is an example of what Alice Marwick describes as 'technopanic' (Marwick, 2008). If you can't write properly, how can you be expected to behave properly? If you share a secret language with your friends, what else might you be up to?

Between 2001 and 2005, Crispin Thurlow carried out a survey of newspaper coverage of issues related to language, young people and new technology. Analysing 101 articles from the UK and the USA, he found a perceived link between digitalese and 'wider social and educational ills'.

> In addition to being described as reprehensible, frightening, depraved, infamous, criminal, jarring and abrasive, apocalyptic, execrable, pointless, and aberrant, [digitalese][2] was often held

responsible for a number of wider social and educational ills. For example, certain journalists and commentators regarded it as being inflicted on the innocent public ... , creating a whole new culture in the country ... , dumbing down the English language ... , and lowering standards all round.

(Thurlow, 2006, p. 677)

While some of these evaluations of digitalese are linguistic ones – the language, for example, is seen as being jarring and abrasive – others constitute thinly veiled moral and social judgements about the *people* who use this language online. It makes no sense to describe a particular language variety as reprehensible or criminal; instead, it is people who are considered as such. This is the case across stigmatised language usages – when we say that a particular accent sounds posh, rustic or stupid, we do so on the basis of our beliefs about the people who speak with those accents. While concerns about language should not necessarily be dismissed out of hand, adults' concerns about digitalese can often be seen as symptomatic of their relationships with, and fears about, young people themselves and their social – rather than linguistic – behaviour.

Myths and misconceptions

As suggested in the above section, the ongoing debate over digitalese also reveals a number of misconceptions that adults have – at least those working in the media – not only about digital communication but about young people. The argument in this section is that these media reports in fact say more about adults' ideas about digital communication than they do about children's or young people's practices (Herring, 2008a).

The first assumption is often that *all* young people (let's say those under 21) use digitalese of the kind described above. In Chapter 9 of this book, I look at studies which report a much lower use of unconventional forms in actual usage than media coverage would like us to believe (e.g. Thurlow and Brown, 2003). In fact, in Britain and the USA at least, it is the media itself that perpetuates the conception of digitalese through its adoption of digitalese forms. In his survey of British and American newspapers, Thurlow reported that almost a third of headlines contained examples of an often 'caricatured' digitalese. Journalistic uses of digitalese include:

If u cn rd ths, u mst b gr8 at txt spk, u gk u! Jk:-.

(*Daily Herald*, March 2001)

A langwidge going from bad 2 worse.

(*Daily Mail*, March 2003)

Y talk? Just txt.

(Geelong Advertiser, January 2005)

I h8 txt msgs: how texting is wrecking our language.

(Daily Mail, September 2007)

OMG! Is FB to blame 4 bad grammar?

(ConnectAmarillo, February 2012)

The second assumption is that digitalese is a fixed and prescribed code which young people have access to and which adults do not – rather as if digitalese was a password with which to get into a party or an illicit chat forum. The assumption that digitalese constitutes a fixed list of spellings is reflected in – and apparently confirmed by – the number of glossaries of digitalese available online (see Task 1.2), as well as translation apps of the kind mentioned earlier in this chapter. In his 2008 book, *Txtng: the Gr8 Db8*, David Crystal also provides lists of reported spelling variants in various languages (pp. 189–229) which include the kind of abbreviated phrases he nonetheless feels are unlikely to occur in 'real' text messages (in English, *AFAIK*, *BION*, *ICWUM*, *PTMM*, *TTYL8R*).[3] And if digitalese features can be isolated and defined in this way, then they can be learnt and used.

There is of course some truth to this assumption, and in Chapter 9 I focus on English to explore the principles or constraints which determine the relatively limited ways in which words can be 'respelt'. Many of the spellings used in online chat, SMS, Twitter and IM originated from the hacker culture of the 1990s, and have become conventionalised in the sense that they are well known, long-established and unreflectively used across social groups. The ways in which people use language online are determined in part by their awareness of the discourses that circulate about digitalese – that is, their interpretation of public and popular statements about what digitalese is supposed to constitute and what it is thought to mean across various social groups. However, as also explored in Section B, Chapter 9, digitalese is also emergent, in the sense that it emerges in the course of actual interaction. It is not, in most cases, imposed on people; instead they make it up and adapt it as they go. If you do not use abbreviations in your SMS text messages to me, I will probably avoid them too. However, if you use abbreviations and if our other friends do, and if we are in sustained, frequent communication by SMS, it is likely that we will begin to develop our own conventions and our own idiosyncratic abbreviations (Rowe, 2011).

The third assumption is that digitalese and 'proper' forms of a language are somehow in competition with each other – that if you use digitalese this will inevitably impinge on your ability to use what would be deemed a grammatically correct form of language. In other words, you can spell the second person pronoun 'you' or 'u', but you will not be able to switch between them, depending on circumstance. In actual fact, of course, people are perfectly able to change their style depending on the context. Most people move between a range of different 'varieties' of the same language, depending on whether they are speaking or writing; whether they are talking to their parents or a stranger on the street; whether they are writing an academic assignment, a note to an employer or an IM to their friends. 'Mistakes' are sometimes made – such as when my Dutch friend accidentally addresses me in Dutch or when children write as though they are speaking (using *and* or commas to run sentences together, for example) – but these tend to be exceptions rather than the rule and can often be addressed at school. When I discuss the txt essay (see above) with students or friends, most people agree that the 13-year-old knew exactly what she was doing, and that the essay was a sign of playfulness, rebellion or disrespect rather than ignorance as to correct spellings. In Section B, I go further than that and discuss the argument that, in order to spell unconventionally in ways that can be understood, awareness of correct spellings and the principles underlying the orthography of the particular written language is needed. In short, the matter is one of appropriateness – young people are generally able to use digitalese in online communications to their friends and standard spelling in school essays. (Indeed, it seems to be adults who often violate the principle of appropriacy by using digitalese in online messages to their children in ways that youth often deride.)

What can we conclude from these misconceptions? One point is the role of the media in amplifying – or in some cases creating – the fears surrounding digitalese. This is not to say that the problems are never real, and helping pupils distinguish between spellings appropriate for texting and those deemed correct for use at school or in job applications is often a difficult task for teachers and parents. The second point, however, is that actions taken to tackle the problems associated with digitalese need be based not on media accounts of often fictionalised or alarmist cases of digitalese, but on descriptions of how people – including young people and children – actually text.

To what extent, then, do media and popular concerns reflect actual practices? In Section B, Chapter 9, I look at how applied linguists have described and sought to understand how and why people *actually* write online. Drawing on linguistics research, I argue that digitalese can be seen as both principled and meaningful (an observation underpinned by new theories of literacy, explored in Section C, Chapter 17). I show that people draw on unconventional spellings in a selective and creative way, and that this may in fact be having a *positive* effect on children's literacy.

Task 1.2

Look up at least one online digitalese glossary. The following were available at the time of writing:

- List of chat acronyms and text message shorthand (Netlingo): http://www.netlingo.com/acronyms.php
- Slang dictionary: text slang, internet slang and abbreviations (No Slang): http://www.noslang.com/dictionary/
- CUA (Commonly Used Acronyms) (Net Nanny): http://www.netnanny.com/learn_center/glossary/acronyms

How many of the entries do you use, or have you seen used? Are there any forms that you use that are not on the list, and why do you think this is? Who do you think uses such lists, why and how? What role do you think such glossaries play in society?

Notes

1 See http://www.textgenieapp.co.uk/.
2 Thurlow uses the term 'computer-mediated discourse' (CMD) here, but his article makes clear that he is talking about similar practices to those we are describing here as 'digitalese'.
3 'As far as I know'; 'believe it or not'; 'I see what you mean'; 'please tell me more'; 'talk to you later'.

2   Has the web changed how we read?

Introduction: why we wouldn't normally print off the whole web

In May 2013, poet Kenneth Goldsmith announced a new project: to print out the entire internet (by which he most likely meant the world wide web) through the power of crowdsourcing (that is, by asking for contributions from the general public). Contributors were asked to mail their print-outs to a gallery in Mexico City and in return they would be listed as contributors to the project. By July of the same year, the gallery had received around ten tons of paper. The exhibition ran until August 2013, during which time the contributions were also read aloud and recorded, and at the end of which Goldsmith's paper version of the web was recycled.

You won't be surprised to learn that many internet users met this outlandish project with a certain amount of outrage, ranging from scepticism regarding the artistic merit of the project to anger about its environmental credentials. However, the project undoubtedly succeeded in fulfilling Goldsmith's real aim, which was of course not to produce a print-out of the web (after all, it was eventually recycled) but instead to raise discussion about the nature of our virtual networks and to make opaque a communication technology that most of us now take for granted.

Goldsmith's project raises a number of issues about how we 'read' the web and how this differs from more traditional ways of accessing information. I want to pick up on some of them in this chapter – the way the web tends to be read non-linearly and in 'snippets' and how this might be replacing any deep engagement in sustained argument; the size of the web and fears of information overload; and the ephemeral, unstable and ultimately less authoritative nature of online texts. Goldsmith's printing project was neutral in the sense that it sought to raise questions rather than prescribe answers; and, in fact, Goldsmith himself revels in the possibilities for literary activities afforded by the internet (see Goldsmith, 2011, for a discussion of the 'uncreative' writing possibilities facilitated by the internet). For many people, however (including teachers and educators), the impact that the web has on how and what we read is a real cause for concern. In the rest of this chapter, I explore these concerns and consider their implications.

> ## Task 2.1
>
> Make a quick list of all the things you read yesterday (however short and inconsequential), and divide them into two categories – those you read online and those you read on paper (or other offline equivalents!). Is most of your reading online or offline? Are there any differences in *why*, *when* and *how* you read online and offline texts?

The decline of reading?

I was discussing Goldsmith's project with a friend, when they made a comment about his printing a particular page out when he got to a particular letter. I was amused at the thought that the web would be printed alphabetically and intrigued as to exactly how that would work (you might argue that each webpage begins with 'w'). The point is that Goldsmith's project of printing out the web makes it very clear that the web is not organised like an encyclopaedia or even a library. That is, printing out the web is ridiculous not only because of its size, but because we don't read the web like we do a printed book.

Online text is structured with hyperlinks – electronic links which connect chunks of text, not only within a particular site (what Jones and Hafner, 2012 call 'internal links') but between different websites ('external links'). Hyperlinks therefore afford readers the possibility of leaving an otherwise linearly constructed argument on one page to follow other paths through the web. On the one hand, this has been seen as increasing reader agency, in the sense that the reader also plays a role in constructing the particular 'text' that they eventually end up reading (with the outcome that no two readers will read the same text); on the other hand, it should be remembered that readers are constrained to some extent by the links that online writers choose to include. As Jones and Hafner (2012) go on to point out, hyperlinks serve an evaluative function, allowing a writer to support or critique the points they make and to embed their argument in a wider discourse. Readers need an awareness of how hyperlinks can work as a persuasive device if they are to effectively critique a writer's argument (a point returned to in Section B). However, the concern often voiced over such hypertext (text structured by hyperlinks) is the effect it may be having on our ability to follow a sustained argument. One proponent of this view is Nicholas Carr, who compares his current reading habits unfavourably with how he used to read a book:

My mind would get caught up in the twists of the narrative or the turns of the argument, and I'd spend hours strolling through long stretches of prose. That's rarely the case anymore. Now my concentration starts to drift after a page or two.

(Carr, 2011, p. 3)

Carr's view finds resonance in Naomi Baron's (2008) description of what she calls 'snippet literacy', which she discusses in relation to her students and their reluctance to read (whole) books. Although one feels intuitively that similar concerns have echoed down university corridors since medieval times, Baron points to particular affordances of digital media, chiefly the search engine and the Find function, which allow students to locate key words and topics. On the one hand, such affordances are useful aids for readers; on the other hand, they discourage deep extensive engagement with the text.

To what extent are these fears justified? As discussed in the Introduction, people's concerns can be seen as natural reactions to change which are paralleled in earlier reactions to earlier technologies. (As Manguel, 1996 shows, silent reading – rather than reading out loud, which was the norm in ancient and early medieval societies – was once considered a sign either of idleness or of dangerous free thought.) Present day concerns about online reading also embody two assumptions that need interrogating. The first is that pre-digital, print reading inevitably involves extensive, close, linear reading (reading from start to finish) in a way that contrasts with online reading. In reality, however, people have always been free to play with the affordances of print just as they can with those of digital media and it is not possible to prescribe or predict a particular reading practice and associate it with books. As Baron points out, 'We can (and do) read Shakespeare's plays silently, and Chaucer could (and did) read aloud his tales to courtly audiences' (Baron, 1998, p. 138). Just because we associate print with linear reading does not mean that people don't follow tangential trains of thought, diligently peruse (or systematically ignore) footnotes, approach a book by looking up words in the index or flip between books.

The second assumption is the idea that hypertext is *replacing* print books and thus the reading practices associated with print – extensive, close, linear reading – are being lost, when in reality it is likely that both forms will continue to exist side-by-side. As the literary theorist Katherine Hayes writes:

As we work towards critical practices and theories appropriate for electronic literature, we may come to renewed appreciation for the specificity of print. ... Books are not going the way of the dinosaur but the way of the human, changing as we change, mutating and evolving.

(Hayes, 2002, p. 33)

In other words, while digital reading may force us to re-evaluate the practices and theories associated with print literacy, this reconsideration may enhance our understanding of, rather than signal the demise of, print reading.

Information overload

What makes Goldsmith's project seem particularly ridiculous is the size of the web, with the ten tons of print-outs received in the space of a couple of months in Mexico City representing, in the *Washington Post*'s estimation, 'not even a sliver of the whole Internet' (Zak, 2013). Its vastness means that potential contributors to the project needed to be highly selective in their choosing which part to print – should they print off and send in their own emails? A newspaper website? The whole of Twitter? What a user chooses to print is likely to be influenced by personal preferences, political ideologies and past internet experience. For example, the *Washington Post* spoke to one contributor who had sent in 32 pages of lyrics by the singer Prince because it recalled one of his first uses of broadband internet. However absurd the options considered by contributors to this project may seem, this selectivity is part and parcel of the decisions made on a daily basis by internet users, who must call on digital skills which differ in important ways from traditional reading abilities and strategies – the ability to search effectively, to filter, to evaluate and to deal with information overload.

Information overload is a common cause for concern, and not without some basis. A study in 2008 by the University of California, San Diego, reported that an average US citizen consumed nearly 12 hours of information in a day, up from 7.4 hours in 1960 (Bohn and Short, 2012). Meanwhile, a survey by NetVoucherCodes.co.uk found that the average British texter will send two million words of text messages in their lifetime, which – as newspapers and online coverage were quick to point out – is twice the size of the complete works of Shakespeare (MacRae, 2013). One culprit responsible for overloading many working adults is email. As technology reporter Timothy Stenovec of the *Huffington Post* puts it:

We live in a culture where email overload is accepted as a fact of professional life – a post-apocalyptic dystopia of over-stuffed inboxes ... and never-ending 'pings' emanating from our computers and devices.

(Stenovec, 2013)

Rosenthal Alves, Director of the Knight Center for Journalism in the Americas, describes the digital revolution in terms of a change in ecosystem – we have moved, he argues, from an information desert or drought (a situation of information scarcity) to a deluge, creating a 'vibrant, lavish rainforest' (MLDF Media Forum, 2010). The problem is not only the abundance of information sources online, but the complex ways in which they connect and interact. The 'problem' may be not so much the amount of information we encounter, as our ability to adapt to the new ecosystem – that is, to manage the input. Stenovec goes on to make a number of useful suggestions for email users, including 'ruthlessly unsubscribe' and 'send fewer emails' – both of which point to our own role in exacerbating the information overload we experience.

Jones and Hafner (2012) point to an important distinction between data and information: it is normal in modern society to be surrounded by data, but our minds can automatically filter it out until we interact with it and try to make meaning from it, at which point the data becomes information (Jones and Hafner, 2012, p. 19). The real problem may be how we decide what to concentrate on, in part because we do not always make those decisions ourselves. When researching online for popular concerns about digital communication for this book, I might be forgiven for thinking the concerns to be limited to the UK and, to a lesser extent, North America – had I not known that Google was helpfully directing me to sites relevant to my computer's Internet Protocol (IP) address. Restricting my online searches to Google does not only limit my global perspective, but it potentially closes my mind to alternative, challenging views – the sorts of issues and arguments, as Baron (2008, p. 205) points out, that we are more likely to stumble across in a library search or in leafing through a book. As Pariser (2011, p. 2) puts it, 'In polls a huge majority of us assume that search engines are unbiased. But that may be because they are increasingly biased to share our own views'. Furthermore, Google's power is gradually being curtailed by what are known as walled gardens being set up by social network sites such as Facebook, whose private content is inaccessible to the search engine. Within such walled gardens, information is not only limited by Facebook's decisions (regarding censorship and free speech, for example) but by the people with whom you interact. People are increasingly accessing information which is channelled to them by the people they know – on the one hand, a useful filtering device but, on the other, another way of limiting our exposure to ideas which challenge or develop what we know. The web is not, then, a problem in the sense of an overload of information. Instead, the apparent wealth of free information obscures the risk that we usually access information we are likely to accept and which is increasingly filtered by people we already agree with.

Information overload finds its parallels in 'constant connectivity' or what Baron (2008) and boyd (2012) call the 'always on' lifestyle: the perception that we are continually bombarded by online messages and posts which we are expected to keep up with. The constant stream of social media input that we receive is highlighted by the different approach to communication heralded by the photo-messaging app, Snapchat. The photos that users take, manipulate and send through Snapchat are automatically deleted no more than 10 seconds after the recipient views them. As a result, argues boyd (2014):

> The underlying message is simple: You've got 7 seconds. PAY ATTENTION. ... In a digital world where everyone's flicking through headshots, images, and text without processing any of it, Snapchat asks you to stand still and pay attention to the gift that someone in your network just gave you.

But for some people, the only way of dealing with the competing and frantic demands on their attention and time is to withdraw from digital communication altogether. This can be done on a regular basis: the Microsoft researcher, danah boyd, advocates (and practises) the need to take what she calls 'an email sabbatical' whereby she informs everyone that she will be unavailable for a period, before setting up an auto-delete for all incoming emails. This can also be done in emergency burn-out situations – author and comedian Baradunde Thurston took a 25-day break from social media in 2012, learning in the process that he had become addicted to information and, more importantly, to being connected.

> Before The Unplugging, I wanted to read every feed and follow all the right sources so I could be connected to every important event ... Only when I dramatically reduced my connectivity did I realize ... that I did not need to sustain that constant high to live well.
> (Thurston, 2013)

But it is tempting to equate 'unplugging' with attempts to purge the body by giving up alcohol for one month of the year; it's a good idea which will probably benefit you, but it shouldn't replace a moderated approach to drinking for the rest of the year; or, in the case of internet connectivity, actively filtering, evaluating and controlling the information stream.

The instability of online texts

As ludicrous as it may seem to print off the web, the attempt reflects a persistent tendency (among some people) to resort to printing as a way of fixing or managing online data – printing off important emails to file or lengthy documents to read (as Sellen and Harper, 2003 suggest in *The Myth of the Paperless Office*, it may be that we are using more paper, not less, in the digital age). In other words, the project highlights the intangible, ephemeral, almost abstract nature of the internet and our desire to anchor it down and to turn it into something we can keep. As individuals, we can have little idea of the size or nature of the web beyond our search returns and little feeling of control or ownership over it (despite its user-generated content).

What is said of the web as a whole can also be said of individual online texts. In a recent paper, David Crystal outlined what he saw as the properties of traditional texts, particularly their definable physical boundaries and their static permanence (Crystal, 2011). The internet draws attention to how fluid, unstable and uncertain these properties actually are. Linguists have established criteria for defining the beginnings and ends of offline texts and for separating one text from another (for the purposes of research), but as Crystal points out they have yet to reach decisions regarding the boundaries of many online texts – is the 'text' what I can see on my screen, or when I scroll? Does it include peripheral or functional elements, such as advertising? The translated version? Is a Tweet a text, or can one text be said to comprise all the Tweets with a particular hashtag? And how do we deal with continuously changing or growing texts such as a blog or a Facebook page? These questions need to be addressed before linguists can consider, for example, the structural features of online texts or how online texts can be distinguished from each other by the different expressions that occur in them. In the course of addressing such questions, the arbitrariness of our decisions regarding the boundaries of *offline* texts becomes apparent – it is, as Hayes (2002) says in her discussion of print literary culture, simply a case that we assumed our distinctions and categories to be self-evident.

With printed or at least published texts, we expect and usually encounter a certain degree of permanence and sameness – or, in Michael Cronin's words, 'identicality', 'the cultural expectation of identical copies' (Cronin, 2013, pp. 76–8). We talk of a written text being a finished product and in our own written texts we can refer to a particular page in another source with the confidence that readers will be able to find the reference if they consult the right edition. However, as mentioned above, many internet texts, such as blogs, wikis or social network sites, were not designed to be considered 'finished products' but to be continuously built on and modified. One problem in education and academia is how these shifting sources can be reliably referenced in written work when they might change or disappear at any time. Even relatively stable texts – such as newspaper articles – can undergo modifications which challenge any notion of permanence – added comments, editor corrections, relocating to a different section of the site. Print texts can of course suffer from anachronisms, whereby language from an earlier or later date is inserted inappropriately into a text (for example, if characters in a novel set in fifteenth-century England say 'okay' to each other, as the word is generally not thought to have emerged since at least the nineteenth century). However, Crystal (2011) describes an additional online phenomenon he calls 'panchronicity' whereby a text can include 'futurisms' – additions to a text, say, ostensibly produced in 2005 but which has additions inserted in 2013. For example, an online newspaper article on censorship in Vietnam contains the following two paragraphs (in a print newspaper, if I had kept the original article, the error would still stand):

> about 20 percent of the world's imprisoned bloggers this year have been Vietnamese. ...
>
> Correction: An earlier version of this post inaccurately reported that 20 percent of the world's imprisoned journalists this year have been Vietnamese. In fact, 20 percent of the world's imprisoned bloggers have been Vietnamese. The post has been corrected.
>
> (Dewey, 2013)

The advantages of the potentially dynamic nature of online text are clear – not only can errors be instantly corrected but knowledge (on a wiki, for example) continually built upon. But at the same time, we are having to learn to deal with the impermanence of – and, in a sense, our lack of control over – online texts and to find new ways to file, reference, organise and appreciate texts. When we print online texts, in a sense we show how we are still bound up with traditional ways of dealing with what we value: as digital librarian and internet activist Brewster Kahle says, 'How do you protect what's valuable? Well, you make copies' (quoted in Zak, 2013).

In Section B, Chapter 10, I look at attempts by applied linguists to understand the specifics of particular genres of online text, and how they need to be read; as well as exploring research seeking to determine how people, especially children, actually fare when reading online and the strategies they adopt. The theories behind these observations are explored further in Section C, Chapter 17.

Task 2.2

Unplug yourself from the internet for a pre-determined length of time. (Know your own capabilities – you could unplug for any length of time from one hour to one week, depending on your level of tolerance, and you could try a complete unplugging or simply avoidance of social media.)

Keep a record, in which you record your changing state of mind over the period; the alternative sources of information or means of communication that you use; and the more general differences it makes to your social relationships and productivity, if any. Then reflect on the advantages and disadvantages of our current 'information overload'.

3 Is the web devaluing what it means to be an author?

Introduction

Hetalia and Hogwarts
England laid [sic] in his own puddle of blood. The red liquid escaped from the whole [sic] in his stomach ...

America let out a big sob as the other nations surrounded their friend. Harry Potter stood outside the circle, depressed and shocked, *I should have been able to do something!*

(by Flameswolf, http://www.fanfiction.net/s/9497950/1/
Hetalia-and-Hogwarts)

Fan fiction – the writing of stories by fans based on the original fiction – is not unique to the internet, and has its origins at least as far back as the Star Trek fanzines of the 1960s (Jenkins, 1992). However, fan fiction has substantially gained in widespread popularity as a result of the affordances of digital technology, which enables fans from across the world to come together and disseminate their work. 'Hetalia and Hogwarts' was posted on fanfiction.net, one of the largest and most popular fan fiction sites. It is a 'Crossover' in that it blends two stories (in this case *Harry Potter* and the Japanese World War II-inspired webcomic, *Hetalia-Axis Powers*) and, like much fan fiction, it comes with a disclaimer which reveals its status: 'I do not own Harry Potter or Hetalia'.

Just as the internet is the perfect tool for fan fiction writers, so fan fiction can be seen as the embodiment of what is understood by online writing. Most obviously, fan fiction represents changing ideas about authorship, as digital communication moves us away from the concept of the writer as lonely genius and towards writing as a collaborative, community-based practice. Related to this shift are changing attitudes towards copying and borrowing (alongside the increasing ease with which both can be done), and the implications this has for both academic plagiarism and legal copyright issues. These changes blur the line between writers and readers, so that both are seen as contributing to the writing process. As well as embodying these characteristics of digital writing, fan fiction challenges popular notions such as the currently perceived decline in reading (Baron, 2008, pp. 201–4) and the alleged lack of creativity in much online production (see Chapter 1), given that fan fiction writers both read and creatively remix what they have read to create new fiction. In this chapter, I explore these issues and lay out the concerns currently circulating about the devaluing of written text and what it means to be an author.

> ## Task 3.1
>
> Go to fanfiction.net and choose a fan fiction story or a crossover which draws on genres and texts with which you are familiar. In what ways does the story build on the existing characters, setting and/or plot, and to what effect? To what extent do you consider this story to be a) creative; and b) original? To your mind, does this story confirm or challenge fears about the 'death of the writer'?

The author as creative genius

The internet is often seen as pivotal in the contemporary redefinition of authorship. The historical importance of 'the author' in the western world can be seen as a consequence of the development of 'print culture' and the laws and principles of copyright that grew up around it. The notion of a print culture emerges not simply as a result of the existence of printed texts (which began in Europe in the 1400s), but rather the use that is made of them, the distinction made between speaking and writing and the value placed on the latter, and the impact that writing has on a society's cognitive thought. In the west, writing came to play an important role in law, politics, science and the arts as a result of the invention of the printing press and moves towards mass education, which led to a society where the majority of the population had direct access to the written word, if not the tools of production. In print culture, writing comes to be seen as a repository of a society's knowledge and a gateway to further discoveries, and the significance of the written word is materialised in the value placed on the physical object of the written text. It thus becomes important to determine 'who owned the author's original manuscript ("copy") and thus had the right to profit financially by replicating it' (Baron, 2008, p. 187). Copyright emerged in the west to protect an author's right to the ownership of their expression of ideas, and to inhibit the ability of others to profit from their work. In turn, copyright encouraged a belief in the need for originality and veracity on the part of authors, and in the notion of the author as a singular creative genius.

There are of course exceptions to this conception of authorship – much scientific writing now tends to be multi-authored; editors and other parties have a substantial but anonymous input into newspaper articles; and many novels have been published anonymously or under pseudonyms, from *Jane Eyre* and *Middlemarch* to *Primary Colors* and *The Cuckoo's Calling* – and authorship is treated very differently in the case of personal, private or transgressive writing such as diaries, photo albums and graffiti. However, cultural expectations surrounding the notion of the authoritative author have shaped contemporary culture. The ideal has not been overturned by the internet – we still value and award good writers and we still see authority in the printed word – but it has been challenged.

The internet serves to contest the traditional notion of an author in the following main ways. Firstly, the world wide web provides a space where anyone can post their work and where it has the potential at least to become publicly available. Mark Boardman (2005, p. 48), for example, comments that homepages appear to be written with the 'sense that the author does not believe many people will read the page – while at the same time daring it to achieve a global profile'. As Baron (2008, pp. 183–4) puts it, 'the outpouring of text fostered by information communication technology may be redefining (some would say debasing) our standards for the written word'. The establishment of wikis – websites written collaboratively by users – such as Wikipedia or Wiktionary, and microblogging sites such as Twitter or Weibo allow anyone with an internet connection to contribute (in different ways) to public debate and ultimately to the world's repository of knowledge. Secondly, the web does not require traditional writing credentials or peer review; instead, 'the legitimacy of web content is self-determining, rather than being imposed by external regulatory bodies: the very existence of the good stuff means that you hang out for it and ignore the rubbish' (Boardman, 2005, p. 41). Thirdly, the web does not demand that you put your name to your work: websites often don't have named authors; many sites allow people to adopt usernames or 'nicks' as they were originally called in the chatrooms of the 1990s; and most Wikipedia users don't look beyond the entries to the 'History' and 'User' pages to see the names behind the edits.

Despite the potentially democratic and open platform provided by the internet, concerns are expressed about its impact on the authority and validity of the written text. Baron (2008), for example, asks whether the intellectual and social value of written texts will be reduced not only by their being freely available (p. 192), but by the reduced attention (as observed by Baron) which is paid to accuracy and carefully constructed argument (p. 198). More importantly, perhaps, the question is whether we can effectively filter the bad from the good – do all internet users possess the ability to 'ignore the rubbish'? Is it always possible to determine the source, status and intention of online texts? In 2012, for example, the Iranian Fars News

Agency jubilantly republished an article suggesting that many Americans would vote for the President of Iran instead of the US President; in the same year, the Chinese *People's Daily* website reproduced an article claiming Kim Jong-un of North Korea to be the 'sexiest man alive'. The original articles in both cases came from *The Onion*, a satirical online newspaper. It is possible that the Chinese website was engaged in its own, highly implicit version of satire (Simon, 2012) but the Iranian news agency eventually apologised for its mistake. The need to filter and evaluate online sites has real implications in academia, where the use of Wikipedia as a source is strongly discouraged but where the existence of the web undoubtedly blurs the line between academically acceptable texts (those which are peer-reviewed, for example) and those which are not acceptable.

Task 3.2

Visit *The Onion* at www.theonion.com. As Dudeney et al. (2013, pp. 198–200) point out, the objective of satirical sites is not to defraud but to 'make people laugh by seeming credible'. What features of the site make *The Onion* seem credible? What features tell you it is satire? Reflect on the more serious implications of sites that intend to defraud, and consider if there are any offline equivalents.

Blurring the line between reader and writer

At the beginning of 2013, *The Onion* published an article entitled 'Internet users demand less interactivity' which purported to report on the results of their poll:

> 'We just want to visit websites and look at them,' users say.
> [W]eb users expressed a near unanimous desire to visit a website and simply look at it, for once, … for a straightforward one-way conduit of information, and specifically one that did not require any kind of participation.
>
> (*The Onion*, 2013)

Ironically, 10,500 readers had responded by posting about the site on Facebook (by September 2013), suggesting they are not yet ready to give up online participation. But the article is timely in its identification of one of the main trends characterising the current state of the internet.

The idea that the line between the writer and the reader is being blurred in digital situations can be understood in two ways. Firstly, and more narrowly, such a blurring can be discerned in relation to the interactive features of many current websites, meaning that readers take on a more active role than that traditionally posited for them.

Readers can, for example, respond directly to the writer of a blog or newspaper article by bestowing ratings or leaving comments. They can respond publicly to a work of fiction by producing and disseminating their own. Also relevant to the active role of readers online is the use of hyperlinks by which a reader actively creates a text by selecting and following links (see Chapter 2). Secondly, the blurring of the writer–reader role can also be meant in the more general sense that the web is increasingly seen as being user-generated, so that it is the users (the 'readers') themselves who are also creating and sharing the content that makes up the web. This is of course generally heralded as a welcome development – as Jay Rosen (2012) claims, 'the people formally known as the audience' can no longer be considered simply as 'eyeballs' fought over by the traditional media. But, as we've seen, a situation in which anyone can become an author raises questions regarding the validity of what they write.

The wisdom of crowds

The kind of collaborative writing seen on Wikipedia also represents another affordance of the internet. As David Crystal said of Wikipedia, the 'fond hope is that by letting everyone have a go, eventually the truth will emerge, and the result will be better than the traditional encyclopedia' (cited by Myers, 2010, p. 130). Bigipedia – a parody of Wikipedia – is the central premise of a BBC comedy sketch show which first aired on UK radio in 2009. In one 2011 sketch (entitled 'The wisdom of crowds'), Bigipedia was asked the question 'What are the colours of the rainbow?' A jumble of voices responds with various colours. Then the voiceover says: 'Consensus: Brown'. The ploy is repeated for various questions, and in each case the outcome is the same – bland, unsatisfying compromises. The consensus? That there are potential problems with the kinds of truths which emerge from a user-generated, collaborative process.

Wikipedia constitutes a marked challenge to the authority of the named author. Each page of the online encyclopaedia embodies a coherent authorial voice, obscuring the thousands of edits made by a range of different editors involved in its production, all of whom remain anonymous to most casual users. The endeavour is truly collaborative in a way that other online communities (such as fanfiction.net) are not, in that contributors work together towards the same goal: that of creating and maintaining an entry. Nonetheless, there are numerous concerns raised about the wiki, summarised by Wikipedia itself:

> The major points of criticism of Wikipedia, an online encyclopedia, are the claims that the principle of being open for editing by

everyone makes Wikipedia unauthoritative and unreliable ... that it exhibits systematic bias, and that its group dynamics hinder its goals.

(http://en.wikipedia.org/wiki/Criticism_of_Wikipedia)

One problem with the fact that Wikipedia is 'open for editing' is that the collaborative nature of Wikipedia attracts experts and non-experts alike, and to most users it is not always possible to distinguish between them. In comparison, sites such as Twitter or Urban Dictionary more obviously display competing, contradictory and individual voices, and disputes are carried out in the open (rather than in Wikipedia's 'Talk' pages). As for its 'systematic bias', Myers (2010) notes Wikipedia's tendency to give too much credence to conspiracy theorists, while Ruth Page (focusing on the Stephen Lawrence case in the UK and the murder in Italy of Meredith Kercher) shows the extent to which entries are influenced by accounts in the traditional media (Page, 2012b, 2013). The group dynamics of Wikipedia become problematic where controversial topics are concerned, and where a community can descend into squabbles and repeated edits and re-edits. Myers (2010, p. 157) suggests that what we are seeing is a tension between different conceptions of knowledge: on the one hand, some contributors attempt to enforce their right (realised elsewhere on the internet) to state their own point of view; while, on the other, the underlying ethos of Wikipedia is to promote knowledge as 'the result of collective discussion and rational persuasion' (Myers, 2010, p. 156). We might conclude that Wikipedia needs to be treated like many online sources: welcomed as a wealth of freely available information, but cautiously consumed.

'Uncreative' writing – or illicit copying?

The internet allows for the dissemination, replication and reworking of people's words (images, videos and so on) on an unprecedented scale and with incredible ease. This affordance has resulted in the widespread movement of internet memes, mashups and remixes. To some, the ease with which existing texts can be remixed and disseminated has worrying implications for notions of originality and novelty. To others, they are acts of creativity rooted in activities traditionally deemed to be 'uncreative', as poet and uncreative writing lecturer, Kenneth Goldsmith, puts it. He gives the example of *Status Update* by Darren Wershler and Bill Kennedy, an art project that harvests users' status updates and randomly replaces each user's name with the name of a dead writer.

Samuel Johnson's socks keep falling down. Day after day, sock after sock. WHY?!?! Emily Brontë and her playstation are overly friendly these days. Jonathan Swift has got tix to the Wranglers game tonight. Jean Cocteau thinks he wants vodka. Iced with a bit of lime.

The project 'taps into one aspect of the current zeitgeist in an intriguing and energetic way', wrote one reviewer (mclennan, 2011)[1], by 'creating an alternative universe where the famous and the obscure are alive, well and reveling in the banal', as another puts it (Davis, 2009). Playing with the notion of the lone authorial genius, literary critic Marjorie Perloff (2010) calls this kind of work 'unoriginal genius': the art of doing new things with existing texts, rather than creating new texts.

Another line of thinking is that online remixes are assertions of identity, as people appropriate from global discourses and reinterpret them for local contexts and immediate purposes (Androutsopoulos 2011; Leppänen et al., 2014), and they are often seen as political statements, whereby the refashioning and recontextualisation of institutional or media messages act as a critique or challenge to dominant views. Take, for example, the video mashup 'AVATAR (Anglos Valiantly Aiding Tragic Awe-Inspiring Races)' by Craig Saddlemire (Saddlemire, 2013), which splices together extracts from a range of US films, including *Lawrence of Arabia*, *Out of Africa*, *Dances with Wolves* and *Avatar*, to highlight Hollywood's obsession with the theme of white Anglo-Saxons rescuing exotic primitive peoples. In many cases, the internet provides a platform and resources to groups of people – the young, the marginalised – who might normally struggle to find a public voice.

One worrying implication of these internet affordances is the enhanced possibility of student plagiarism. This is a concern that echoes down school and university corridors. The internet not only provides access to numerous websites filled with commentaries and summaries and the ability to easily cut-and-paste, but it also hosts sites where students can buy made-to-order essays. The problem, perhaps, lies as much in the nature of the tasks being set as in the easy solutions available. Digital communication has ushered in a different approach to information – with the web, there is no need to memorise information (to *know* it); rather, one needs to know where and how to find it. Thus, essay questions asking students to regurgitate facts lend themselves to plagiarised work, and it may be that some parts of academia need to respond to changes in how students can access and use information.

Perhaps the more serious implication is for existing copyright laws, which were laid down in a print culture somewhat different from what we see, and what we can do, online; and which, some would argue, have yet to catch up with current practices or expectations about free content. The problem here is not only the ease with which works can be replicated or remixed, but also the fact that the internet makes public acts of appropriation or creativity which previously would have been private and beyond the reach of commercial regulations. As the legal scholar Lawrence Lessig explains:

> For the first time in our tradition, the ordinary ways in which individuals create and share culture fall within the reach of the regulation of the law, which has expanded to draw within its control a vast amount of culture and creativity that it never reached before.
>
> (Lessig, 2004, p. 8)

Moves to provide open access to online property include the GNU General Public Licence, which makes available open source software, and the Creative Commons Licence, which allows online writers to specify the rights they would like to have over their own work, from 'Attribution' (which lets others do what they like to your work as long as they attribute it to you) through four other licences of increasing restriction to 'Attribution-NonCommerical-No-Derivs' (which only allows others to share your work). But tensions are likely to remain between publishers, artists and other interested parties on the one hand and, on the other, the generations who work on the presumption that online content should be freely available, fuelled partly by the initial ethos of the web (see Chapter 1) and partly by people's experience of freely downloading music and films from the internet.

How concerned should we be?

To what extent are these apparent changes to ideas of authorship and the written word real – and to what extent should we worry about them?

As with all concerns about technology (see the Introduction), we should be cautious in positing an overly dystopian view. Although anyone can post online and, in Baron's words, debase the good stuff out there, it is necessary to acknowledge that online mechanisms exist for filtering and evaluating the data. These mechanisms include the filtering work carried out by our own social networks (as, for example, when someone you trust retweets a Twitter post or comments on an article on Facebook); as well as user ratings and reviews (entries in Urban Dictionary, for example, are rated by other users); and censorship and moderation from the site owners themselves. (The latter does not always work smoothly – Google, for example, has been criticised for going along with the Chinese government's demands for censorship.) Often, however, the controls come from users themselves, as embodied in the concept of folksonomies – taxonomies created by users as they tag photos and posts and in this way organise web content. With respect to Wikipedia, although it might seem that, as Crystal put it, the site lets 'everyone have a go', in fact there are strong controls from the implicit but strong sense of shared goals and principles which favour a 'neutral point of view' (NPOV) and 'no original research' (NOR) (Myers, 2010); and from the monitoring activities of some editors – edits made by 'vandals' seeking to disrupt the site, for example, are typically reversed within two minutes (Viégas et al, 2004). And as Myers points out, it is important to understand the purpose of Wikipedia – the encyclopedia is not concerned with generating new knowledge, but in collating 'currently prevalent representations of knowledge about the world' (Bruns, 2008, p. 148, cited in Myers, 2010, p. 148).

However, claims that the internet has brought about a revolution in our ideas and practices – in this case, in relation to authorship and the value of written texts – must also be considered with caution. Political remixes have been traced back to the early decades of the twentieth century in Russia and East Berlin (McIntosh, 2012). Appropriated poems also have a long history – Charles Reznikoff's 'Testimony', for example, was a 'found poem' comprising thousands of court testimonies from between 1855 and 1915 written as close as possible to the words of the witnesses themselves (discussed in Goldsmith, 2011). With respect to the blurring of the distinction between reader and writer, we might argue that digital communication simply highlights a phenomenon that has long been recognised, in media and literary studies alike. At a recent literature festival in Cheltenham, UK, the British author Ian McEwan discussed his experience of one of his books, *Enduring Love*, being on the school curriculum. McEwan noted how the children of authors whose books were on the curriculum rarely benefited from their parents' insights (being told in one case that they'd misunderstood the writer's intentions), and he praised *York Notes* – English literature revision guides – as having analysed the book in ways he never considered. What emerges from his anecdotes is the evident point that readers (and critics) are always active in the process of constructing meaning from a text. What the internet does is to build the readers' choices into the very architecture of the site and make very obvious what has always been the case – the meaning of any text emerges from its interaction with both the writer and reader.

In Chapter 11, I discuss the research carried out by applied linguists into two of the online writing spaces discussed in this chapter – the fan fiction community and Wikipedia – to highlight how these sites shape and are shaped by particular language and literacy practices. Overall, the message coming out of applied linguistics research in this area is that we need to redefine what we mean by 'writing' (and 'copying') in order to understand and embrace online practices. Chapters 17 and 19 in Section C are relevant in explaining the theories behind the research.

Note

1   mclennan spells his name in lower case.

4 Does the internet further the global dominance of English?

Introduction

English is commonly called the global lingua franca: used in international business, academia and commerce, disseminated via multinational brands such as McDonalds, and popularised through American films and music. The worldwide reach of English can be seen as a force for both good and bad. On the one hand, a lingua franca allows people to communicate ideas, conduct trade and reach political agreements across linguistic barriers; on the other hand, the dominance of one language over others can be seen both to reflect existing inequalities and to perpetuate them. English extended across the globe in the eighteenth and nineteenth centuries because it was the language of a colonising power, Britain, and it has spread since then as the language of the commercial and political leader, the United States. In countries where English is a second or foreign language, access to the language tends to be reserved for the elite, the powerful and the educated. In these countries, the poor or marginalised who do not have access to English may not always be able to enter national and international job markets, travel abroad or access the best information, thus maintaining or exacerbating their poverty and social disadvantage. Meanwhile, the spread of English as part of economic and cultural globalisation is often seen as a threat to other languages: people learn English and thus abandon their own languages. This process is bound up with wider changes, as people abandon traditional ways of life and adopt those of the dominant culture. The loss of language is both indicative of these wider changes and an integral part of what is being lost.

Thus it would seem to be problematic that the internet is similarly dominated by English language websites and that it is seemingly often accessed in English. In 2012, the digital marketing agency Greenlight asked people across the world how many languages they used and found that a majority (76 per cent) searched in more than one language. People from English-speaking countries such as the USA and UK tended to search only in one language, while 100 per cent of Belgians, Italians and Spanish participants claimed to search in multiple languages (and over 90 per cent of the Portuguese, French, Dutch and German respondents). Multilingualism might be expected in a country like Belgium with three official languages, the study suggests, but the implication for other countries which don't have multiple national languages was that people were using English alongside their native languages. In this case, the wealth of English-language material on the web appears to be encouraging people who wouldn't normally use English in their daily lives to search in English. (In comparison, there cannot be many offline activities that 100 per cent of Spaniards could be expected to do, even rarely, in English.) The multilingual searching uncovered by the survey was not, then, a sign of linguistic diversity but rather evidence for the global status of one language (English) and for the role that the internet – given its importance in providing information and connecting people – may be playing in furthering its global dominance. This is the issue that I want to explore in this chapter – to what extent does this occur to the detriment of other languages?

Task 4.1

Before reading on, consider how many languages you use online, how and why.

1. Do you ever conduct searches in another language (the question asked by Greenlight)? Regularly, sometimes, rarely or never? What would motivate you to choose one language or another?
2. What languages do you write in online, for example on a social network site or a blog?
3. In how many languages do you read online, on newspaper websites for example?
4. Where do you think you fit in the aforementioned survey?

Central to this question is the fate of minority languages online (and thus the implications for their offline existence), rather than, or as well as, 'big' or 'super' languages like Spanish or Italian.[1] The assumption made by Greenlight that Spanish and Italian users are switching to English to conduct online searches is a perfectly valid one given the benefits of searching in a language so well represented on the web, but it skates over the fact that both Spain and Italy are home to people speaking numerous regional languages (including, in Spain: Galician, Catalan/Valencian, Basque, Aranese, Astorian, Leonese; and in Italy: Albanian, Catalan, German, Greek, Slovene, Croatian, Firulian, Ladin, Occitan, Sardinian) as well as various languages spoken by immigrants. The online presence of minority languages is important, on the one hand, because the internet can be a useful tool for maintaining them and strengthening their national or global position;

on the other hand, the digital fate of minority languages is so important that their presence and vitality on the web is often inextricably bound up with – it both reflects and perpetuates – the offline status of the groups who speak them. This is a second question I want to explore – to what extent should we be concerned that the internet is perpetuating deeper social inequalities?

The term 'minority language' covers a wide range of contexts, uses and speakers, but can be defined generally as a language spoken by a minority group within a particular territory. Minority languages can therefore be official languages – Irish in Ireland; Catalan and Basque in Spain – and 'big' languages can become minority languages in particular contexts – French in Canada; Bengali in the UK; Turkish in Germany. When we talk of minority languages we usually mean those spoken by disadvantaged or peripheral groups, and those that are often (because of changes to the lifestyles of these groups) 'threatened' or 'endangered' by extinction. This is often termed 'language death' (e.g. Crystal, 2000) though more accurately it involves the death of the last speaker. A UN report in 2013 forecast the loss of half of the world's estimated 6,000 or so languages by the end of the twenty-first century (Izsák, 2013).

Since at least the start of the twentieth century, there have been various movements aimed at actively reviving and supporting minority languages through a mixture of educational measures and the use of mass media. After years of decline in the nineteenth century, for example, Welsh is now an official language in Wales alongside English, is learnt by children in Welsh schools, and is spoken on the Welsh television channel, SC4. Other languages are less fortunate: despite attempts to maintain it, Manchu in China is now spoken by only a handful of people, due to the influence and power of the dominant Han majority (Blanchard, 2010). The importance of maintaining minority languages is not primarily linguistic but concerns threats to culture and identity, and proponents (activist and linguistic alike) often talk of 'language rights': that is, the right of a person to speak 'their' language (e.g. Skutnabb-Kangas, 2008).

To paraphrase the title of an influential essay by Daniel Cunliffe, digital communication has brought new threats and new opportunities to those concerned with maintaining minority languages (Cunliffe, 2007). In Niall Mac Uidhilin's words:

> The challenge is that dominant languages are becoming even more pervasive as new forms of media and technology enter into our daily lives. The opportunity is that new technologies have lowered the barriers to producing and publishing many forms of content and have enabled many-to-many communication and collaboration.
>
> (Mac Uidhilin, 2013, p. 146)

In the rest of the chapter, I'll explore these two claims: that 'dominant languages' are becoming more pervasive through the internet; and that, in Crystal's words, 'an endangered language will progress if its speakers can make use of electronic technology' (Crystal, 2000, p. 141).

English and other dominant languages online

What we know about the distribution of languages online comes primarily from large marketing or political surveys, such as those carried out by the UN's International Telecommunication Union (ITU) and by Nielson Online. Internet World Stats (http://www.internetworldstats.com/) has collated the data from one such survey, thus giving an indication of the languages spoken by internet users over the first decade of the twenty-first century, culminating in 2011.

Some interesting points emerge from the figures. The first is that the internet is dominated by a few 'big' languages – 82 per cent of all users can speak one of the top ten languages listed, all of which are politically strong national (or regional) languages. The role of speakers of the 'rest of the world's languages' is marginal (17.8 per cent of total internet users) and, bearing in mind that this category could include up to 6,000 languages, the low figure here shows that individual minority languages make up a tiny proportion of internet users. The data also highlights the small proportion of speakers of other languages that are online (15 per cent of all speakers of other languages). In comparison, over a third of the big language speakers are online (36 per cent), as are nearly 80 per cent of Japanese and German speakers.

Another observation concerns the shifting fortunes of these big languages. Although English-speaking internet users in 2011 outranked even Chinese (the language with the most 'native' speakers), the number of internet users that speak English is not increasing as quickly as those that speak some other languages, notably Arabic, Russian and Chinese. Other languages which appear to be slowing in growth are Korean, Japanese and German. The reasons for this lie in population size and inequalities in wealth and online development. Korea, Japan and Germany are all technologically advanced countries with small populations which began by dominating the internet before reaching market saturation and being overtaken by languages with more speakers (Japanese, German and Korean are the only languages represented in the data for which over half the population have internet access). The implication for English is that, despite its initial domination, other languages are catching up. But the implications for linguistic diversity online remain pessimistic – if Chinese overtakes English in the near future (or if it already has), this does not increase the number of languages online, but merely represents the replacement of one super language with another.

If we compare internet users to website content, the picture becomes more complex. While English users make up nearly 27 per cent of internet users, the percentage of web content in English is much higher (57 per cent). In contrast, the amount of web content in Chinese is much lower than the proportion of Chinese-speaking internet users would suggest (only 5 per cent); and the number of 'other' languages on the web is also lower than the proportion of their speakers (10 per cent). This suggests firstly that speakers of other languages are likely to be accessing English language websites; and, secondly, that in terms of web content (if not users), English will remain a dominant presence online for some time.

The dominance of English online can be put down to three main factors. One is the global status of English as an international lingua franca, and the fact that it now plays a role, official or unofficial, in most countries – of the 1,302,275,670 population estimate for English, probably no more than 500 million speak English as a first language (although such figures are hard to pinpoint) (Crystal 2012, p. 153). I now explore the other two factors: the history of internet technology, and the political and economic status of the various countries involved.

Technological factors affecting language choice online

> What can and what cannot be expressed when it comes to electronic communication is, in the end, determined by the underlying and in many respects invisible infrastructure of standards that enables (and, at the same time, constrains and restricts) such communication.
> (Pargman and Palme, 2009, p. 181)

The internet and later the world wide web were designed by North American and British engineers and scientists who had laudable goals of facilitating global communication but somewhat limited notions as to which languages people would want to communicate in. The standard initially used on the internet was the ASCII character set, which was based on the English language and, thus, in some people's eyes, a form of typographical imperialism (Pargman and Palme, 2009). The use of ASCII had different implications for those using languages other than English online, depending on which language – and which script – they wished to use. As Paolillo (2007, p. 413) points out, small languages such as Indonesian, Yoruba and Guarani which used the Roman script were able to 'piggy-back' on the Anglo-centric approach and gain an early presence on the internet. In some cases, languages that use unsupported scripts are also commonly written in other, encoded scripts, meaning that they can be used online (The Unicode Consortium, 2013). However, for speakers of languages written in the Roman script, it was not always possible to access all the language's characters online (e.g. Spanish ñ and Swedish ö). Neither was it possible to write other languages – Chinese, Greek, Arabic – in their traditional scripts. One solution for speakers of these languages was to switch to English – the language that many were already using to communicate and trade internationally. It is unlikely that the use of English online (and elsewhere) will pose a serious threat to these 'big' languages (in fact, it is probably more likely that languages like Mandarin Chinese or Arabic will threaten other minority languages in the same region) but it is possible that the dominance of English will restrict the domains in which these other languages are used. The fact that scripts such as Arabic and Chinese were originally unavailable also encouraged internet users to develop a Romanised version of their language (Danet and Herring, 2007, pp. 9–11) – that is, to write the language using Latin characters based on phonological or visual similarity to the sounds of the language.

> 9ba7 el-'7air Mona. Asfa ma raddet 3aleech ams, kent nayma. Tabeen shay?
> [*Good morning Mona. Sorry I didn't answer your call yesterday, I was sleeping. Do you want anything?*]
>
> (Haggan, 2007, p. 440)

The example shows how Arabic numbers are used for sounds not represented by Roman letters in the English language (see Chapter 12 for further discussion of this practice of creative Romanisation). Such practices are negatively perceived by people concerned about the linguistic purity of Arabic (Al-Issa and Dahan, 2011), particularly as Romanisation has continued despite the more recent adoption of Unicode, a standard for encoding text which potentially allows for the use of all languages online.

Unicode has so far resulted in the encoding of around one hundred languages, including all the 'big' languages and an increasing number of smaller languages (Anderson 2005, p. 27 explains that languages were chosen for inclusion based on the number of speakers). Although, as documented by the Script Encoding Initiative (2012) at the University of California, Berkeley, some scripts still wait to be encoded (including Kpelle, Loma and Newar), those who hope all languages will soon be represented online have cause for optimism.

Political and economic factors

As mentioned above, the distribution of dominant and minority languages online is important because it both reflects and potentially perpetuates global inequities. Cunliffe (2007, p. 134) points out, 'As digital exclusion tends to follow existing patterns of social exclusion, where minority language communities are already socially excluded, they are also likely to be digitally excluded'. The digital age is often said to be cleaved in two by the digital divide, a term that presupposes 'a division between nations or communities who have access to communication technology and those who don't' (Thurlow et al., 2004, p. 84). On the one side stand the 'information haves' or the 'information rich', and, on the other, the 'information have nots' or the 'information poor'. In reality, of course, the divide is rather a cline, from those with multiple devices and fast, strong internet connections at home to those who rely on access to PCs in libraries or internet cafes, or on cheap mobile devices, now a mainstay in the global south (Ling and Horst, 2011). Internet use tends to be higher in developed nations (in Asia, Europe and North America) and lower in developing countries (in Oceania, the Middle East and Africa) (Internet World Stats, 2013). But the digital divide also cuts through nations along economic and class lines. The divide is no longer chiefly perpetuated by a lack of infrastructure in a particular region but by the varying abilities of local communities to access it (Norton et al., 2013).

The digital divide does not simply reflect, but also perpetuates, existing inequalities. Firstly, in a world where services, information and connections are increasingly to be found online, not having access to the internet is becoming a huge disadvantage. Bonny Norton and colleagues, for example, describe a programme for teaching young Ugandan women from rural communities how to access information about sexual health, which not only enables them to make informed choices but also empowers them to reconstruct themselves as 'knowledgeable people', as one participant put it (Norton et al., 2013). Secondly, if over a billion internet users speak English, then more than three-quarters of them do not. As Crystal (2012, p. 155) points out, we need not 'travel far into the hinterland of a country – away from the tourist spots, airports, hotels, and restaurants – to encounter this reality'. And, finally, a presence on the internet is likely to raise the profile and prestige of a minority language (Buszard-Welcher, 2001), encouraging as well as enabling its community to use it.

Opportunities for minority languages online

The likelihood that speakers of minority languages may not always have internet access or digital literacy skills qualifies any discussion of using the internet as a way to promote minority languages: as Cunliffe (2007, p. 133) says, 'Any discussion of Internet media, in terms of production or consumption, must be grounded in the realities of access and use'. Despite this caveat, studies suggest that language minority communities are effectively using social media to maintain their languages (e.g. Dołowy-Rybińska, 2013 on Kashubian; McClure,

2001 on Assyrian; Villa, 2005 on Navajo; Wagner, 2013 on Luxembourgish; Warschauer, 1998 on Hawaiian).

The particular affordances of digital media may change the way in which minority languages are supported. Typically, as Michael Cormack points out, language maintenance meant 'top-down activity – language planners trying to encourage the language or particular versions of it' (Cormack, no date given, p. 1). However, unlike traditional media campaigns involving public broadcasting and the press, anyone with digital access can establish a web presence without incurring costs and without mediation, approval or monitoring from an official body; and anyone with an internet connection can not only access the material but help produce it. As Cunliffe (2007, p. 137) puts it:

> the real potential of the Internet lies not in the replication of traditional media and the formation of passive communities of minority language media consumers, but in the formation of active communities of collaborative language producers.

As Dołowy-Rybińska (2013) points out in relation to Kashubian in Poland, young people were not really using the language, particularly in its written form, until the internet provided a space for informal writing. Whilst in the early days of the internet, its text-based nature may have been a problem for languages with no written form or limited literacy practices, the availability of media-sharing sites such as YouTube now allows for oral representations (e.g. Cunliffe and ap Dyfrig, 2013).

The internet also allows for communication between same-language speakers who may be geographically dispersed, and for the development of the notion of a 'networked community' in relation to minority language groups (see Chapter 21). Thus the internet can bring together (physically and conceptually):

> native speakers living within a territory that is predominantly minority language speaking, native speakers living outside that territory but still using the language regularly, irregular users of the language, fluent non-native speakers living within the territory, fluent non-native speakers living outside the territory, learners within the core language territory and learners living outwith the territory (a category with potentially a global range).
>
> (Cormack, 2013, p. 258)

At the same time, the internet raises a number of challenges yet to be resolved. In some contexts, Cormack points out, information posted online may not seem as credible as that published or broadcast in a top-down fashion. One distinctive feature of the internet is that, because content is not policed or planned, challenges arise for linguistic standards of accuracy and purity, which have historically been important in minority language maintenance. This may also have implications for the perceived authenticity of online postings, given that there is no central authority; as Cunliffe (2007, p. 141) points out, giving people their own voice will inevitably lead at times to competing ones. A more practical problem is that 'establishing a presence on the Internet does not guarantee that it will attract users' (p. 136). Cunliffe and ap Dyfrig (2013), for example, reveal the difficulties involved in relying on users' tags, titles and descriptions when searching for Welsh language videos on YouTube, and they conclude 'While there is undoubtedly a quantity of Welsh language material on YouTube, it is difficult to argue … that there is a coherent Welsh language media space' (p. 142).

As Cormack suggests, the internet may challenge us to radically rethink what minority language maintenance means: 'The question is not "How can we use social media for language planning" but rather, "How can language use be encouraged in an era in which language planning is obsolete?"' One change may be that the onus to maintain minority languages now falls on the users rather than the language planners:

> Minority cultures and languages should not be viewed simply as victims of the Internet or as passive recipients of Internet technology, services and content. Instead it should be recognised that they have the potential to be active shapers of this technology, able to create their own tools, adapt existing tools to the local needs and to create culturally authentic, indigenous Internet media.
>
> (Cunliffe, 2007, p. 147)

Conclusion

English had a head start in terms of gaining a foothold on the internet due to the technology on which the internet was built, but ultimately it is its status as a global lingua franca and ongoing political and economic inequities that sustain its online dominance. At the same time, the internet is simultaneously (as we have seen) a huge opportunity for those seeking to maintain and revive minority languages. Furthermore, the broad claim that English dominates the internet brushes over the more complex picture of language use that has emerged in this chapter.

The surveys we looked at towards the start of this chapter rest on the assumption that the internet – be it in the form of internet users or website content – can be categorised into one distinct language or another. But we've also seen that 'English speaker' more often than not refers to second- or third-language English speakers, who can be assumed to use English alongside other languages (as in the Greenlight survey). Minority language speakers would not typically be expected to use only – or even primarily – their minority language online, but English or another regionally or locally dominant language. This has implications for what it means to be a 'speaker' of a language when it comes to internet use – for example, if you acquired Finnish as your first language but learnt English at school and now invariably use English online, how would you categorise yourself? And how about if you switched equally between Finnish and English online? Internet surveys tend to rely on website material (rather than email or online chat) and assume that they will be written in one language which can then be 'counted'. When we look away from these relatively static, formal sites and towards real-time, informal chat-based spaces – such as Skype chat and instant messaging – we find users drawing on various resources, from various 'languages', that defy straightforward categorisation.

In Section B, Chapter 12, I look more closely at the realities of language use online, and in particular the practices of code-switching – moving back and forth between languages – that has been seen to characterise much online interaction. And in Section C, Chapter 18, I explore recent developments in the theorisation of multilingual practices and repertoires.

Note

1 I follow practice elsewhere in using the term 'big language', but do not mean to imply any linguistic superiority by the term. Instead, big languages are defined in social and political terms, as languages with large populations and relative political and economic security.

II

Social issues and social media

5 From anonymity to self-promotion

Are we ever ourselves on social media?

Introduction: two sides of the online coin

<Thunder> sssssssssss *passes joint to kang* ...
<Kang> thanx dude *puff* *hold* > :-)
<Thunder> kang exhale ... you will die :-)
<Kang> *exhale*
<Kang> ;)
<Kang> :|
<Kang> :|
<Kang> :\
<Thunder> heheheh
<Thunder> heheheheh
<Thunder> that was great
<Thunder> :-Q :| :| :\ sssss :)

(Internet Relay Chat data, from Danet et al., 1997)

The participants in the Internet Relay Chat (IRC) chatroom are simulating a party, and in particular the smoking of a joint. Their performance highlights two seemingly contradictory concerns about individual identity in the age of social media. On the one hand, the simulation underscores the perceived triviality of much internet interaction, and the apparent focus on presenting oneself as sociable, happy-go-lucky, and popular. Kang and Thunder might be said to be showing off in this public forum, competing with each other to produce yet more complex and creative deployments of graphic symbols. Thunder simulates the exhaling of smoke through repetition of the letter {lthan}s{gthan} , while Kang represents the actions of holding and exhaling through a series of smileys, and Thunder responds with his own, more elaborate performance of someone with a cigarette in his mouth, who holds and exhales in a line of {lthan}ssss{gthan} and then smiles: :-Q :| :| :\ sssss :). Through their performances, Kang and Thunder create the illusion of a relaxed, informal situation, and they construct themselves as playful, daring party-goers. On the other hand, the point is, of course, that they may in the offline world not be any of these things. 'Kang' and 'Thunder' are both 'nicks' (nicknames), and it is impossible for other participants to know how old they are, where they are from, or whether they are male or female. The potential for this kind of anonymity worries many people, who see it as facilitating a range of dangerous activities from terrorism to paedophilia. So, we have two almost contradictory concerns: those involving the effect of anonymity on social behaviour; and those centring on the use of the internet for egocentric self-promotion. However, both relate to a similar concern: that people are not really themselves on social media. In this chapter, I explore each in turn.

Online anonymity

Anonymity can be ensured online in two main ways: firstly, in that people can use usernames or nicks rather than their actual names; and, secondly, that they reveal fewer of the social cues conveyed through handwriting, accent or appearance (Herring, 1993). However, the *perception* of anonymity afforded by the physical distance between interlocutors may be just as important in providing participants with a sense of safety and liberation, even where it is possible to trace the identity of an online participant (Herring, 2002; and see Chapter 7).

Like any possibilities afforded by the internet, online anonymity is not a problem *per se*: the problem lies in how people choose to take advantage of it and how these choices are perceived by others. In the early 1990s, the internet was celebrated as a liberating place where people were free to discard and adopt identities at will, a perspective illustrated by the now famous *New Yorker* cartoon of 1993 which claimed 'On the internet, nobody knows you're a dog' (1993). The wearing of online 'masks' was, and continues to be, seen as contributing to the playful, carefree atmosphere of many internet domains (Bechar-Israeli, 1995; Danet et al., 1997; Deumert, 2014). Deumert (2014), for example, describes how South African teenagers who are not involved with local gangs adopt gangster-related nicks online, mainly for fun, but also to transgress norms and reflect a local identity. In the 1990s, it was also widely assumed that anonymity would contribute to the democratising effect of the internet, in that gender, class, race and other social differences would be left behind and participants would communicate on an equal footing (Graddol and Swann, 1989). People would be free to say what they liked, and would be judged only by the content of their posts. As Sherry Turkle wrote:

> You don't have to worry about the slot other people put you in as much. They don't look at your body and make assumptions. They don't hear your accent and make assumptions. All they see are your words.
>
> (Turkle, 1995, p. 184)

The initial optimism regarding online democracy and equality has faded somewhat (e.g. Schuler, 2003), partly because of changes in how we use the internet. In the 1990s, the internet was associated with anonymous chat rooms in which offline strangers came together around common interests. Ten or fifteen years later, the internet has become synonymous with social media, epitomised by social network sites such as Facebook which work on the basis of existing relationships – people tend to connect with people with whom they have some kind of offline relationship (boyd and Ellison, 2008) and they tend to use them in part to document (and organise) events and activities in their 'offline' lives. These changes are illustrated in spoofs of the *New Yorker* cartoon, in which dogs sit in front of computer screens displaying messages such as 'On Facebook, 273 people know I'm a dog. The rest can only see my limited profile' (Cottingham, 2007). Increasingly then, self-presentation online is less about creating new identities and more about playing with and foregrounding particular aspects of an 'authentic' offline identity – a point I explore in relation to applied linguistics research in Chapter 13.

The potential to be anonymous online continues, however, to be beneficial for those who have sinister reasons to hide their activities or facets of their identity: stalkers, groomers of young children, cyberbullies and others who engage in online harassment. Three types of online activity which involve an interesting form of identity play are spamming (sending a message indiscriminately to a large number of users usually to sell something), phishing (purporting to be a message from a legitimate user or corporation to trick users into clicking on links which compromise their accounts or to obtain sensitive personal details), and other online scams designed to elicit money from users. These practices were not born with the internet – letters from Spanish prisoners purportedly imprisoned during the country's civil wars were sent to unsuspecting Britons throughout the nineteenth century, for example, and 'only differ [from internet scams] in their method of delivery' (Whitaker, 2013). However, digital communications have undoubtedly raised them to a new level in terms of scale and scope. Back in 2009, for example, Microsoft revealed that more than 97 per cent of all emails were spam (Waters, 2009); while Twitter revealed that 10 million of its 200 million users could be spammers, robots or other 'bogus' users (Spangler, 2013).

A huge amount of research in the social and computational sciences – too much to detail here – has sought to identify phishers, spammers and scammers, using content clues (Bergholz et al., 2010), and language (Schaffer, 2012) among other methods in a bid to improve filtering and detection rates. Much of the research into Twitter spam focuses on the behavioural patterns and network connections of the spamming accounts (e.g. Ramachandran et al., 2007). On Twitter, spammers do not target users (as email spammers do) but instead 'latch on to' a trending topic (Yardi et al., 2010). Yardi et al. (2010) captured nearly 20,000 tweets containing the hashtag #robotpickuplines, and estimated that spammers constituted 14 per cent of the tweets. They found that spam tweets were more likely to contain multiple hashtags and spammers to have three times as many friends or followers as legitimate users. As they point out, however, many legitimate users will also exhibit these characteristics and the chance of accurately targeting spammers is low: the number of likely false positives is too high.

Unlike most spam and phishing, scammers often purport to be ordinary users who need money, for reasons ranging from setting up a money-making scheme to paying medical bills or getting home after being mugged in a foreign country. Some users respond by engaging with scammers in a practice known as scambaiting. The aim is to engage the scammer for as long as possible in order to waste their time and resources, and often to get as much information as possible from them to pass on to the authorities. Scambaiters may ask scammers to complete elaborate tasks (one scammer travelled 3,000 miles across Africa to pick up a non-existent $500,000) or they may pose as experienced scammers and give 'newbies' dubious advice (Cheng, 2009). According to psychology professor Daniel Simons (in interview with On the Media, 2012), this may be the most effective way to tackle scamming: in a paper entitled 'Why do Nigerian scammers say they are from Nigeria?', Cormac Herley from Microsoft Research argues that scammers' unlikely tales of African princes deliberately aim to stop less gullible users (who are unlikely to actually send money) from replying and to target only the most gullible; that is, those likely to eventually pay. In other words, scammers too want to weed out false positives (Herley, 2012). Websites such as 419 Eater (www.419eater. com) list amusing and provocative stories detailing scambaiters' attempts and successes.

While activities such as spamming and phishing have received near-universal condemnation, the exploitation of online anonymity by oppressed users may be welcomed by those interested in democracy and freedom of speech. Such users include gay or lesbian people in countries where homosexuality is banned, for example; and political dissidents, campaign groups and activists who can communicate and organise online without the repercussions of doing so openly. In her book, *Consent of the Networked* (2012), the journalist and internet policy specialist Rebecca McKinnon describes the potential of the internet to empower the oppressed and those seeking to change the status quo in countries such as China, Iran and Turkey. Online anonymity is not, in these cases, in the interests of the relevant authorities: the Turkish government, for example, moved to prevent 'fake accounts' on social network sites following protests in Gezi Park in 2013: 'If someone is opening up an account, everybody should know the person who opened the account' said Deputy Prime Minister Bekir Bozdağ (*Hürriyet Daily News*, 2013).

Anonymity does not inevitably lead to dangerous, immoral or illegal acts, but can also lead to the protection of those seeking to combat injustices and liberate those who are disempowered offline. This is not, however, to ignore the fact that the potential to hide or distort who you are remains a cause for concern.

The narcissistic self

By 2013, the art of the selfie – taking a photo of yourself to share online – was so deeply entrenched in internet culture that the term became the *Oxford English Dictionary*'s 'word of the year'. You'll probably recognise the practice, even if you don't know the term – the outstretched hand, the odd angle, the pout – and you may have heard some of the hype surrounding celebrity selfies (from Obama's daughters snapping a group selfie at their father's swearing in to model Kelly Brook breaking her own ban to stop herself obsessively taking selfies). Selfies can be uploaded onto Facebook or photo-sharing sites such as Flickr, Tumblr and Instagram (a search for #selfie on Instagram retrieves many millions of photos). The rise of the selfie illustrates a number of current concerns about how we present ourselves online, including our self-obsession and our ability to manage how we appear to others. In the rest of this chapter, I explore these issues in relation to the selfie and other relevant forms of digital communication: webcam and the status update.

Firstly and most evidently, selfies illustrate the apparent self-absorption of internet users who are obsessed with creating – and managing – their own image. What could be more narcissistic than repeatedly taking photos of oneself and posting them online? Of course, there is also recognition in the media that selfies may not always be so much about narcissism as insecurity. As one Instagram user was reported in the press as saying, 'there's a real feel-good attitude towards selfies, and as vain as it may be, you know that if you're not feeling great, there's someone who will "like" your photo and tell you you're pretty' (Coulthard, 2013). Posting a selfie is in this sense not so much showing off as seeking reassurance from one's online network.

In their study of the use of webcam – online communication via a video camera, such as that provided by Skype – on the Caribbean island of Trinidad, anthropologists Daniel Miller and Jolynna Sinanan report an unpredicted yet unsurprising outcome – the webcam users they observed tended to spend more time looking at the image of themselves than they did looking at their interlocutors (Miller and Sinanan, 2014). As the researchers explain, webcam offers users the first opportunity to see themselves as others see them in interaction, rather than frozen in a photo or posing in front of a mirror. Like the mirror and photography, then, webcam may be having an impact on how we see ourselves (and how we perceive others to be seeing us) and thus on our sense of self. But Miller and Sinanan (2014) do not put this down to narcissism among the islanders, in part because of the way in which Trinidadians value physical appearance. In the west, one's appearance is not seen to reflect one's true identity; in Trinidad, in contrast, appearance is thought to be a direct indication of one's true self – how you choose to decorate or compose yourself comes from within and shows the world how you want others to see you (Miller and Sinanan, 2014). The use of webcam is seen not as increasing self-egotism, but in facilitating a project that people are anyway engaged in – that of presenting themselves as coherent reflections of who they think they are. This is not to say that Trinidadians are necessarily more likely to look at themselves when Skyping; rather, their argument highlights the fact that any apparent self-obsession is likely to be more interpersonally complex than it might at first appear.

Nonetheless, a second concern about the selfie relates to the kind of self-image that is usually put across. Key to the process of disseminating a selfie is the concept of image management – that is, people's ability to manage their image or to shape how they come across. The photos may look as though they've been taken in a casual, ad hoc manner but they are generally posed and often carefully managed, and those that appear online are undoubtedly carefully selected. Writing in the British newspaper the *Guardian* in early 2013, self-professed selfie practitioner Bim Adewunmi suggests 'Look at enough and you start to realise the key to a good selfie – nonchalance. Whether you're showing off or looking less-than-"perfect", you want to look like it doesn't matter' (Adewunmi, 2013). A study by Westfield Carindale shopping mall which surveyed 1,000 Australian women aged between 18 and 35 found that most took photos of themselves on holiday (32 per cent) or at social events (21 per cent). As one participant pointed out, 'You're not going to be taking an image of yourself in tracky dacks [a tracksuit], watching TV, like I am seven nights a week'.

Similar observations have been made of the Facebook status update which tends to be delivered in an upbeat, light-hearted way. This is what Baron (2008) refers to as the 'my best day' approach to self-presentation. Deumert (2014) relates this to the adoption of 'a particular Facebook persona' or mask, which her students describe in terms such as 'funny', 'joyful', 'happy go lucky' (Van Blerk, 2008). Teenagers in a study by McLaughlin and Vitak (2011) in the US felt there were unwritten rules or social norms that status updates on

Facebook should not be used to express grievances. One participant, Lana, said: 'Some people talk way too much about their feelings and I'm like "you should probably keep that private. I don't need to know every detail about what's going on in your life"' (p. 308); that is, the messy, sometimes uncomfortable or painful details that come out in a face-to-face conversation. When one of my friends reported his failure in a job interview on Facebook, we sympathised but winced slightly – did he have to tell everyone?

One effect of this implicit social norm is that we're presented with a skewed impression of other people's sunny, carefree lives. Another of McLaughlin and Vitak's (2011) teenage participants, Lindsay, said:

> I think there's probably a disproportionate amount of me, of pictures of me at parties [on Facebook] … you know people aren't gonna take pictures if you're just hanging out and even though that's much more my speed … if someone was only to look at my Facebook profile to get an impression of me, they would think that I go out way more than I do.
>
> (McLaughlin and Vitak, 2011, p. 306)

The fact that photos posted on sites like Facebook might authenticate a 'false view' of an individual can have important consequences. For example, a 2012 survey by the British charity Anxiety UK found that over half of the 298 Brits they interviewed felt social network sites influenced their behaviour in a detrimental way, in part because they would negatively compare themselves to others. The effect on young people may be similar to that produced by pictures of celebrities and models in glossy teen magazines, except that the unobtainable lifestyle being displayed is that of a peer.

There have been some moves to counteract the perceived obsession with perfection online, prompted by recognition of the potential harm such images can have on viewers. One of these is the 'Bad Picture Monday' selfie, a project begun in 2011 by poet Sonya Renee and which, along with other sites such as PrettyGirlsUglyFaces[1] on Reddit (a news and entertainment website), can be seen as something of a movement. Renee was motivated to start the project by her realisation that although she campaigned for women to accept their bodies, she still carefully monitored her own selfies (Mapes, 2013). Whilst one may challenge the extent to which 'ugly photos' in fact depict people as truly ugly (they are generally posted by people not otherwise considered ugly, often shown next to a more attractive pose, and are usually obviously unflattering photos), the ugly selfie 'sort of deconstructs our obsessive relationship with showing only our perfect selves', as blogger Joanna Schroeder (2013) put it.

Of course, it's important to note that elements of the 'selfie' didn't originate with photo-sharing sites such as Flickr or Tumblr, or even with the advent of the internet. People have always taken shots of themselves (the first cameras with self-timers being available as early as the 1880s) and shown them to others (there was, for example, a craze for exchanging self-portraits in the form of photograph cards, or 'cartes de visite' as they were known, in late-nineteenth-century Europe and America). As with the other practices and performances described in this book, digital technology facilitates both the production and the dissemination of people's self-portraits. Never has it been easier for so many people to play with their identity and to do so in front of so large an audience.

In Section B, Chapter 13, I look more closely at the role language plays in such identity performances and what applied linguistics research can tell us about self-presentation in the twenty-first century. In Section C, Chapter 20, I look at the way in which identity has been theorised in applied linguistics research.

Note

1   http://www.reddit.com/r/PrettyGirlsUglyFaces/

6 What are the implications of social media for privacy?

Introduction

In an interview at the Crunchies awards in 2010, Facebook founder and CEO Mark Zuckerberg described how he had watched people's willingness to share information online develop:

> people have really gotten comfortable, not only sharing more information and different kinds but more openly and with more people. ... that social norm is just something that's evolved ... our role in the system [is] to constantly be innovating and updating ... to reflect what the current social norms are.
>
> (Zuckerberg, 2010)

Within this short statement, Zuckerberg made two controversial claims about privacy. The first is that social norms regarding openness and sharing have changed throughout the early years of the twenty-first century (since he invented what was to become Facebook in his Harvard dorm in the early 2000s). This claim chimes to some extent with popular opinion on the subject of privacy online, as expressed at least in the media, but while Zuckerberg describes current social norms in neutral terms (new perceptions of privacy are 'just something that's evolved'), the focus in the press is rather on the damaging implications of our apparent willingness to share 'more openly and with more people', as Zuckerberg puts it. The concern is that people – and particularly young people – are no longer able to make reasoned decisions about what can be made public and what should be kept private, and that this exposes them to potential harm (ranging from social embarrassment to dismissal at work and even criminal charges). Zuckerberg's second claim appears to be that social network sites (SNSs) like Facebook have played no part in those changes, but are instead following wider social developments. This, again, is not exactly how the public view it. Facebook's commitment to open sharing is sometimes seen rather as a self-serving smokescreen for their own ambitions regarding advertising revenue and their position as a major global SNS, with little consideration for the potential harm facing their users.

In this chapter, I explore these concerns and evaluate them in light of questions raised by internet researchers: what does privacy really mean in a digitally networked age? How can privacy concerns be balanced with the social benefits of being connected? What strategies do people have for ensuring privacy and protecting their identity? These are areas for which, as we shall explore in Chapter 14, applied linguistics has much to offer.

Concerns about privacy online and our struggle to manage it

It is misleading to assume that a clear boundary ever existed offline between what is public and what is private (think of the village gossip, for example). However, the novelty of sharing practices on social media has created a general perception that a boundary is being eroded. Trying to find the balance between public and private is difficult on sites like Facebook, where on the one hand you are invited to share and in doing so maintain connections with people from your life; but on the other, you are aware that your posts may persist online indefinitely and be accessed by people to whom you did not intend to disclose. This is what social researchers Nicole B. Ellison and colleagues at Michigan State University call the balance between gaining 'social capital' – the resources or benefits derived from one's relationships with other people – and maintaining privacy (e.g. Ellison et al., 2011). A prolific status updater and friend of mine highlighted this tension when she admitted that she felt torn posting so much about her baby; she did so because he was a big part of her life and it would seem odd not to mention him; at the same time, she did not want to attract criticism from Friends for putting her baby on public display.

The problem is not only a question of revealing information about ourselves. As social researcher danah boyd says, 'Our data – and with it, our privacy – are increasingly networked. What we share about ourselves tells heaps about other people' (boyd, 2012, p. 348). In other words, it is no longer possible to view privacy as an individual matter. In McLaughlin and Vitak's (2011) study of American teenagers, they found that not posting inappropriate photos of their friends was an implicit norm that guided behaviour on Facebook, violations of which received condemnation. One teenager, Lana, said:

One of my friends tagged a picture of another friend … and she was hammered and her skirt was up and her underwear was showing in a not-very-flattering way at all, and she tagged her. I'd be pissed if someone tagged a picture like that of me.

(McLaughlin and Vitak, 2011, p. 308)

In most cases, however, McLaughlin and Vitak noted 'a norm of consideration or privacy among friends' (p. 307), with another teenager, John, reporting 'My friends are considerate of me and I'm considerate of them, so I haven't had any trouble with [Friends posting inappropriate content to my page]' (p. 308).

Task 6.1

Reflect on your attitudes and the experiences you've had regarding your own privacy on social network or other sites, as well as that of your friends. Take notes on the following questions.

1. What kinds of personal information do you post, and what if anything do you hope to gain from it?
2. What, if anything, would you not post about on a social network site, and why?
3. Where do you draw the line between what is private and what can be shared publicly? Can you think of any occasions when somebody has overstepped the line you draw?

Although, as mentioned above, it is misleading to assume that a clear boundary has ever existed between what is public and what is private, perceptions of our eroded ability to maintain a line between what is private and what is public are undoubtedly reinforced by media coverage of the issue, and in particular by extreme cases where, for example, jobs are lost because of social media postings. A Google search using the term 'fired over social media posting' on 12 August 2013 brought up the following cases (the list goes on):

- Employee fired after posting pay cheque on Instagram (New York, reported on www.smartcompany.com.au, 8 August 2013).
- Nursing home workers fired over inappropriate photo (Des Moines, Iowa, reported by *USA Today*, 3 August 2013).
- TV reporter fired over blog 'didn't think it would come to this' (Alabama, reported by Today.com, 30 July 2013).

The stories suggest that users can misunderstand the potentially public reach of their online postings, a suggestion that is supported by social research (e.g. Debatin et al., 2009). In many of these and other cases, what the fired employee has posted may be perfectly acceptable in the eyes of friends and family, or indeed people who do not know the employee, but is interpreted differently when read in a work or professional context. The problem is twofold: firstly, on social network sites, a user's audience can often be fairly large and diverse and what is intended for a particular individual or group can in fact be heard by everyone and interpreted in various ways in the context of different news feeds. This is what danah boyd and colleagues describe as 'context collapse' or 'social convergence' – the bringing together of different audiences into one space (e.g. boyd and Marwick, 2011). Secondly, online postings can easily move from one online context to another, through direct copying, remixing and quotation. The replicability and persistence of online postings, to use boyd's terms (see Introduction), makes it difficult for a user to predict or control who will see a post, a photo or a video, when, and how they will interpret it.

Another problem concerns differing perceptions as to whether social media should for legal purposes be considered private or public. This has emerged most strikingly in cases involving Twitter, where someone's apparent use of the microblogging site as a private space conflicts with the authorities' perception that Twitter is public. In January 2010, British man Paul Chambers set in motion what has come to be known as the 'Twitter joke trial' when, annoyed that snow might thwart his flying plans, he posted a tweet reading 'Crap! Robin Hood airport is closed. You've got a week and a bit to get your shit together otherwise I'm blowing the airport sky high!!'. Two and a half years later Chambers was finally cleared of intention to menace, with the judge suggesting it should never have come to court and most journalists scathing of the whole process. However, what the trial did achieve – at the cost of over two years of Chambers' life – was to make it clear that Twitter is to be considered a public space where private jokes can have serious consequences. Subsequent cases in the UK of a potentially defamatory or malicious nature suggest that its privacy status is still being negotiated and contested.

It seems that people are increasingly aware that what they write may be taken out of context and/or accessed in an unintended context, and are trying to find new ways to manage their online information. The difficulties this can involve are illustrated by the following internet meme. In 2012, Facebook users began posting privacy notices on the site in response to the public flotation of the company which it was felt would further compromise users' privacy. The variant that reached me read as follows:

> In response to the new Facebook guidelines I hereby declare that my copyright is attached to all of my personal details, illustrations, graphics, comics, paintings, photos and videos, etc. (as a result of

the Berner Convention). For commercial use of the above my written consent is needed at all times!

The post went viral. However, what these users presumably did not realise was its lack of any legal status – posting a disclaimer through a status update did not change their agreement to abide by Facebook's Terms of Service. However, the viral message serves to highlight the tension regarding online privacy – on the one hand, that privacy is a concern for many people and that social media companies such as Facebook are often seen as untrustworthy in that regard; but, on the other, that many people have only a basic understanding of the law and of these companies' privacy policies, and about what they can do to preserve their privacy. As Chester Wisnieski of Sophos (the online security services developer and vendor) pointed out in response to the notice, 'taking control of your identity is not as simple as making a declaration on your Facebook wall' (Wisnieski, 2012). Any perceived privacy violations that occur can be attributed to the fact that it is not possible, as boyd (2012) points out, to manage absolute control over our data.

Google: good or evil?

An advertiser's dream ...

Facebook is not the only online corporation facing problems with how they manage privacy issues. Google's practices have also been criticised in this regard.

Most of these concerns surround the amount of data that search engines such as Google are seen to amass about individuals using their services – or, to put it another way, the amount of information that users are seen as giving away in return for the services provided. Writer and internet activist Cory Doctorow describes this as 'the worst deal ever' (Doctorow, 2012). Individuals go along with it, he argues, in part because of our inability to weigh up possible future aggregated costs against immediate individual benefits – that is, to really appreciate the impact that one search can have when added to thousands of others and used as data.

Google's ambitions to go beyond being a search engine have added to the concerns. As of 2013, when using Google's web browser, Google Chrome, signing in using a Google username and password allows Google to 'synch' your services. It also enables Google to synch its privacy policies, so if you were (unwittingly or otherwise) signed into just one service, this gave Google access to use data accrued from across your Google services. Alarm surfaced over the fact that your passwords can be retrieved by anyone using your username in Chrome (if, for example, you left your computer on with Chrome running), and over Google's alleged claim that users of its email service should not expect privacy in the first place.

The internet abounds with suggestions of ways to get around Google's attempts to keep track of your searches across its services, ranging from 'Don't use Google' to 'Don't log in to your search engine', 'Block cookies from your search engine' and 'Don't Google Yourself' (e.g. Eckersley et al., 2006; McCarthy, 2012). While it's tempting to assume that the worst outcome will be more ads targeted at what Google thinks you want to buy, law professor and online privacy expert Daniel J. Solove argues that data collection is never innocuous (Solove, 2013).

… or a cure for flu?

There are arguments to counteract the negative portrayal of Google's data collection. On the one hand, it could be argued that targeted searches are necessary to filter the vast amount of information available on the web – if I search for 'Birmingham' I probably do mean the city in the UK (where I live), rather than in Alabama, the United States.

On the other hand, the web tool Google Trends compiles anonymised data from 100 billion searches every month and allows researchers to predict flu epidemics – 'wherever people are Googling "flu symptoms", an outbreak is imminent' (Grossman, 2013) – and, in one case, to show that although child abuse cases in the US reported to the authorities had gone down, searches for 'My dad hit me' or 'child abuse signs' had gone up (Stephens-Davidowitz, 2013).

We might conclude that the ends either justify (in the case of child abuse research) or condemn (in the case of making money from advertising) the means.

Managing your privacy

Users' attempts to manage privacy challenge the notion that privacy involves a clear dichotomy between what is private and what is public. For example, when Facebook introduced the News Feed in 2006 – a page which brought together and displayed to a user their Friends' recent activity – there was a torrent of complaints about the effect of this on their privacy (boyd, 2008). The paradox was that all the information collected and shown in users' News Feeds was available to them anyway – the feed simply pushed it to them rather than requiring them to pull (boyd, 2008). As boyd explains, the reaction reflected earlier opposition to the introduction of a search function on Usenet, an internet discussion system popular in the 1980s and 1990s, even though all the searchable information on Usenet had always been public. These stories highlight that privacy is concerned less with the actual visibility of information than with people's sense of the power they have to make decisions about it. In privacy theorist Irwin Altman's words, privacy is the process of ensuring 'the selective control of access to the self' (Altman, 1975, p. 24); in other words, privacy is an inherently social phenomenon that involves interpreting and negotiating the control of boundaries (Margulis, 2011, p. 11). In relation to the News Feed case, boyd explains:

> Information is not private because no one knows it; it is private because the knowing is limited and controlled ... When snippets and actions were broadcast to the News Feed, they were taken out of context and made far more visible than seemed reasonable.
>
> (boyd, 2008, p. 18)

In order to incorporate the News Feed feature into their social interactions (which, placated by the Facebook company, users eventually did), users had to shift their expectations to assume that any of their posts could be accessed by any of their Friends, rather than those who deliberately hunt out their page (boyd, 2008, p. 15) and to adapt their strategies for defining and ensuring privacy accordingly. This is not necessarily because people do not care about privacy but rather that they are weighing up the risks and benefits of social connection (Debatin et al., 2009; Livingstone, 2008) and carefully managing and negotiating the line between the public and the private as they seek to remain connected. In the next section, I look at the strategies that users adopt to enable them to do this.

Using privacy settings and other privacy strategies

Users of social media sites have various resources to draw on in seeking to control their information flow, categorised as technical controls, limits on disclosures and social strategies. I discuss each below.

Facebook, like other SNSs, incorporates various privacy settings and functions into its site architecture. The most obvious is that of the Friends list, coupled with the ability to restrict the visibility of your posts to Friends. In some respects this is a straightforward and effective strategy. boyd and Hargittai (2010), for example, observe some young people's refusal to 'friend' their parents on social media sites. The strategy is never completely foolproof, not least because posts and photos can become visible to Friends' Friends. It is not always possible to refuse requests for friendship – without seeming rude, for example – and an overly restricted Friends list constitutes a rather blunt instrument which undermines the social benefits of sites like Facebook.

Other structural strategies available to users include the audience selector function, which can be used to select the audience for each post; the deletion of posts; and the untagging of photos. A survey by the Pew Internet and American Life Project found an increase between 2009 and 2011 in the number of people who reported untagging photos, deleting comments or 'unfriending' Friends (Madden, 2012). While these tools provide a more nuanced approach than the privacy settings, boyd (2012) notes that one drawback is that users – or at least the American teenagers which she studies – tend not to trust them. This is unsurprising given the frequency with which the tools can change, leaving a user suddenly (and perhaps unknowingly) exposed. The history of privacy on Facebook, for example, has involved constant redesign, inevitable backlash from users and commentators (followed eventually by acceptance), increased complexity (until the company was forced to respond to complaints by simplifying its privacy settings in 2010) and a continued insistence on sharing as broadly as possible.

A second strategy is that of not disclosing, which appears to be an increasing trend. Recent studies identify a correlation between high privacy concerns and low levels of disclosure (Krasnova et al., 2010; Stutzman et al., 2011) which appeared not to be the case a few years earlier (Acquisti and Gross, 2006). A study carried out in New York found that the amount of information New Yorkers revealed on Facebook – including personal details in their profile – fell dramatically between 2010 and 2011 (Dey et al., 2012). As argued above, however, lack of self-disclosure may limit access to social capital and thus, as a privacy strategy, it works to reduce the possible social benefits of sites like Facebook (Ellison et al., 2011).

A final approach to maintaining privacy involves what boyd and Marwick (2011) call 'social strategies'. In her studies of teenage American users, boyd notes that instead of relying on structural features built into the site, many users 'work to limit access to meaning' (boyd, 2012, p. 348). By this she means that the language used in any one post is designed to be understood by certain individuals and to exclude others. boyd explains how the teens:

> use pronouns and in-jokes, cultural references and implicit links to unmediated events to share encoded messages that are for all intents and purposes inaccessible to outsiders ... Only those who are in the know have the necessary information to look for and interpret the information provided.
>
> (boyd, 2012, p. 349)

Of the examples provided by boyd and Marwick (2011), my favourite is the story of 17-year-old Carmen and her interfering, over-reacting,

Spanish-speaking mother. When Carmen broke up with a boyfriend, she wanted to let her friends know without informing her mother, so she posted the lyrics to 'Always look on the bright side of life' on her Facebook page. Her friends knew that this was an ironic song, originally sung by someone about to die, and they immediately responded with sympathetic, enquiring text messages; her mother did not know this and took the words literally.

The importance of social strategies lies in users' ability to manage privacy issues – at least those pertaining to interference from individuals whose immediate access can be predicted – whilst maintaining the social benefits which sites like Facebook are designed to provide. And it is here – in exploring how users utilise and adapt their language resources to achieve this – that applied linguistics has a vital role to play. I explore this in Section B, Chapter 14.

7 Is social media making us less social offline?

Introduction: the end of society as we know it

The year is 2068. Two British survivors from one of the 'greatest disasters to befall mankind' have lived to tell the tale – of the internet. They recount how they lost years of their lives looking at pictures of cats, or waiting for video clips to buffer. As one survivor explained, 'at first you could still get milk ... but soon the shops just shut down ... once high speed broadband hit the rural areas, the farmers stopped producing food'. All offline activity ceased in March 2017 and it was not until May 2018 that a group broke into the national grid and cut the power lines, and the internet ended. People ran out into the streets to celebrate, only to find that London was destroyed and most of Britain had reverted to forest.

This nightmare vision of the end of society was created by Sarah Campbell of The Poke, an online satirical website (www.thepoke. co.uk). Like all good satire, the video is grounded in real-world issues that its viewers can relate to – that is, the apprehension that many people feel regarding the perceived breakdown of face-to-face interaction and local community, and the role of the internet in this social decline. The media frequently expresses fears that we are forgetting how to interact face-to-face in social situations or even at home with loved ones because we are becoming too used to communicating at a distance via texting and social network sites like Facebook.

> Social Media – is it killing real life human ties and interactions?
> (*The New Times*, Rwanda, 8 August 2013,
> in Mwai and Umutesi, 2013)

> Smartphone mania to impact social skills
> (*Light Reading*, India, 14 December 2012, in Singh, 2012)

> Without social media, 18% of teens would stop communicating
> (*Mashable*, US, 20 July 2012, Price, 2012)

Is social media paradoxically making us more unsociable? And should we worry that something like the future scenario presented by The Poke could ever come to pass?

In this chapter, I want to start by exploring the anxieties that people have about the effect of digital communication on social interaction, and then go on to unravel these concerns and to consider more objectively the attitudes and rationales behind them. I highlight three related matters: firstly, the concern that constant access to the internet through smartphones is affecting the way in which we interact with people around us; secondly, that we are forgetting, because of the amount of time we spend in virtual encounters, how to carry out face-to-face conversations and relationships; and, finally, the concern that digital communication is altering how we organise our offline lives.

People's uneasiness about the effects of the internet on social behaviour and our ability to communicate is also fuelled by antisocial aspects of digital communication such as flaming, trolling and cyberbullying. These are discussed in Chapter 8, leaving the current chapter to focus on the way in which the internet is seen to have an impact on offline communication and relationships.

When the phone in your pocket (or the laptop in your room) takes priority over the people around you

If you believe the popular press, digital means of communication would seem to be replacing face-to-face spoken conversation, with dire consequences. Surveys quoted in the press suggest that we are favouring written (digital) communications over spoken interaction in ways that have not been documented before. For example, the British media watchdog Ofcom reported in 2012 that, while mobile phones continued to trump landlines, they were increasingly being used to text or (in the case of smartphones) to access online communication sites, rather than to talk. In relation to its findings, James Thickett, Ofcom's director of research, pointed out that communication patterns were changing due to 'newer forms of communications which don't require us to talk to each other' (Plunkett, 2012). What his comment overlooks is the long history of written communications – letters, telegraphs, postcards – but there may be something in the argument that, due to smartphones, written communication has never been so easy and convenient for so many people.

One consequence of the perceived move towards managing interpersonal relationships through written communication at a distance (bearing in mind that we have long communicated by letter) is the way in which it interferes with our offline encounters; that is, with how we interact with the people who are physically around us. I see teenagers meet up with each other and then sit around typing messages to other people. People update their online status to tell others what a great time they're in the process of having. Pupils text in class. I often find myself stuck behind someone on the street who is dawdling as they type, or who has obstructed a doorway by stopping to operate their phone. In my experience, social norms regarding the use of phones in public are still developing. Not so long ago, it felt inappropriate to get your mobile phone out during a public event such as a conference talk, meeting or lecture, but more recently the practice of 'live tweeting' an event (posting about it on the microblogging site Twitter as it occurs), not to mention the myriad other roles a phone may play, has made it acceptable for people to use smartphones in such situations. I certainly find I cannot concentrate on what is being said while I type into my phone; at best, my attention is divided. The same is true when we multitask in other ways (reading a book at breakfast and only half-listening to the family conversation), but it could be argued that the smartphone embodies an unprecedented variety of distractions and that it tends always to be on our person, strengthening the likelihood of its impacting on our behaviour.

Internet theorist Nathan Jurgenson takes this further to suggest that our repeated digital interactions are also changing us in more fundamental ways; that is, reshaping not only what we _do_ but also who we _are_:

> If the hardware has spread virally within physical space, the software is even more insidious ... social media give us a surfeit of options to tell the truth about who we are and what we are doing, and an audience for it all, reshaping norms around mass exhibitionism and voyeurism. Twitter lips and Instagram eyes: Social media is part of ourselves; the Facebook source code becomes our own code.
>
> (Jurgenson, 2012)

As one consequence of the way in which social media pervades our lives, we are forgetting essential conversational and interactional skills (according to popular media accounts). In the hairdresser's the other day, I read in a glossy woman's magazine about how to have a conversation. The journalist had been to a conversation specialist and revealed some top tips (one was to properly listen rather than butting in; another to avoid staring too intently at the person you're listening to). What struck me, however, was the premise for the piece – it is the time spent online that has such a detrimental effect on our conversational skills. The assumption here is that online communication does not require the kinds of interpersonal skills needed for offline interactions – and it is true that online communication does not involve eye contact, physical proximity or the ability to read facial expressions;

nor does it always require the 'social niceties' of most face-to-face conversations.

The problem of social awkwardness is apparently taken to its extreme in Japan, where the internet has become implicated – among other effects – with the social phenomenon of *hikkomori*; that is, the withdrawal of young people from social life into isolation and confinement and onto the internet and online games. In a particularly extreme case, the Japanese media reported that a *hikkomori* had stabbed five members of his family after they cancelled his internet contract (Gamo, 2010). Internet addiction, however, is not confined to Japan. Media reports from countries across the world highlight the social problems that too much time spent online can cause:

> Lee Chin-hei, who is in charge of Christian Service's Online Addiction Counselling Centre, said his team received up to a dozen calls a week from parents seeking help with their children's computer addiction. This was about three times as many calls as two years ago, he said.
>
> (Tsang and Kao (2013),
> writing in the *South China Morning Post*, 15 August 2013)

> The National Information Society, or NIA, estimates 160,000 South Korean children between age 5 and 9 are addicted to the Internet ... Such children appear animated when using gadgets but distracted and nervous when they are cut off from the devices and will forgo eating or going to the toilet so they can continue playing online.
>
> (Lee (2012), writing in *The Huffington Post*, 28 November 2012)

> Internet addicts who log on to chat rooms for long hours are advised to quit the habit in stages and instead take part in sports activities, read the Holy Quran or visit relatives and friends.
>
> (Shaghouri (2003), writing in the *Gulf News*, UAE,
> 27 February 2003)

Children are accused of spending too much time on offline activities like watching television. However, the addictive nature of the internet is something that I suspect many of us can sympathise with. Like many adults who use email for work, I tend to check my inbox on a regular basis. When I wean myself off checking my email in preparation for a holiday, I can feel myself gradually lose the urge to do it. And it's something that's harder and harder to control, given the extent to which the internet pervades our lives. For example, I recently read a blog post written by journalist Patrick Garratt, in which he vowed to cut down on his all-consuming use of Twitter (Garratt, 2012). At the end of the post, the reader is confronted by the tagline:

Follow Patrick Garratt on Twitter: www.twitter.com/patlike.

A final concern is the role that text messaging and mobile communication play in altering how we organise our lives. Chief amongst my concerns would be that these days there is increasingly less need for making definite plans. Because we are 'always on' (the term used by Naomi Baron in her 2008 book to refer to the fact that, in a digitally connected world, we are always available to others), there is no need to commit to a plan a week in advance, or even a day in advance; instead, the details of an arrangement take shape as a plan is being put into effect. This is what Richard Ling and Birgitte Yttri call 'nuanced instrumental coordination' or the 'progressively exact arrangement of a meeting'. As they put it, '[w]ith the use of mobile communication systems, one need not take an agreement to meet at a specific time and place as immutable. Rather, those meeting have the ability to adjust the agreement as the need arises' (Ling and Yttri, 2002, p. 139). Any mobile phone inbox is presumably filled with text messages such as the following, sent on the move to micro-coordinate ongoing arrangements.

> Hey babes. Guess ur still in meeting. Give me a buzz wen ur out. Xxx
>
> Hey don't forget to pick me up xxx
>
> Walking down to club now. See ya up there xxx
>
> Sorry m8 still at work will text you in like 2 hours when i finish sorry bro x x
>
> Hey baby i'm gonna head straight into town. Gimme a call wen u get here. Hope work was fun! Xxx
>
> (Tagg, 2009)

What I find potentially problematic about this way of organising activities is not so much the uncertainty of any arrangement, but the lack of commitment. People do not have to commit to being somewhere at a particular place. What this change shows is the impact that digital technology can have not just on how we interact and what we say, but on how we organise our lives and who we are.

Task 7.1

Reflect on the ways in which digital technology shapes the way you communicate with others, both on- and offline. Does online technology ever intrude into what you are doing offline? Consider also the aspects of other people's behaviour which you find irritate or inconvenience you. To what extent do you see digital technology as having a negative impact on the patterns of communication around you?

Unpacking the problems

Having acknowledged and laid out the various assumptions and prejudices around communication and digital technology, it is important as scholars to step back and consider more objectively the rationale behind the attitudes we hold. In this section, I challenge two assumptions: firstly, that a distinction can be made between the offline and the online; and, secondly, that there has been a decline in social or communicative standards at all.

Firstly, the notion of an 'offline' world that is real, normal and under threat is no more than a response to the perceived dangers (or simply the novelty) of the internet. The 'offline' has been created as a counterpart to the 'online' in a false dichotomy, so that 'time spent online means less spent offline' (Jurgenson, 2012). In reality, Jurgenson argues, the fact that we are often 'online' shapes our perception of the world when we are 'offline' (we might update our status or check in to an online location-based social network site during a day out, or use Google to resolve a face-to-face debate), just as we never leave behind the 'offline' when we go 'online'. As boyd and Ellison (2008) point out, on social network sites, we tend to connect with people we know offline; and we also use the site to post updates on, and photos of, our offline activity. In Jurgenson's words, 'Facebook doesn't curtail the offline but depends on it'. The suggestion that our use of new media is replacing or destroying our offline lives falls apart when we consider the extent to which technology is embedded into the physical experiences and activities in which we engage, and may in some cases enhance our offline experiences (such as when friends go through Facebook photos together).

Secondly, judgements about present-day problems are often strongly shaped by the tendency to assume that they are symptomatic of a marked change – and usually a decline – in behavioural standards regardless of the historical evidence (see the Introduction). For example, I complained above about the current tendency to conduct virtual conversations whilst in the middle of face-to-face ones, but the issues involved in managing multiple interactions or contexts are not new. In a pre-digital world, there were social and politeness norms involved in deciding whether and when to butt into a conversation (and when to break off to address someone hovering nearby, anxiously trying to catch your attention). Similarly, you may sometimes be frustrated when someone serving you in a shop stops to answer a landline; and I was frowned at by a waiter whom I tried to beckon when he was serving another table. These offline norms are, like online ones, often implicit – apart from your parents, nobody explicitly tells you what is polite or not. Instead, these social norms are negotiated – you try something and it offends so you alter your behaviour. Digital technology may increase the possibilities for multiple interactions and thus decrease the social norms that mitigate against them, but it does not represent a fundamental break with the past.

Similarly, the argument that we are losing our ability to converse rests on the assumption that people once had more sophisticated conversational skills. Let's consider more closely whether conversational skills are likely to be in decline. Firstly, we might ask what being an effective conversationalist entails. There are myriad ways of answering this, but answers perhaps fall into two general categories: the attentive listener and the eloquent speaker. To the expert interviewed in my hairdresser's magazine, being a good conversationalist involved showing engagement (listening and thinking up relevant questions) and managing the physical encounter (not staring the person in the eyes). But it seems that often those bemoaning the loss of conversational skills are in fact referring to something different – they refer to someone able to put on a witty, eloquent and informed performance. To what extent can we know how people in the past 'performed' in conversation, in order to make meaningful comparisons with conversationalists today?

It is very difficult if not impossible to know what spoken conversations were like in the past, prior at least to the invention of recording equipment. Our only sources are by necessity written accounts or re-creations of spoken interactions, ranging from such contexts as Old Bailey trials to theatre plays or novel dialogue; or style guides prescribing best practice. Comparing accounts of the conversational skills of Coleridge or Samuel Johnson with the oral acuity of the average internet user is hardly a fair comparison, and it is unlikely – given comparative levels of education and world knowledge – that a typical person on the seventeenth-century street would be any more eloquent or informed than one on the twenty-first. In fact, you might assume they'd be less so.

The internet as problem or panacea?

Even assuming that the above premises were true – that once-sophisticated oral skills are being lost – the arguments still rest on the premise that digital technology is at fault for this. In other words, the assumption is based on a cause and effect relationship – communication via digital technology is directly responsible for a decline in conversational skills. A more likely scenario may be that both digital communication and changes in offline communication patterns feature in modern-day trends towards informalisation, brevity and multitasking – trends now associated with digital communication but which predate them. It may even be possible that increasing pressures on people's time, combined with greater mobilisation and wider networks, are themselves responsible for people's ready reliance on digital means of communication – reversing the cause and effect relationship to make a breakdown in traditional community structures the reason for people's increasing use of digital communication.

This may be the view of Brazilian businessman, Humbert Camacho, who in 2011 opened a nightclub in Epitaciolândia, Brazil and called it Facebook (Philips and Engle, 2012). His idea was to bring the advantages of online socialising to the offline world:

> The Facebook concept is about sharing ideas, adventures, friendships, parties and photos with your friends … So what we wanted to do was to build a nightclub with this concept, where people could come and share things with their friends.
>
> (Humbert Camacho, quoted in Philips and Engle, 2012)

The popular belief that online communities may in fact be the antidote to contemporary social problems represents what Thurlow et al. (2004, p. 108) call the other 'extreme' position towards technology. They argue that, in popular and media accounts of community (as well as some academic treatments), people tend to fall into one of two opposed camps: those who see the internet as destroying society and those who see digital communications as saving it. In reality, the truth may lie somewhere in the middle. As internet scholar Nancy Baym points out:

> It is fundamentally reductionist to conceptualize all 'virtual communities' as a single phenomenon and hence to assess them with a single judgement … [there are] countless thousands of online groups that vary tremendously. Some groups are surely bad for offline life, but there's certainly no reason to believe that most are.
>
> (Baym, 1998, p. 63, as cited in Thurlow et al., 2004, p. 110)

In Section B, Chapter 15, I explore the work that applied linguists have done in identifying and describing the affiliations that people establish in online contexts, and the various connections that many people seem to feel with those they may only ever meet through the mediation of digital technology. The ways in which affiliations and communities have been theorised are explored in Section C, Chapter 21.

8 What can be done about trolls and online bullying?

Introduction

There are so many stories in the media about online aggression, abuse and bullying that it is hard to know where to begin. Acts of antisocial behaviour in digital communication are as old as the internet itself but, as social media extends its reach across our lives, stories of online aggression and how it impacts on people's lives are increasingly hitting the headlines. The apparent pervasiveness of aggressive behaviour online has led many to identify and blame features of digital communication – chiefly physical distance, anonymity and reduced social cues. Thurlow et al. (2004, p. 70) identify 'a tendency to portray the internet as a problematic communication environment where people feel free to, or even compelled to, behave in extreme and inappropriate ways'. There is some truth in this portrayal of digital communication, but I want to argue in this chapter that it is ultimately not the technology that causes antagonism but the social situation – including the intentions and purposes behind the aggressive behaviour, the ways in which it is interpreted, and the relationships between participants (Thurlow et al., 2004). It is important to be aware of this if we want to understand online aggression in order to effectively tackle it. In this chapter, I look at three very distinct forms of online antisocial behaviour – flaming, trolling and online bullying – in order to consider the motivations behind them, the extent of the problem and the ways in which applied linguistics can shed light on the matter.

> ### Task 8.1
>
> Reflect on your own behaviour online. Do you find it easier to get annoyed at emails or other online posts than you would in most face-to-face situations? Do you ever find yourself responding more aggressively than you would in offline interactions? If so, why do you think this is? And what do (or might) you do to avoid such situations getting out of hand?

Flaming

Flaming can be defined as 'aggressive or hostile communication occurring via computer-mediated channels' (O'Sullivan and Flanagin, 2003, p. 70). The term has been used widely to include incendiary, rude or insulting messages, 'vicious verbal attacks, nasty and often profane diatribe, derogatory, obscene or inappropriate language, overheated prose, and derisive commentary' (Thurlow et al., 2004, p. 70). (Trolls and bullies, as we shall see, draw on various forms of flaming for their particular ends, although they may also use more subtle methods.) Empirical studies of flaming tend to suggest that acts of aggression occur more frequently than in face-to-face communication (e.g. Castellá et al., 2000; Dyer et al., 1995; Siegel et al., 1986) and this has led to attempts in academic and popular circles to isolate what it is about the internet that encourages such behaviour. This freedom or compulsion to act badly is most usually put down to a lack of inhibition – that is, a reduction in the degree to which social norms, personal embarrassment and the judgements of others regulate an individual's behaviour (Joinson, 1998). Disinhibition is generally seen to be encouraged by three characteristics common to much digital communication which I mentioned above: reduced social cues, physical distance and anonymity.

Reduced social cues refers to the fact that internet users do not typically have access to the paralinguistic features (the tone of voice in which something is said, for example), or to the facial expressions, gestures and body language of their interlocutors. The implications of what is often thought of as 'impoverished' or deficient interaction are that people cannot express themselves as effectively as in spoken interactions; they are more likely to experience misunderstandings; and they are likely to feel less inhibited when it comes to confronting their unseen interlocutors. People are seen to compensate for the lack of paralinguistic features through the use of graphic devices such as case (HELP), punctuation (!!!), smileys (☺) and other emoticons; and, in more recent years, through online photos, videos and links. Thus the internet smiley was invented (by Scott E. Fahlman at Carnegie Mellon University in 1982) as a way to disambiguate users' intended meanings on a university online bulletin board. As Fahlman (cited by Baron, 2009, p. 4) put it:

> a good many of the posts were humorous (or attempted humour). The problem was that if someone made a sarcastic remark, a few readers would fail to get the joke, and each of them would post a lengthy diatribe in response. That would stir up more people with more responses, and soon the original thread of the discussion was buried.[1]

The smiley was suggested as a 'joke marker', so that jokes did not misfire. In the following text messages (dating from around 2006), the smileys similarly indicate that an utterance should not be taken seriously (the first two examples below) and to soften an otherwise demanding request (the last example).

> Yeh do u like it and no u cant lend borrow or pinch it ! :)

> Lessons were fine - nice groups. We'll have to meet up Friday or sometime to do your holiday snaps - hope you took some ... And hope your Japanese was up to it ;)

> Are u home?If so,what door number&put the kettle on!Ta :-)
>
> (Tagg, 2012)

Online writing, then, quickly developed from the text-only interactions that characterised very early computer use to become multimodal (that is, with users drawing on various modes alongside writing, such as case, punctuation and so on). This can be seen to some extent as an attempt to replicate the richness of spoken language and to replace the various modes available to speakers – intonation, facial expressions, laughter, shaking hands. One problem with this view is that the written modes are much more than simply an attempt to replicate spoken language, a point made by Baron (2009), among others. If emoticons emerge from an attempt to fill the gaps left by carrying out a spoken conversation through writing, that presumes that users consider themselves to be engaging in such a conversation. Research, however, suggests a more complex picture, with users drawing on features associated with speech *and* with writing, and moving away from 'textese' to embrace a range of styles, including an elaborated prose more clearly characteristic of written texts (Baron, 2009).

To Sproull and Kiesler (1986, and see Kiesler and Sproull, 1992), it is not misunderstandings that cause aggression, but the fact that interacting online reduces the effect of the social norms that normally regulate behaviour and thus lowers people's inhibitions. This is down to the sense of anonymity and physical distance afforded by the mediation of the computer – potential flamers or bullies may not see their 'victims' as people but as lines of text (and in static photos and so on). Anonymity and physical distance appear to work together in powerful and complex ways to contribute to situations in which people are no longer inhibited from becoming aggressive and where they do not feel themselves to be accountable for their actions. What is interesting here is that where 'anonymity' is seen as leading to aggression it need not, and often does not, refer to a state of being completely anonymous (i.e. where nobody knows or can find out who you are). Instead, an enhanced sense of being anonymous – even in situations where one's identity can be traced or is to some extent known – can be sufficient to reduce inhibitions and accountability (Wallace, 1999). Studies in fact suggest that people using pseudonyms (what used to be known as 'nicks') may in some situations act more aggressively than people acting anonymously without invented identities (e.g. Tsikerdekis, 2012). The explanation is that people use pseudonyms to project a persona from which they can disassociate themselves and through which they feel free to act in ways that the user would not in offline situations (acting, perhaps, on thoughts or desires they cannot in their everyday lives). In extreme cases of disassociation, the user may feel that the actions of their online persona have no implications in the real world.

How convincing is the reduced cues theory for explaining aggressive behaviour? The problem comes when we assume that features of the internet inevitably lead to bad behaviour. In reality, the internet is also associated with empathy and community, allowing people with shared interests or concerns to interact and support each other with positive effects for people's sense of empowerment, well-being and self-confidence (Barak et al., 2008). Physical distance might encourage cruelty – but it can also give people a safe space in which to self-disclose and share personal information they might be reluctant to share face-to-face. Rather than being implicated in disassociation, an online persona may become an extension of how people perceive themselves (Bechar-Israeli, 1995) and, like all digital communication, be deeply embedded into their offline lives (Lee, 2014).

As Thurlow et al. (2004, p. 61) point out – and this comes back to the argument made in the Introduction to this book – blaming aggressive behaviour on a computer and an internet connection risks indulging in technological determinism – the idea that we are passive victims of technological development, rather than active agents able to use the technology to our own purposes. The question, then, is why some people choose to take up the affordances offered by the internet for the purpose of flaming and aggression. To answer this question, we must seek to understand the interactional norms and social relationships within a particular context, to determine what participants perceive as aggressive, what motivations seem to underlie the aggression and what functions aggression is seen to fulfil on the site (O'Sullivan and Flanagin, 2003). It is here that applied linguistics work can make a contribution, as we shall see in Chapter 16.

Trolling

More than the embodiment of the internet hate machine, trolls are the ultimate hero, trolls fuck shit up. Trolls exist to fuck with people, they fuck with people on every level, from their deepest held

beliefs, to the trivial. They do this for many reasons, from boredom, to making people think, but most do it for the lulz [defined in turn as 'laughter at someone else's expense'].
(Encyclopedia Dramatica, cited in Coleman, 2012, p. 111)

I make a distinction between a 'troll' (a kind of online post) and a 'troller' (the person who posts such a post). Although not a distinction made in the above quotation, it is useful (and it suggests the origins of the term not in Scandinavian bridge-dwelling monsters, but a method of fishing whereby a hook is trawled behind a boat).

What is a troller, why do they act as they do, and to what extent should we be worried about their behaviour? The above definition of trolls in the words of the trolling community (as represented in the online 'Encyclopedia Dramatica') highlights central characteristics of the online troller – someone who deliberately disrupts online forums with the primary purpose of getting pleasure at the other participants' expense. Trollers typically post a controversial message (a troll), then sit back and enjoy the outrage that follows. Trolling may involve flaming but more often than not it constitutes a more sophisticated strategy ensuring that other participants believe that the troller is being sincere in their stated opinions (Hardaker, 2010, pp. 237–8). In other words, the troller may not be overtly aggressive, but instead causes disruption through deception.

Whether or not an act of trolling is considered harmful, then, depends very much on the context in which it takes place: it is dependent not only on the object of the troll (who or what is being targeted) but also the reactions of the people involved and their interpretations as to the troller's intentions. Some targets of trolling – such as Facebook memorial pages set up in the memory of deceased users – are likely to be universally condemned (outside of trolling communities). The activities of a subset of trollers, 'griefers', can vary in their moral acceptability. Griefers seek to disrupt virtual worlds and games through pranks that range from stopping other avatars from bathing in a virtual swimming pool to gatecrashing the funeral for a player who died in real life and killing the avatars present (Coleman, 2012, p. 110). Meanwhile, trolling on discussion websites such as the following example on TED.com (the video-hosting platform) might generally be considered fairly harmless, in that they do not target particular individuals or cause undue upset. Some studies suggest that trolling in such cases may even be conducive to group bonding, in the sense that recognition of, and collective action against, trolls can function to signal group membership and define the boundaries of the group (Tepper, 1996).

T.D.:   Molecules are deadly poisonous, if there were any in your food, it [sic] would kill you.

Monsanto has been experimenting with putting molecules in food for years, the test subjects always die horribly.

J.S.:   Everything is made of molecules, from you, to food, to the desk in front of you. Everything is a chemical, some are dangerous (H2SO4) and some are not (H20).

T.D.:   @ J.S. surely you are not suggesting that dihydrogen monoxide is safe!?

A.B.:   So true. It can kill you in minutes if one breathes it. I been trying to ban it for years now. Glad you are on the cause too.

(Drasovean, 2012)

As Drasovean (2012) explains, although J.S. fails to read the irony in T.D.'s (the troller's) words, A.B. not only recognises the utterance as trolling, but also builds humorously on it, claiming that he has been trying to ban water – dihydrogen monoxide – 'for years'. Pranks like this are apparently harmless, and can serve such functions as distinguishing new from old members of the group, and defining the boundaries of what the community feels is acceptable.

These user comments, posted on an online newspaper site, illustrate the various ways in which trolling activities are perceived and evaluated:

'Most trolls are too easy to spot (often they start with a general point then quickly try to get down to absurd minutiae), and it's just not worth debating with them.'

'I disagree with the suggestion that one should never reply to trolls sincerely. An argument can be valid no matter where it originates and there are always more people reading than just the respondent and the troll. If a troll brings up an interesting point, run with it.'

'I am frequently accused of being a troll, simply for expressing (broadly) right wing comments on these (broadly) left wing boards. I genuinely don't think I am a troll, but some of my critics would doubtless say that I was in denial.'

(comments posted in response to an article on trolling by Abrahams, 2011)

What these comments confirm is that trolling is not necessarily viewed as a 'bad thing'. While the first commenter criticises trollers for arguing for the sake of it ('down to absurd minutiae'), the second applauds the value of argument and debate, and refuses to rule out engaging with arguments simply because they are deemed as emanating from someone with bad intentions. The final comments raise the question as to how a troll can be identified in the first place and the extent to which a troller is in fact no more than a person with an opinion which differs from your own or who enjoys playing devil's advocate.

To conclude, although the actions of trollers can in some cases be offensive and upsetting (and thus unforgivable), trollers should not always be seen simply as trouble-makers. It may be useful in counteracting the negative impacts of their behaviour to understand better how acts of trolling are realised and – of particular importance – how they might be stopped from escalating into cyberbullying.

Online bullying

Acts of flaming or trolling can develop into cyberbullying if the aggressor begins to repeatedly target one person (or group of people) with the intent of causing them (often personal) harm. The relationship between bully and victim is likely to be characterised by a power imbalance – Smith et al. (2008, p. 237), for example, define the bully's victim as someone 'who cannot easily defend him or herself'. (We would be unlikely to describe the hacktivist group 'Anonymous' as bullies in their targeting of powerful institutions such as the government or the Church of Scientology, but we might expect targets of bullying to include children, employees and the emotionally vulnerable.)

Drawing on a survey of existing literature, Tokunga (2010, p. 278) offers the following inclusive definition of cyberbullying:

> Cyberbullying is any behavior performed through electronic or digital media by individuals or groups that repeatedly communicates hostile or aggressive messages intended to inflict harm or discomfort on others.

All bullying hurts, but cyberbullying has the potential to hurt more than face-to-face bullying because of its reach – it can, to paraphrase the title of Tokunga's (2010) survey, 'follow you home from school' – and because of the anonymity that may in some cases be afforded the bullies (or at least a protective sense of anonymity). A worrying type of cyberbullying is that which concerns children and teenagers, particularly given the lack of (adult) supervision and regulation online. However, although most research into cyberbullying focuses on children and adolescents (Tokunga, 2010, p. 280), adults can also be victims of what is in their case most commonly known as 'online harassment' or 'cyberstalking'. The rising Canadian tennis star, Rebecca Morino, for example, cited cyberbullying as one reason for her withdrawal from the sport in 2011 (she returned in 2013). She told *The New York Times* that Twitter users would write 'You gave that match away, you cost me such-and-such amount of money, you should go burn in hell' or 'You should die' and that she found it 'really scary'

(Rothenberg, 2013). British radio presenter Richard Bacon and his family became the object of one cyberstalker who claimed to dislike the programme that Bacon hosted and whose acts of online aggression included 255 abusive tweets over three months and a blog dedicated to abusing Bacon (Ford Rojas, 2012). Online attacks were also aimed at Bacon's wife and mentioned his five-month-old baby.

Cyberbullying is an unacceptable behaviour which by definition brings harm to vulnerable individuals with sometimes catastrophic consequences. Like face-to-face bullying, cyberbullying can have real outcomes, ranging from depression and other affective disorders, to academic problems, substance abuse and suicide. However, anxiety about online bullying is driven to no small extent by the high-profile cases of teen suicide reported by the press and the public reactions that follow. These media reports thus have the effect of obscuring the actual extent (probably much lower) and nature (less extreme) of online bullying. Despite newspaper headlines proclaiming cyberbullying as an 'epidemic' of 'national' proportions, 'silent' and 'growing' (Sabella et al., 2013), studies have yet to confirm how many children experience cyberbullying. Research suggests anywhere between 10 per cent and 40 per cent of schoolchildren may experience some form of cyberbullying (e.g. Shariff, 2005; Tokunga, 2010), but accurate estimations are hampered by the need to rely on self-reports and on varying definitions of cyberbullying. One 2012 UK survey found that only 2 per cent of internet users reported having been the victim of threatening behaviour online in the past year (Chalabi, 2013). As Sabella et al. (2013) point out, the hysteria around cyberbullying can have deleterious consequences: it can lead children and parents to overuse the term in describing their own experiences of what they see as unfair or unpleasant online behaviours (thus driving up the statistics); it can suggest to young people that such behaviour is the norm; and it can add to adults' misunderstanding of youth (see Chapter 1) and lead to unwise or overblown 'solutions' to the problem.

While bullying is always wrong, the motivations behind bullying and the kind of people who indulge in it – like that of flaming and trolling – are extremely complex (Sabella et al., 2013). Cyberbullying is likely to be facilitated by the disinhibiting effect of anonymity and physical distance. For example, the nature of digital communication would seem to be implicated in actions by bullies which Willard (2007) labels 'inadvertent' – those bullies who seem not to see the serious nature of what they are doing and report that they are doing it for fun. However, online disassociation is not always the motivation. Sabella et al. (2013, p. 2706) suggest that some cyberbullies perceive their bullying as a retaliation for a wrong caused by the victim, and because they feel 'angry, frustrated, or otherwise emotionally distraught'. According to Wilton and Campbell (2011), children and adolescents who bully others may do so because of peer pressure – perhaps the internet is the new cool place to be seen bullying.

What can be done?

Solutions to online harassment abound in the literature and in various public responses to high profile cases. As Sabella et al. (2013, p. 2707) point out, avoiding certain devices or platforms is generally not a solution, given the way they are embedded into our lives. Nor have zero-tolerance policies been greeted with much enthusiasm, because these tend to criminalise young people (Shariff, 2005) or threaten free speech,[2] and may therefore have opposite effects to those intended. For example, boyd et al. (2011) found that, in response to inflexible age restrictions imposed by many sites, parents in the US will often help their children circumvent them, and that a more effective approach would be to require parent consent (as intended by the Children's Online Privacy Protection Act), and to provide space for adult–child discussion: that is, 'to help parents and their children make informed choices' (boyd et al., 2011).

Preferred solutions at present involve technological adaptations and attempts to educate parents and young people. The former include in-built affordances such as buttons which allow users to report suspicious or offensive posts. In 2013, for example, Twitter UK responded to a series of allegations of abuse on the site by setting up an in-tweet report abuse button. In a separate case of a suicide apparently provoked by online abuse in the UK in 2013, British social worker Danielle Adler went further to call for sites to add 'I'm being bullied' buttons so that young people can connect immediately to online counsellors (Adler, 2013). Schools need to play a role, by implementing violence-prevention programmes, writing up clear policies, educating parents and staff, directly training pupils through lessons and peer helper programmes (Sabella et al., 2013, pp. 2707–8) and by 'fostering inclusive and positive school environments' (Shariff, 2005, p. 462). It is clear that a multifaceted and informed response is necessary to tackle the complexities of cyberbullying.

Applied linguistics cannot solve the problem of cyberbullying, just as it cannot stop trolling or acts of flaming. But, by contributing through linguistic analysis to our understanding of how and why people behave aggressively online and with what effects (and in highlighting the complexity of these phenomena and processes), applied linguistics can help us move towards a solution which, to paraphrase Tsikerdekis (2012, p. 2), doesn't just heal the symptoms but tackles the underlying cause. In Section B, Chapter 16, I describe contributions made so far.

Notes

1 See also 'Smiley Lore :-)' on Fahlman's homepage: http://www.cs.cmu.
  edu/~sef/sefSmiley.htm. Accessed: 10 August 2013.
2 See, for example, responses to Nova Scotia's Cyber-Safety Act: http://www.
  thestar.com/opinion/editorials/2013/08/11/nova_scotias_crackdown_on_
  cyberbullying_goes_too_far_editorial.html. Accessed: 29 September 2014.

Section B

Interventions

Section 8

Interventions

I

Digital language and literacy

9 Why digital communication may be good for literacy

Introduction

In Chapter 1, we saw that concerns about the unconventional spelling used in digital communications tend often to be based on scare stories in the media which feed into adults' natural fears about and misunderstanding of what young people are doing. Applied linguistics researchers have drawn on empirical research – research grounded in analysis of online data – to reach conclusions about digital spellings which challenge the media hype. Firstly, spelling variants (or textisms) occur much less frequently than is often assumed; secondly, the textisms usually used are not randomly deployed but follow orthographical principles, thus reflecting spellings used in other kinds of writing; and, thirdly, these spelling variants can be seen as an important meaning-making resource – that is, the choice of an unconventional spelling over the standard form conveys meaning. Meanwhile, experimental research shows that engagement in digital communication correlates positively with strong spelling skills. The argument in this chapter is that if children are able to play with spellings when communicating by SMS text message or the internet, this may signal a strong grasp of the underlying orthographic principles – they have to know the rules before they can bend them.

I start by looking at the last finding mentioned above – the correlation between digital communication and good literacy skills. Literacy, in this chapter, is used in a rather narrow sense to refer to the ability to spell and to manage other basic writing skills – in Chapters 10 and 17 I take an increasingly broader view of literacy. I explain this correlation by exploring how people use language to express themselves in digital communications and how these practices relate to spelling patterns in non-digital texts.

Digital communication and literacy – a positive correlation?

Since around 2007, a growing body of linguistics and psychology research has explored the correlation between digitalese (or the use of textisms) and the literacy skills of children (aged between 8 and 12), adolescents (12–17), and young adults (18–25). The focus is on SMS text messaging, with some attention paid to instant messaging (IM) platforms (Geertsema et al., 2011; Rosen et al., 2010; Spatafora, 2008; Varnhagen et al., 2010; Winzker et al., 2009), but findings are likely to be relevant to recent applications such as WhatsApp, Line and Facebook which similarly encourage synchronous conversations. The research covers various English-speaking countries, chiefly the UK, USA, Australia and Canada, with some work carried out in Malaysia (Shafie et al., 2010), South Africa (Winzker et al., 2009; Geertsema et al., 2011) and Ghana (Dansieh, 2011). As this list suggests, the main focus is on native speakers of English, but there is some consideration of non-native speakers (Winzker et al., 2009; Shafie et al., 2010) and other languages, including Finnish (Plester et al., 2011) and Dutch (Radstake, 2010; Spooren, 2009). However, there is very little English-language research into languages other than English. Methodologically, the research is divided into two approaches – a few studies adopt a *user-informed approach* to ascertain participants' perceptions of the effect of digitalese on literacy (e.g. Geertsema et al., 2011), but the majority take a *data-driven approach*, where SMS are elicited through translation tasks (with participants asked to translate from standard English into digitalese and vice versa) or through invented scenarios (where participants are asked to write SMS appropriate for given contexts). The limitation of this work is that people may act differently in experimental contexts than in naturally occurring situations. Only a handful of studies collect naturally occurring SMS (Varnhagen et al., 2010; Wood et al., 2011) – that is, those sent as part of everyday communicative practices. In terms of findings, the research can be divided into studies reporting negative correlations, those reporting no clear correlation and those reporting positive correlations, the latter representing the majority of studies (Verheijen, 2013).

The user-informed studies tend to support anecdotal evidence by suggesting that teachers and students see digitalese as having a negative impact on literacy, as in Geertsema et al.'s (2011) South Africa study, which used questionnaires to ascertain what secondary-school teachers of English thought about the influence of digital communication on their students' writing. Dansieh (2011) notes similarly negative attitudes among teachers and students in a Ghanaian university, where students were generally found to have a weak grasp of English. Drouin and Davis (2009) find that many students (in an American college) report a negative effect on their literacy practices, even where no such impact could be found by the researchers. However, only a limited amount of the experimental research comes to a similar conclusion. The use of digitalese is linked to weaker spelling and reading skills among American college students in one study (Drouin, 2011) and, in another, high-school students and undergraduates in Australia (De

Jonge and Kemp, 2012). In some cases, existing levels of low literacy may explain the negative correlation (Rosen et al., 2010; Shafie et al., 2010). In their study of young American adults, Rosen et al. (2010) conclude that those with less education were more likely to 'unintentionally' transfer the practice to other types of informal writing, although this was not the case with more formal writing. Notably, no negative outcomes are reported for children's literacy abilities (those aged 8–12).

Overwhelmingly, the research suggests that digitalese either has no impact at all on literacy or may actually lead to improvements. Studies reporting no correlation include those focusing on the spelling abilities of young adults from the States (Drouin and Davis, 2009; Massengill Shaw et al., 2007), Canadian adolescents (Varnhagen et al., 2010), and South African high-school students (Winzker et al., 2009). Positive correlations between the use of digitalese and good literacy skills have been found predominantly among children (Bushell et al., 2011; Kemp and Bushell, 2011; Plester et al., 2008; Wood et al., 2011) although also adolescents (Kemp, 2011; Durkin et al., 2011; Powell and Dixon, 2011). Methods and findings vary, but the generally positive conclusion 'speaks against media claims that text messaging has a detrimental effect on spelling' (Bushell et al., 2011, p. 34). For example, Bushell et al.'s (2011) study of 227 Australian children used questionnaires and translation tasks to ascertain their awareness and use of digitalese and measured their spelling ability with standardised spelling tests. They found that children who did better on the spelling tests produced more textisms in the translation task. In the UK, Plester et al. (2008) asked schoolchildren to translate between standard English and digitalese, and found similarly positive correlations between the number of textisms used and the scores achieved for verbal reasoning and spelling. The finding from across these studies is that children and adolescents appear able to move between digitalese and standard English. In other words, although mistakes are made, there is recognition among children that textisms are not appropriate in formal writing and should be avoided.

The question as to whether children and young people are able to play with their spelling because they can spell well, or whether playing with spellings improves their general spelling skills, is not something that all studies can address. This is because they find only a correlation between digitalese and literacy, rather than being able to specify whether there is a causal relationship and, if so, what causes what. Kemp (2011, p. 65), for example, speculates that the effect may be both ways:

It seems likely that young adults with stronger linguistic skills can better employ these strengths to create and decipher textisms than those with weaker linguistic skills. It is also possible that the language 'play' encouraged by extensive practice with textisms ... helps to boost interest in language and thus scores on language tasks.

Regression analyses carried out by Beverly Plester and colleagues in the UK – analyses that allow them to explore the relationship between variables – suggest that digitalese may improve spelling. Wood et al. (2011), for example, collected SMS sent at the beginning and end of the school year and found that textism use at the start of the year could predict spelling ability throughout the year, but that children's initial spelling ability could not predict variance in textism use at the end of the year. They concluded that digitalese was leading to improved spelling ability, rather than the other way around.

One interesting illustration of the informal learning that digital communications enable can be found in Blommaert and Velghe's (2014) study of a severely dyslexic South African woman called Linda. Her problems with dyslexia were compounded by the poverty and marginalisation of the South African town in which she grew up: she dropped out of school and was unemployed at the time of the study. Her friends introduced her to the South African mobile IM platform, MXIT, which quickly became an important part of her life. Blommaert and Velghe note two interesting aspects of Linda's learning of 'textspeak': firstly, it was scaffolded and 'collective'; and, secondly, it impacted on her wider literacy skills. Linda's friends helped her to compile a repertoire of phrases for use on MXIT and they responded to her messages in the spirit in which they were sent: as indicators of belonging and friendship, rather than in terms of their linguistic correctness. Linda invested a huge amount of time and effort in copying phrases she encountered on MXIT into notebooks (found 'all over the house'), to use in her own MXIT posts. Linda's offline writing increased alongside her online use of textspeak and became highly purposeful to her, and her writing skills were thus stimulated and expanded (Blommaert and Velghe, 2014).

To sum up, the conclusions drawn across the literature are somewhat mixed, due in part to the varied research designs (Verheijen, 2013, pp. 596–7). Nonetheless, the positive correlations found between digitalese and literacy skills are sufficient to challenge the assumption that digital communication is necessarily having a negative impact on literacy, and should encourage us to carefully consider the assumptions mooted in the press.

Spelling variants as a meaning-making resource

One question left largely unaddressed by the above studies is why there should be a correlation between digitalese and basic literacy skills. To address this question, we turn to descriptive linguistic studies seeking to categorise and explain spelling choices. What emerges is that very little spelling variation can be categorised as 'misspelling'; instead, textisms are rule-based, reflect pre-digital patterns in spelling variation, and are thus better described as respellings (Sebba, 2007) – a neutral term for unconventional spelling that avoids the assumption that a word is misspelt and allows for the possibility that the spelling is meaningful.

Between 2004 and 2007 – perhaps the height of concern over spelling in SMS – I collected and analysed a corpus of over 11,000 SMS ('CorTxt'). Although the SMS were not sent by children but by people ranging in age from 18 to their 60s, evidence suggests that their spelling reflected younger age groups (Shortis, pers. comm.). The texters were speakers of British English and texted almost entirely in English, and studies suggest a similarity in patterning across varieties of English in Nigeria (Chiluwa, 2008); South Africa (Deumert and Masinyana, 2008); Malaysia (Hassan and Hashim, 2009) and several Arab countries (e.g. Al-Khatib and Sabbah, 2008) as well as across different languages, including French (Anis, 2007; Fairon and Paumier, 2006); Swedish (Hård af Segerstad, 2002); Hebrew (Borochovsky-Bar-Aba and Kedmi, 2010) and Romanised Arabic (Haggan, 2007). Interestingly, users of some languages and non-Roman scripts have been more resistant to playing with them. For example, while the South Africans in Deumert and Masinyana's (2008) study played with English spelling, they initially saw isiXhosa as too pure and traditional to allow language play, although their attitudes and practices were seen to change (Deumert, 2012).

Words that were respelt tended to be frequently occurring words in my corpus, CorTxt. This is observed elsewhere (Grinter and Eldridge, 2003) – texters don't usually create complex, obscure acronyms out of lengthy statements; the words they respell are short, common ones whose meanings can be easily retrieved. The table below lists the fifteen most frequently occurring words in CorTxt which also appear in a respelt form (the bracketed numbers refer to the number of times each form occurs).

We might start by asking whether these spelling variants can be explained away as mistakes. The list reveals a few variants that might best be described as 'typos' – <ot> for *to*, <hte> for *the*, <jurt> for *just*, <iin> for *in*, <annd> for *and*, and perhaps <uu> for *you* (although one *uu* occurs in the utterance, 'Okay, see uu then then!', suggesting language play), while <im> for *I'm* might occur because people are confused about where to put apostrophes (although concerns about apostrophes do not usually cite this particular form) or because they don't bother to add them. However, the number of occurrences of typos is very small – in most cases, people aren't making typos. It seems unlikely that the repeated uses of <4> for *for* or <tomo> for *tomorrow* are misspellings.

Table 9.1 Respellings in CorTxt

Headword	Respelt forms
you (4560)	u (3043)
	ya (256)
	yer (14)
	ye (9)
	uu (2)
to (4283)	2 (690)
	ot (3)
x (2161)	xx (833)
	xxx (635)
	xxxx (11)
	xxxxxx (3)
	xxxxxxx (2)
	xoxox (1)
	xxxxx (42)
the (3511)	d (21)
	da (6)
	th (8)
	hte (3)
	te (2)
	ze (2)
and (2956)	n (182)
	an (19)
	adn (10)
	amd (2)
	annd (2)
in (2385)	iin (2)
for (1698)	4 (357)
	fer (2)
have (1868)	av (8)
	hve (6)
	ave (5)
	hav (106)
be (1192)	b (375)
are (1054)	r (422)
	ar (2)
good (1197)	gud (40)
	gd (25)
	goodo (3)
see (1007)	c (248)
just (1214)	jus (18)
	jst (6)
	jurt (2)
I'm (936)	im (280)
so (1152)	soo (1)
	sooo (5)
	soooo (1)

Source: adapted from Tagg, 2012, p. 53.

It is evident from the above that words are respelt in different ways – *you*, for example, can be respelt as <u>, <ya>, <ye> or <yer> – and it is here that we see differences in what texters might *mean* by their respellings. Empirical research shows us that the possible ways of spelling a particular word constitute a fairly constricted set of options. In fact, in a study where colleagues and I standardised the spelling in a sample of 2,430 SMS from CorTxt (Tagg et al., 2013), we found most spelling variation was accounted for by a small number of letter and number homophones (where a letter or number stands for the word it resembles phonetically). In particular, the letter homophone <u> used to mean *you* accounted for over a fifth of all variants. The implication is that textisms are 'relatively homogeneous and linguistically circumscribed' – so that texters tend to repeat the same respellings. As we shall see, respellings are in fact regulated by 'a finite set of orthographic principles' (Shortis, 2007a, p. 24; and see Shortis, 2007b). In other words, the ways in which words can be respelt are limited by the underlying principles of English orthography (what is possible according to English spelling norms).

If users are selecting from a restricted set of possible respellings, what is the significance of choosing one rather than the other? Returning to our example of *you*, the forms <ya>, <ye> and <yer> all represent various ways in which *you* can be respelt to reflect how it might be spoken. Colloquial contractions – reduced or contracted written forms which reflect informal or regional pronunciation as well as suggesting emotions of anger or affection – are widely used in non-digital writing, from song lyrics ('I wanna hold your hand') to dialogue in literature:

> Knock, knock, knock! Who's there, i'th'name of Belzebub? Here's a farmer that hang'd himself on th'expectation of plenty: come in time; have napkins enowa about you; here you'll sweat for't.
>   (The porter in *Macbeth*, Act II, Scene III)

Table 9.2 Most common spelling variant normalisations in CorTxt

Respelling	Frequency (out of 3,166 respellings)	Standard form
u	666	you
2	187	to
r	95	are
4	85	for
ur	75	your
tomo	74	tomorrow
its	71	it's
b	69	be
c	52	see
im	43	i'm

Source: adapted from Tagg et al., 2013, p. 377.

As the example from *Macbeth* suggests, colloquial contractions are not primarily about reflecting pronunciation, but about capturing what someone's pronunciation tells us about their social identity – their background, level of education, their ignorance or disobedience. In other words, their function is primarily indexical – they are language features which relate directly to personal or social characteristics of the user. This argument is reinforced by eye dialect. Unlike colloquial contractions, eye dialect does not alter the pronunciation of a word – <what> and <wot> are pronounced the same, as are <says> and <sez>. (Unlike <you> and the colloquial contraction <ya>, where the latter spelling reflects an altered pronunciation.) Instead, the respelling constitutes a 'default' sound-spelling correlation (Carney, 1994). That is, *what* is respelt <wot> because the letter <o> is the most frequent pronunciation of the sound /o/ as in pot, toggle, forgot. The respelling of *what* as <wot> actually draws on underlying orthographic principles. And like colloquial contractions, eye dialect can point directly to a particular social identity. Eye dialect forms are often used to indicate an act of transgression or difference (in graffiti, for example), or they suggest a lack of education or social status (as with *Macbeth*'s porter), in that the phonetic spellings can be interpreted as mistakes made by people who write what they hear.

If colloquial contractions and eye dialect can signal social status and education level, what effect might homophones have? Again, the use of homophones and phonetic spelling has a long history. In the early 1900s, Pound (1925) identified a 'kraze for K' among advertisers: KitKat, Kleenex, Rice Krispies; other advertising techniques include consonant reductions such as Protex, double-consonant reductions such as Hot-Stuf (Jacobson, 1966; Praninskas, 1968) and homophones in Spud-U-Like, Toys R Us and Phones 4U. These phonetic spellings work to attract consumers by grabbing their attention as the unexpected spellings contrast with the rest of the text (Jaffe, 2000, p. 510). In other words, the impact of these respellings lies in their divergence from expected norms. This connotation can also be used to signal transgression, as Androutsopoulos (2000) noted in his investigation of German punk fanzines, where spellings like <punx>, <thanx>, <lyrix> and <demnaxt> (*demnachst* or 'soon') mark a fanzine as part of the radical subculture. We might speculate that homophones in SMS similarly create a modern, dynamic, eye-catching effect.

When we look at digitalese through the lens of earlier research into spelling variation, it is evident that the textisms can be categorised according to a small number of existing patterns of non-standard spelling, with implications for the effect they might be intended to have. Table 9.3 contains the categories identified in CorTxt.

Importantly, respellings are seen not to work if they do not follow certain patterns. For example, as Crystal (2003) points out, the meaning of consonant writing is much more easily retrievable than vowel writing would be: compare these two spellings of *please*: <pls> and <eae>. Similarly, if in eye dialect you don't choose a recognised sound–spelling correspondence (a permitted way to spell a sound), the result may be retrievable from context but will not have the same impact. Sebba (2007, p. 31) illustrates this with the difference between 'Down with skool!' and 'Down with zgüül!'.

How does all this relate to literacy? Empirical studies of digitalese reveal that textisms are in fact realisations of rule-based patterns of spelling variations which cannot always be explained as misspellings – instead, they are more accurately described as <u>re</u>spellings used, as in graffiti or literature, as a meaning-making resource. If you use textisms, it is not because you don't know the correct spelling; it is more likely that you not only know how to spell the word but you also know the parameters within which you can play with it.

Table 9.3 Categories of respelling in CorTxt

Category of respelling	Examples in CorTxt
Colloquial contractions (Weber, 1986)	< n>, <av>, <yer>, <wiv>, <goin>, <bin>, <allo> and <fink>
Other colloquial respellings	<goodo>, <pleasey>, <nope> and informal variants of *yes*: <yep>, <yeah> and <yup>
Regiolectal respellings (Androutsopoulos, 2000)	<summat>, <summort>, <sumfing> and <summing> for *something*; and <wid> and <dis> for *with* and *this*
Phonetic respellings	<2>, <4>, <u>, <b>, <c>, <gud>, <woz>, <coz>, <thanx>, <wot>, <nite>, <cum>, <luv>, <fone>, <cud> and <wud>
Abbreviations	<tomo>, <cause> and <bout>; while the final letter is omitted from a number of words including: *are, have, will, just, all* and *back*
Consonant writing	<gd> (*good*), <jst> (*just*), <thks>, <thnx> or <thx> (*thanks*), <bk> (*back*), <frm> (*from*), <wk> (*week*), <lv> (*love*), <pls> or <plz> (*please*), <cld> (*could*), <wld> (*would*), <nxt> (*next*), <txt> (*text*) and <wknd> (*weekend*)
Omission of apostrophes	<im> (*i'm*) and <ure> (*you're*) (categorised as a type of abbreviation)
Visual morphemes (Bolinger, 1946)	such as the symbol *x*, alone or repeated, representing kisses and used to sign messages off, occasionally alongside *o*'s which represent hugs.
Mistakes or typos	*thrus, iin, adn* and *jurt*

Source: adapted from Tagg, 2012, p. 58.

Spelling variants occur less frequently than currently supposed

This chapter ends on an important caveat. The focus throughout has been on spelling variation, which is particularly associated in the public mind with SMS and, to a lesser extent, IM. However, despite this deeply rooted association, studies of online data find that spelling variants are relatively infrequent, even in SMS (Doring, 2002; Grinter and Eldridge, 2003; Tagg, 2009). Thurlow and Brown (2003), for example, report that although 82 per cent of the 19-year-old university students participating in their study claimed to use textisms, they found only an average of three per SMS (which they describe as 20 per cent of message content). In an attempt to standardise the spellings in a sample of SMS from CorTxt, we found only 7.66 per cent of words were respelt and half of the SMS (1,217) contained no spelling variants (Tagg et al., 2013). According to Taylor and Harper (2003), abbreviating to avoid sending more than one SMS can in fact lower the perceived value of an SMS among friends, because the sender is seen as begrudging the cost or effort of writing in a standard form.

Instead, as Crystal (2008) points out, SMS (and by extension other forms of digital communication) are likely to be characterised by diversity in style, shaped not only by the sender's preferences but by contextual factors such as the purpose of the message, how quickly it is sent, and what the sender is doing at the time (standing at a crowded bar or watching television). See, for example, the following SMS taken from CorTxt (Tagg, 2009):

Where r u? The others r here

Bloody hell I'm definitely going to have to get my skates on! Quite literally!Just lying on the sofa with a hangover watching Morse and eating chocolate trifle not terribly athletic!

Other forms of digital communication may exhibit even less spelling variation. Although it is often assumed that Twitter is a bastion for poor spellers (see the UK *Daily Telegraph* article 'Twitter users can't spell', discussed in Chapter 1), Baron et al. (2011) found much less spelling variation in their corpus of Tweets (posted mainly by celebrities) than in my SMS corpus. In terms of message length, Tweets and SMS are similarly restricted. The difference in respelling was therefore put down to differences in users' perception of audience: in SMS, texts are generally aimed at one named individual whom the texter knows well; celebrity Tweets in the Twitter corpus were likely targeted at a wide, largely unknown audience who could not be expected to share the same kind of background information. This comparative research emphasises the fact that social considerations – such as whom you are writing to – may have just as much impact on people's online spelling practices as technical constraints, and that in some cases social motivations may be dominant.

Task 9.1

Collect some data from your SMS or IM inbox, your Twitter stream or your Facebook. (If you use messages sent or posted by other people, you will need to ensure the data and the analysis are not accessible to others; and it would be advisable to get the contributors' consent beforehand.) Analyse the spellings in the data using the list of respelling categories in this chapter (including colloquial contractions and consonant writing). Then compare the most frequent forms (e.g. <u>) and functions (e.g. homophones) of spelling variation in your data with the most frequent in CorTxt (Tables 9.1 and 9.2). Can you explain any differences?

If spelling variation, as a meaning-making resource, is employed less often than people assume, then this draws attention away from spelling and towards other possible features and resources. Other language features explored in the applied linguistics research include typography, morphology (including the shaping of new words), syntax and discourse structure (Herring, 2012). Examples include Hård af Segerstad's (2002) analysis of grammatical ellipsis such as first-person-pronoun omission in Swedish SMS; my own investigation of the 'speech-like' nature of the clausal structure in texting (Tagg, 2012); the occurrence (or otherwise) of openings and closings in French SMS (Bernicot et al., 2012); and the use of utterance breaks in instant messaging (where a user hits 'send' while typing a message in order to send it in bits), which Baron (2010) found was motivated by the expectation that users be brief.

In subsequent chapters, I go beyond spelling to look at other features of digitally communicated texts, including the strategies used by bloggers to engage their audiences (Chapter 10) and the ways in which fan fiction writers use the conventions of story genres to explore sensitive issues of significance to their lives (Chapter 11). And in Section C, Chapter 17, I look at the literacy theories behind the empirical observations made in this chapter about the meaning-making potential of online spelling.

10 Exploring digital literacies

Introduction: what does it mean to be digitally literate?

Research into web texts, and the skills and strategies required to read them, serves to address concerns about online reading by enhancing our understanding of *actual* texts and how readers *actually* deal with them. Things have moved on since computers were first used as a tool in reading classes. In 1966, educational psychologists Richard C. Atkinson and Duncan N. Hansen reported on their proposed programme of computer-assisted reading for children at Stanford University. The report prompted the following response from George Spache of the University of Florida:

> the implications seem appalling to the reading specialist or classroom teacher accustomed to thinking in terms of classroom life. ... The definitive trial proposed to test the system is apparently to be conducted in a separate building which carefully isolates the learning of reading from the contaminating effects of class-room life and the ineffectualness of live teachers.
>
> (Spache, 1967, p. 101)

As this spat shows, the use of computers in literacy instruction is far from new; the history of computer-assisted instruction (CAI) research can be traced back to at least the 1920s (Pagliaro, 1983). The objections raised by Spache also draw attention to how much things have since changed. One recent innovation is the embedding of computers in many or most people's daily lives. In the mid-twentieth century, computers were seen as a useful tool for enhancing reading instruction, in the sense that they allow children to work at their own pace and provide instant feedback (Atkinson and Hansen, 1966). In the twenty-first century, it is necessary for children to learn how to read digital texts, as well as printed ones: reading on computers is now a goal in itself rather than simply a tool (Coiro et al., 2008). This means that children (and adults) are now learning how the conventions and expectations around new online genres differ from their offline antecedents.

Another innovation is the internet itself, which by connecting computers has revolutionised what technology means for how we read: as we saw in Chapter 2, we must learn to access, filter and organise information from a huge web of networked resources; and to navigate our way through hyperlinked text (hypertext). This means that readers of new online genres must learn a new set of skills and strategies (Coiro and Dobler, 2007). In contrast to the isolation described by Spache, the internet also allows users to make connections with other users, and to exploit social and professional networks online.

The term 'digital literacy' emerged in the 1990s from these developments, and was popularised by Paul Gilster (1997). Educational researchers have since sought to understand 'digital literacy' by identifying and categorising the various skills needed to effectively access information and participate online (Calvani et al., 2009; Eshet, 2004, 2012; Lankshear and Knobel, 2008; Pegrum, 2011). Two main points emerge from such attempts. Firstly, it is evident that being digitally literate involves many of the skills and strategies also associated with print reading: for example, to understand an online text, skilled readers will draw on what they already know about the topic (to interpret meaning, make predictions, and read between the lines) as they would to read print texts (Coiro and Dobler, 2007). Secondly, underlying the attempts to identify digital literacy skills is the understanding that digital literacy is not simply a question of mastering the technology (to turn on a computer and operate a mouse) but of developing a range of cognitive, personal, social and cultural strategies. As Calvani et al. (2009, p. 154) put it, 'the competence we are dealing with entails a critical understanding of technologies, a cognitive and cultural appreciation, and in particular the ability to select and manage information, along with relational and ethical awareness'. Rather than technical expertise, what is central to most lists of digital competences is the need for reflection and critical awareness – the ability to filter, evaluate, understand and use multiple sources of information. Although researchers tend to foreground different aspects (Leu et al., 2004, for example, focus on accessing and sharing knowledge; Buckingham, 2007, on a critical approach to digital media), it is evident that these various skills come together in a complex interplay when a person reads and writes online.

Task 10.1

Imagine you are planning a weekend trip with a friend based in another town, and you have agreed to research possible destinations and report back. Compile a list of the actions you would be likely to take, including finding information, reading it, taking notes and sharing the information with your friend. Then reframe the list in terms of the skills required – what do you need to know or be able to do in order to carry out this everyday task?

One recent and comprehensive list of digital skills is that produced by e-learning researchers Mark Pegrum, Nicky Hockly and Gavin Dudeney (e.g. Dudeney et al., 2013; Hockly, 2012; Pegrum, 2011). They divide digital skills into four main categories: language, search, connections and remix, which I have recategorised to include a fifth, technology. You might want to consider your response to Task 10.1 in terms of the following.

1. Focus on technology

a. *technological literacy*: the ability to use computers and access the internet, and to find solutions to technical problems
b. *mobile literacy*: the ability to handle 'the emerging mobile web, underpinned by wireless technology and mobile devices' (Dudeney et al., 2013, p. 15)
c. *code literacy*: the ability to adapt, 'mod' or mix programmes (Jones and Hafner, 2012, pp. 99–103)

2. Focus on language

a. *texting literacy*: recognising and using 'textese'
b. *print literacy*: recognising and using online genres
c. *hypertext literacy*: navigating new media texts; and inserting hyperlinks into texts
d. *visual and multimedia literacy*: interpreting and exploiting images/ sounds

3. Focus on information

a. *search literacy*: searching effectively for information, for example using search engines
b. *tagging literacy*: labelling information so that it is findable, for example using **bookmarking sites** like delicious.com
c. *filtering literacy*: identifying relevant information and managing information loads
d. *information literacy*: critically evaluating information and sites

4. Focus on connections

a. *personal literacy*: presenting yourself online, and managing your digital identity
b. *network literacy*: using social networks to filter information (Pegrum, 2010)
c. *participatory literacy*: creating and producing digital content
d. *cultural and intercultural literacy*: working with others

5. Focus on remix

a. 'macro' literacy that involves the ability to rework existing content, from copying and pasting and avoiding academic plagiarism to remixing YouTube videos.

(adapted from Dudeney et al., 2013)

Chapter 9 explored research into 'texting literacy' (respelling and its effects on literacy). In this chapter, I focus more broadly on 'language' (particularly print literacy and hypertext literacy) and on information (chiefly search literacy, filtering literacy and 'information' literacy), highlighting the findings of empirical research into the description of online genres and the development of online reading strategies. Chapter 11 looks at remix literacy, while Chapters 12 and 13 focus on 'connections'.

Applied linguistics and online genres

Print literacy encompasses traditional skills needed to construct and decode written text and an awareness of online genres (Dudeney et al., 2013, p. 8; Hockly, 2012, p. 108). Online genres identified by linguists generally correspond to popularly used labels for particular platforms or media (emails, blogs and wikis might all be considered examples of genres). Crucially, however, genres are defined not by the technology but by what users achieve with them; in other words, genres are 'types of texts that share certain features because their users share certain purposes' (Myers, 2010, p. 15). The focus on communicative purpose means that the use of any media is not wholly predetermined by its infrastructure but by how users choose to exploit them (see the Introduction) and in principle that any one platform may be exploited differently by users at different times.

Early studies by applied linguists seeking to identify and deliminate online genres often highlighted the ways in which users drew on their existing knowledge of spoken and written conventions (Baron, 1998; Collot and Belmore, 1996; Gains, 1999; Yates, 1996). For example, Naomi Baron outlined the linguistic features that characterised email as a language variety in the 1990s, describing informal emails as 'speech by other means' and comparing formal emails to 'letters by phone' (Baron, 1998). She concluded that email was at that time a variety in transition, with relatively novice users divided over whether to treat it as a written or spoken medium but not yet ready to treat it as a genre in its own right. In a comparison of academic and business emails, Gains (1999) reached similar conclusions, finding that academic users treated the medium as a form of conversation while business emails followed traditional conventions for formal letters. Both the site users and the linguists studying them understood online genres in the light of their offline equivalents.

As the digital world has grown in complexity and become more familiar, applied linguists have moved away from describing online language in terms of its resemblance to speech or writing to explore how various features of different online contexts – both technological and social – shape the language used and the practices engaged in. Susan Herring's multifaceted framework identifies a range of contextual factors relating to the medium ('technological facets') and to the context ('social facets') (Herring, 2007; see also Crystal, 2011, pp. 33–4) and shows how these factors combine in complex ways to determine the language used. Technological facets include how long a message persists (Snapchat messages are deleted after ten seconds; websites are usually fairly stable), the number of characters allowed, and the possibilities for adaptation (whether the message can be copied, modified and/or forwarded); social facets include participant characteristics such as age, gender, purpose and norms of organisation.

The link between contextual and linguistic features has proved useful in understanding the language of online genres. I illustrate this with reference to applied linguistics research into one such genre – the blog. The blog illustrates how online texts provide us with a different kind of reading experience from that with which we are familiar offline, and engage and reward us in new ways.

Blogs – an online genre

Blogs – websites which comprise regular entries or posts displayed in reverse chronological order, so that the most recent post appears at the top – are often considered a unique or 'emergent' online genre (Crowston and Williams, 2000); one without a counterpart or antecedent in the offline world. Applied linguistics research throws light on the ways in which the blog genre is characterised by its interconnectedness (through its use of hypertext) and by the way bloggers handle the simultaneously highly personal and yet potentially public nature of the genre.

The importance of hypertext to blogs can be traced back to their original function of providing links to websites or 'filtering' information from them (Blood, 2002). These early 'weblogs' (a term coined by Jorn Barger) might be seen as successors to the list posted online in 1991 by Tim Berners-Lee of all the websites then available (something impossible now). However, empirical analysis suggests that filtering may no longer be the predominant function of blogs. In a quantitative analysis of 203 blogs, Herring et al. (2005) found that blogs were often not concerned with external content or knowledge-sharing but instead functioned as personal journals (expressing 'the author's subjective, often intimate perspective on matters of interest to him or her', p. 152). They concluded that many blogs drew on the historical tradition of handwritten diaries, travel journals or even photo albums (and probably also from the personal homepages of the 1990s, Boardman, 2004). In other words, blogs combine elements that are unique to the web ('emergent') with those that are 'reproduced' from other texts and practices (Crowston and Williams, 2000). However, although blogs have developed from 'filters' to something akin to public diaries, bloggers continue to draw on hyperlinks as an affordance to achieve certain communicative purposes (Myers, 2010, p. 45).

Through links to external sites, bloggers align their views with others, place their text within the context of wider discussions, and support, extend or otherwise comment on their claims. The challenge for readers, as Jones and Hafner (2012, p. 38) point out, is that the intended association is often implicit – bloggers (and other writers) do not usually explain why they have made a particular link, although it can usually be assumed that a blogger will link to like-minded sites (Myers, 2010, p. 30). In his study of blogs, Myers (2010) identifies the following kinds of associations suggested through hypertext:

Giving more information on a topic raised in the linking text, e.g. 'A LOOK AT Barack Obama and Supreme Court appointments' (Instapundit);

Providing evidence for a claim by the blogger, e.g. 'Just as the government retains a stronghold over many areas of our lives, the BCCI retains its monopoly over representative cricket' (India Uncut);

Giving someone or something credit, e.g. 'Link to NATURE page, Link to BBC Radio 4 profile of Nicholas from 2003 (Thanks, Vann Hall)' (BoingBoing);

Urging the reader to take action, e.g. 'You can support their campaign by reading and agreeing to a pledge' (Bitch PhD);

> Solving a puzzle posed by the lack of information in the original post, e.g. 'I'VE ALWAYS FOUND THE SMELL OF FAKE-BUTTER POPCORN NAUSEATING, but who knew that it could also be deadly?' (Instapundit);

> **Creating contrasts, through irony for example**, e.g. 'There will be many smaller fluctuations that do just as well; the minimal one you might imagine would be a single brain-sized collection of particles that just has time to look around and go Aaaaaagggghhhhhhh before dissolving back into equilibrium' (Cosmic Variance, linking to a Monty Python sketch).

> (Myers, 2010, pp. 38–42)

Reading a blog requires awareness of these possible meanings. As Myers suggests, 'users of blogs orient to these affordances, developing a reading style that may involve moving to another text, and maybe back again, to try to figure out what the blogger is trying to say, and what stance the blogger is taking on this new text' (Myers, 2010, p. 46).

Blogs are also shaped by a combination of the personal and the public – as Boardman (2004, p. 41) says of personal homepages, they are a 'curious hybrid of secret diary and public revelation'. Bloggers may express intimate feelings or opinions with potentially large and usually unknown audiences that they would hesitate to share in conversation (Chandler, 1998). The combination of the personal and the public has implications for the way in which bloggers address and manage their perceived audience. It is not usually possible for bloggers to know exactly who is reading their posts and so, like broadcasters, bloggers are likely to imagine what their audience is like (see Chapter 14 for more on imagined online audiences). Myers (2010) explains how bloggers in his study engage with a largely unknown audience in a personal and intimate way by creating an 'audience-in-the-text' (Myers, 2010, p. 77) – that is, constructing an audience through their language use and simultaneously interacting with it. Bloggers have various linguistic devices at their disposal in doing this. One overt way is to construct an imagined conversation with readers:

> I received Christmas presents as a kid. I am a Hindu and agnostic (shut up people. I can be both like my Jewish secular friends, heh)
> (comment on the blog Sepia Mutiny, in Myers, 2010, p. 85)

Another is to directly address the audience (or particular segments) with pronouns such as *you* and *we*:

> What do you guys think? Can we raise that much?
> (Bitch PhD, p. 80)

A similar device is the use of (rhetorical) questions or directives (illustrated respectively in the following examples):

> Does your dog do that? Hop on and off your bed, over and over again, because he is part Labrador, part douchebag?
>
> (Dooce, p. 83)

> Yes, go sign up now, but come back here to read the rest of the post when you're done. Thanks!
>
> (Climb the stairs, p. 83)

Despite the 'reputation of bloggers and commenters for casual rudeness', as Myers (2010, p. 89) puts it, the language of the blogs that Myers looked at suggests that bloggers are very concerned with politeness and face-saving techniques. This is indicated by a high use of hedges (words or phrases used to soften or mitigate a statement), as in the following post:

> If you have a moment, it may be worth glancing at Dr 'Abd al-Shafi's famous speech from the Madrid talks.
>
> (Raising Yousuf, p. 90)

Similarly, although the blogs contained a high degree of stance-taking, Myers notes that bloggers carefully flagged their assertions as personal opinions:

> It is my personal feeling that the blogosphere has elements which may change us all, when we can indulge in peering into the souls of those affected by current events.
>
> (IsraeliMom, p. 101)

In short, applied linguistics investigation of this online genre highlights how the language of blogs is shaped not only by technology but by communicative purpose and interpersonal considerations. The technology must be seen as providing affordances which are exploited in various ways (avoiding a technological deterministic stance). For example, hyperlinks may or may not be taken up by bloggers – Myers (2010) compares blogs that use hyperlinks for 'incidental support' to those that frequently use them as 'an essential part of each entry' or 'are built entirely around links' (p. 29). Links can be used in humorous, subversive or unexpected ways, as seen earlier in 'Aaaaaagggghhhhhhh', where a science blogger linked to a comedy sketch (Myers, 2010, p. 42). As with bloggers' language use more generally, such creative uses can be seen as attempts to engage with the potentially huge audience afforded by the internet, and to tread a careful line between unbridled self-expression and the maintaining of face.

Online reading skills and strategies

Literacy education researchers show that reading online requires many of the same strategies as print reading, but that contemporary readers are also adapting these and adopting new, particularly complex strategies (Aflerbach and Cho, 2009; Cho, 2013; Coiro and Dobler, 2007; Goldman, 2010). Those working on reading strategies see reading not as a passive activity but as a strategic process of meaning-making, or as 'constructively responsive'; that is, the text itself is constructed through the act of reading as readers predict and evaluate what they read, and relate it to previous experience and background knowledge (e.g. RAND Reading Study Group, 2002). This view encourages us to see the reading of hyperlinked text as an extension of existing reading practices, rather than radically departing from them.

One such study by Coiro and Dobler (2007) explored the reading strategies used by accomplished readers aged around 11–12 years. The eleven informants were asked to carry out online reading tasks which involved locating information within an interactive website ('5 Tigers: the Tiger Information Centre'), whilst 'thinking aloud' their decisions and motivations, and they were interviewed before and after the task. The researchers found that the children drew on recognised reading comprehension strategies but that they did so in more complex ways than previously noted for offline readers.

To take the example of inferential reading strategies – involving predictions about the current text based on previous experience – the online readers drew on those associated with printed texts (they used structural cues within headings and boldfaced words; and they matched words on the website with those on the question sheet they were working through). However, the researchers found a particularly strong reliance on forward inferential reasoning, seemingly motivated by the use of hyperlinks to organise information. Hyperlinks mean that readers cannot always rely on scanning or inferential strategies to determine relevance but must instead make predictions about what they expect to find. In other words, whenever readers came across, or considered clicking on, a link, they were encouraged to make predictions as to the content and relevance of the linked page. For example, in one think-aloud, Marina said:

> Marina: [skimming a website for information about what would make a hurricane lose power] Well, we can eliminate already that we don't want the facts of it [referring to one link], and we don't want to protect buildings from it [a second link], and we're not talking about warnings [a third link], and so we have three left. And since this one [a fourth link] has more of the context of the power of the

storm, it's connecting the words with the question, so this
one [a fifth link] would probably be better to look at.
(Coiro and Dobler, 2007, p. 233)

While readers of printed texts can constantly check their predictions
against the linear text, online readers use their predictions to follow
hyperlinks and thus reshape the text. Therefore, as Coiro and Dobler
(2007, p. 242) point out, 'inaccurate predictions about upcoming text
may cause some readers to get lost or disorientated' (Coiro and Dobler
2007, p. 242). The point, however, is that the children were not lost or
disorientated, but were prompted by the online context to exploit their
existing reading strategies and draw on their experience of being online
to effectively and purposefully navigate the links.

As Coiro and Dobler acknowledge, the greater complexity of online
reading may mean that weaker readers struggle with online texts. A
Canadian study of high-school students' search skills (Julien and Barker,
2008), for example, criticised the participants' reliance on Google as a
search engine, their 'unsophisticated' searching techniques (including
their use of limited search terms and their reliance on the first few search
results) and evaluation skills (they relied only on domain names and
seemed not to evaluate the content). Such data can be used to make
recommendations to promote effective teaching strategies (Julien and
Barker, 2008, pp. 15–16; Pellegrin et al., 2001; RAND, 2002). Most
importantly, however, the point must be made that online reading is in
many ways similar to or an extension of print reading; and while weak
readers may struggle particularly with online text, good readers are able
to develop the reading strategies necessary to successfully navigate it.

Conclusion

Public concerns over the impact of the internet on reading fail to take
into account the fact that reading online texts requires an awareness of
conventions and expectations as much as offline ones do, and that –
like offline texts – these can be picked up or explicitly taught. Applied
linguistics research into online genres highlights similarities between
online and offline texts and carefully identifies and explains where the
technology allows writers to do things differently. Educational research
suggests that strategies needed to navigate online text may be more
complex than for offline reading, but that they build on and extend the
kinds of strategies required of all readers. Both strands of research
highlight the particularly complex relationship between reading and
writing online – blog readers, for example, create their own text as
they navigate through hyperlinks; they can leave comments; and they
can become blog writers themselves. The next chapter looks at the
process from the writer's viewpoint.

Task 10.2

Choose a blog with which you are familiar and analyse the language used. Start by noting some contextual features, such as topic and purpose, and the social characteristics of the blogger. Is it a filter blog or a personal diary? Then look for the following linguistic features:

- the use of hyperlinks (how many? internal or external? if external, what kinds of evaluations or stances do they imply? what kinds of linguistic items are linked from?);
- strategies used to engage the reader and to interact with them (imagined conversations; pronouns *you* and *we*; questions and directives);
- politeness and face-saving techniques, including hedges.

To what extent do you feel the blogger has 'assure[d] readers that they are in the right place, and that it might be completely reasonable to interact with this total stranger on the other side of the world, by commenting or linking or quoting' (Myers, 2010, p. 93)?

11 Using the web as a space for writing

Introduction

> There's a lot more goes into making a remix than you might think. You actually have to have a goal in mind, like what message you want to convey, and then using all the different [rhetorical] methods we've been learning about, deciding what will be most effective to get the message across.
>
> (Mike, first-year student of 'Political rhetoric and new media', in Dubisar and Palmeri, 2010, p. 79)

In Chapter 3, I explored concerns surrounding online writing and remixing: the demise of the author in the digital age, the questionable validity of many online texts, the ease with which texts can be copied, and the potential implications for plagiarism and copyright infringements. In the face of these concerns, the chapter concluded by highlighting various grassroots mechanisms that exist to control and manage online content, from community norms to site moderators; and it suggested that the internet does not constitute a radical change from the past but brings to the fore tendencies and practices that pre-date digital technology. In other words, caution is needed before the internet as a space for writing is labelled an unprecedented free-for-all. Empirical language-related research is useful in exploring the kind of writing that actually takes place online.

In this chapter, I look at applied linguistics research into two online writing spaces – Wikipedia and fan fiction – and at how their different social purposes, norms, regulations and technological affordances shape and are shaped by users' language practices. What is important about this empirical research is that it seeks to describe, explain and understand what is going on in these relatively new sites, rather than jumping to hasty or evaluative conclusions. Having said that, in explaining why users engage so enthusiastically with such sites, the research tends to highlight the benefits for contributors and other internet users, describing Wikipedia as a space for productive collaboration with shared norms and values; and fan fiction as a site for supportive, informal learning. In other words, researchers assume users are writing online for positive reasons, rather than presuming the worst. As such, the research identifies opportunities for developing traditional 'print' literacy skills as well as the acquisition of 'remix literacy' (Dudeney et al., 2013), as in the case of the student quoted at the start of this chapter.

Wikipedia

Studies suggest that Wikipedia entries are both stylistically similar to and as accurate as printed encyclopaedias such as the *Encyclopaedia Britannica* (Elia, 2007; Giles, 2005) and the Columbia Encyclopedia (Emigh and Herring, 2005). In Giles' (2005) study, for example, experts compared 42 entries from Wikipedia with the *Encyclopaedia Britannica* and found a similar number of errors in both. These similarities appear to emerge because of, rather than despite, the collaborative nature of Wikipedia. For example, a study by Wilkinson and Huberman (2007) found the number of edits and editors to correlate with the quality of the article (the more edits and editors, the better the article). As the authors point out, this finding contrasts with received wisdom about large-scale collaborations, which tend to report less positive outcomes than smaller endeavours. In relation to this paradox, language-related empirical research has drawn attention to aspects of Wikipedia which shape the nature of its collaboration and ultimately its articles: firstly, the Talk pages and other places which facilitate discussions; secondly, the degree and nature of (often implicit) controls which operate on the wiki; and, thirdly, the existence of relatively small communities of dedicated editors whose values dominate the site. I touch on each below.

Talk pages are sites for discussion among editors which exist for each specific Wikipedia article (they can be accessed by clicking on a tab in the top left hand corner of each article). Viégas et al. (2007) highlight the growing importance of the Talk pages in planning and coordinating amongst editors. In an earlier study, the researchers had used data visualisation methods to plot the evolution of articles and to analyse patterns of collaboration and dispute (Viégas et al., 2004). In 2007, using the same visualisation methods, they found that the Talk pages and other spaces devoted to coordination constituted the fastest growing part of the site. They note that the Talk pages are not only used for resolving disputes following contested edits (that is, 'retroactive resolution') (Viégas et al., 2004), but for collective planning and the enforcement of norms (Viégas et al., 2007), and thus the establishment and enhancement of information quality (Stvilia et al., 2005). Specifically, Viégas et al. (2007) found that over half of all contributions in their sample of Talk page discussions (58.8 per cent) constituted requests or suggestions for editing coordination, highlighting the role that the Talk pages serve in providing a space for editors to 'discuss their editing activities in advance, to ask for help, and to explain the reasons why they think specific changes should be made' (p. 8): in other words, to collaborate in planning and organising intended edits.

The researchers also conclude that the Talk pages constitute an informal but very necessary mechanism for educating new users about, and generally enforcing, Wikipedia policies and norms. A further 7.9 per cent of the contributions to the Talk pages analysed in the study made explicit reference to Wikipedia guidelines, suggesting that they are being actively used and enforced by editors. As Myers (2010) points out, although it is hard in practice to reach a consensus on what, for example, constitutes NPOV (Neutral Point of View), the principles provide a 'useful basis for arguments, because one can expect other participants to recognise them' and not to 'reject them outright' (p. 147). In another 5.4 per cent of contributions, editors justified arguments through reference to precedents on the site:

> As an experiment, I'm going to semi-protect this page for a bit so only logged in users can edit it. This appears to be done more on Wikipedia of late due to increasing vandalism. (However, opinion is very split over this, just see here [Wikipedia_talk:Semi-protection] and here [Wikipedia:Village pump (policy)]. If anyone has a problem with this please let me know.
>
> (Viégas et al., 2007, p. 9)

A community or communities of editors adhering to the (often implicit) values of Wikipedia can be said to dominate and shape the site. As Emigh and Herring (2005, p. 9) point out, editors who adhere to these values, and who seek to enforce them, tend to devote more time and energy to the site, and thus have more control over it, than casual users, which include those seeking to vandalise the site. Similarly, Myers (2010) also notes a tendency for articles (at least the less controversial ones) to be edited mainly by a group of dedicated and active editors who appear to take some responsibility for the entry. The suggestion that pages are managed by different 'communities' of editors with particular areas of expertise also receives some support in Emigh and Herring's (2005) observation regarding stylistic variation between some pages – Ben Hogan's page at the time being written in a narrative style, while Karl Marx's was 'interlarded with expository statements of a philosophical, abstract nature' (Emigh and Herring, 2005, p. 7).

Drawing on a corpus of 365 discussions taken from 47 Wikipedia Talk pages edited between 2002 and 2008, Bender et al. (2011) show how various claims to authority – statements 'made by a discussion participant aimed at bolstering their credibility in the discussion' (p. 48) – are also a feature of Wikipedia Talk pages, with 32 per cent of editors making authority claims across 21 per cent of turns in the corpus. Editors drew on the following sources of authority:

- Credentials (reference to education, training, or work experience)
- Experiential (reference to involvement or witnessing event)
- Forum (explicitly citing site policy)
- External (based on an outside authority or source of expertise)
- Social expectations (based on wider community norms).

Interestingly, Bender et al. did not find claims in the Talk pages based on Institutional authority (an individual's position within a powerful organisation), suggesting that editors do not appeal explicitly to their status within Wikipedia. However, editors with different statuses tended to formulate different claims – unregistered editors were more likely to make external claims and less likely to put forward forum claims; while administrators were more likely to make forum claims and less likely to defer to external authorities (p. 55). A related finding was that the more integrated into the community the editors were, the more authority claims they would make. In short, authority claims played an important social and discursive role in the Talk pages, as well as contributing to a sense of community.

At the same time, editors also drew on linguistic resources to hedge their authority claims and thus defuse potential conflict. Myers found that the editors often drew on discourse markers more commonly associated with spoken conversation or online discussion forums, such as 'well', 'hmmm' and 'pfft' (an observation also made by Emigh and Herring, 2005), which served the interpersonal function of 'marking the response as casual, offhand, not claiming the authority of a full written case' (Myers, 2010, p. 154); that is, to avoid provoking antagonism by appearing overly authoritative. Interestingly, the speech-like feel of the Talk pages contrasts with the formal style of the actual entries (Emigh and Herring, 2005), suggesting that editors are able to move between styles deemed appropriate for the different parts of the site. This and other research begins to suggest that collaboration on Wikipedia is 'based partly on some explicit principles and procedures, but more on an implicit sense of how they [contributing editors] should interact' (Myers, 2010, p. 130).

To show how 'behind the scenes' negotiation can result in the construction of an effective article, Myers analysed the first 100 edits as listed on the History pages of two 'Featured articles' (those rated highly by Wikipedia editors): one on the city of Manchester, and one on the World Trade Center. Both articles gradually built up through a series of *additions* (whereby information is added) and *changes* (whereby information is altered), and from an initial stub rather than from an extended essay by one person (suggesting that these articles are collaborative from the start). At the same time, by the time the articles reached the status of 'featured articles', they still retained a great deal of the initial focus and wording established in the early edits. However, the process for the two articles was a little different: while the Manchester article was uncontroversially added to by editors, every addition to the World Trade Center was potentially intended or interpreted as supporting one of two contrasting viewpoints: that the building was deliberately destroyed or accidentally fell on 11 September 2001. However, even with the more controversial articles, Myers shows how extreme or minority opinions tended to be subsumed by the consensus view (or relegated to the Talk pages – that is, behind the scenes of the main article).

In fact, what emerges from this empirical research is whether, in its similarities to expert-produced, traditional encyclopaedias, Wikipedia is defeating the purpose of online collaboration, with its potential for fostering diverse, unconventional and overtly evaluative views. In Chapter 3, I cited a parody of Wikipedia where the question 'What are the colours of the rainbow?' is met with the consensus, 'Brown'. The research discussed in this chapter points to an element of truth in the joke; not in the sense that Wikipedia is inaccurate or misleading, but because the nature of the collaborative process tends to produce uncontroversial, single-voiced articles. This:

> is at odds with the goal of the wiki (and user-created content) movement to create content incorporating diverse perspectives, and more generally to foster new and better communication practices. Notably, it suggests that a few active users, when acting in concert with established norms within an open editing system, can achieve ultimate control over the content produced within the system, literally erasing diversity, controversy, and inconsistency, and homogenizing contributors' voices.
>
> (Emigh and Herring, 2005, p. 9)

This in turn has implications for the question as to whether students should cite Wikipedia (Warschauer and Grimes, 2008, p. 12). The question should be considered in the light of studies showing a tendency for undergraduate students to draw inappropriately on online sources which lack 'rigor, objectivity, authority and transparency', or ROAT (e.g. Radia and Stapleton, 2009). Radia and Stapleton (2009) put forward the argument that while many web sources, including Wikipedia, lack ROAT in a traditionally defined sense, such 'unconventional sources' may 'harbour a type of information that stimulates both ideas and originality of thought, while also enhancing critical analysis' (p. 156) and, furthermore, prepare students to deal with the kind of collaborative, unverified and fluid sources that increasingly characterise the digital age. Their study involved the analysis of essay assignments by 16 largely East Asian students at a Canadian university, who also provided a commentary on the sources chosen in writing the essay and (in three cases) were interviewed. Student A, for example, whose essay was on Canadian multiculturalism, justified his citing a blog magazine by asserting that 'as a public medium it provided further insight into the often ambiguous arguments surrounding multiculturalism' (Radia and Stapleton, 2009, p. 161); another student used an online Arabic news site in her essay on masculinity to show that 'beauty expectations differ across cultures and are manipulated differently by non-western media' (p. 161). The researchers propose that the 'judicious' use of such sources alongside more conventional ones can enhance critical enquiry.

In their practical book for teachers, Dudeney et al. (2013) outline a number of activities for developing students' critical literacy – or what they call 'information' and 'filtering' literacies (see Chapter 10) – within class. One activity, which they call 'Fun facts', involves students looking online to verify some odd-sounding facts such as 'Ants don't sleep'; 'A pregnant goldfish is called a "twit"'; and 'Cows give more milk if they listen to music' (and see mysterytopia.com). The researchers suggest students first discuss whether they think they are true, before carrying out an investigation into their veracity across a number of sites. The same activity would presumably work well with 'urban myths', 'housewives' tales', stereotypes and conspiracy theories. Such activities work to develop students' awareness of the status of different sites and encourage them to take a critical and reflective approach when gathering information online.

Fan fiction

Applied linguistics studies of young fan fiction writers reveal fan fiction sites to be a rewarding space for learning and personal development. In this section, I report on an ethnographic study of the anime section of the international fan fiction site, FanFiction.net (FFN) by Rebecca W. Black. Black explored the extent to which adolescent English-language learners used the site to improve their language and literacy skills in ways that both reflected and departed from school-based ways of learning. Black used participant observation to fully understand the site (in that she herself participated as a writer), collecting fan fiction stories as well as reader reviews, and conducting interviews with her focal participants. Given the increasingly important role of collaborative online writing in people's professional and personal lives, Black's argument is not that fan fiction is a threat to traditional schooling, but that schools have a lot to learn from informal learning spaces like fan fiction sites.

One of the strengths of FFN as a learning space is that participants are highly self-motivated to participate and improve. In Black's study the participants shared a passion for a particular anime series, Cardcaptor Sakura, as well as for creating fan fiction. One of Black's participants, Nanako, discovered the site soon after moving from China to Canada, and firstly her 'avid' reading and subsequently her 'successful and wildly popular' writing were pivotal in her acquisition of English (Black, 2006, p. 173). Because the internet allows people with similar interests to come together, the communities that form are very heterogeneous, spanning various national backgrounds and life experiences (Black, 2007a, p. 389), potentially creating a rich and diverse social and learning space. In both motivation and heterogeneity, Black argues, online spaces like fan fiction are markedly different from traditional school environments.

Fan fiction may, argues Black (2006), offer scaffolded writing practice in the sense that a framework – plot, genre, characters – already exists, thus relieving 'the pressure of having to create a wholly new setting or cast of characters' (p. 124). As well as the structured writing practice that fan fiction affords, various forms of feedback on learners' writing are offered by the site. For example, the opportunity for readers to review fan fiction stories is built into the site – Black (2009), for example, records that Nanako had at that time received 9,400 reviews of her stories. As Black (2007b) explains, reviewers adopted a variety of techniques, ranging from pulling apart sentences or paragraphs and making grammatical and stylistic improvements to what Black calls 'OMG standards' consisting of 'enthusiastic statements of appreciation for the fiction' prefaced by 'OMG!' (Black, 2007b, p. 124). While the former provide targeted and useful feedback, the latter serve to boost the learners' confidence. Indeed, Black (2006, p. 126) comments on the generally positive nature of feedback on the site, which not only boosts confidence but also allows fan fiction writers to take on identities as successful writers. Furthermore, the site also affords opportunities for collaborative writing, in the sense that people receive feedback whilst writing their texts, which directs the future course of their stories. Black's participants also took advantage of beta readers – 'a person who reads a word of fiction with a critical eye, with the aim of improving grammar, spelling, characterization, and general style of a story prior to its release to the general public' (FanFiction.net, 2008, cited by Black, 2009, p. 691). As such, fan fiction sites offer language learners the opportunity to develop their print literacy skills (see Chapter 10): the basic conventions and skills associated with a particular genre.

Fan fiction writing also offers opportunities for developing new digital literacy skills such as multimodal and technological literacies, and information literacies (Black, 2009). Focusing on three participants,

Black (2009) explains how they moved from being fairly unskilled computer users to setting up and maintaining their own websites and social network accounts, and using multiple modes of meaning-making such as colour, image, movement and sound. Black puts this down to their involvement in the fan fiction site: 'through participation in fan spaces, all three focal participants have developed skills in designing webpages; using various software programs; creating videos; and manipulating online, multimodal texts to effectively communicate and convey information' (Black, 2009, p. 693).

On fan fiction sites, new members ('newbies') inhabit the same space, carry out the same practices and have access to the same resources that expert or experienced users have (Black, 2007a, p. 389). Not only were the participants treated as 'legitimate participants' – full members of the community – but their texts were seen as 'meaningful contributions to the "fanon"' (fan additions to the canon) (Black, 2009, p. 692). In contrast, school-based practices rarely allow students to go beyond critique to actually create or add to the existing canon. In fact, Black (2006) found that English language learners on FNN who struggled with English were often sought after for other skills. For example, writers of anime fan fiction often post messages asking for Japanese translations of certain words to authenticate their texts (*kawaii* [cool or cute] and *arigatou* [thank you]) or request information about Japanese or Chinese customs and practices to make their anime more realistic. This meant participants taking on the status of 'expert' and enjoying a sense of belonging and of renewed confidence, as well as allowing them to see themselves as legitimate English-language users (Black, 2009, p. 692).

Black's research has implications for how literacy can be taught in schools. Again, Dudeney et al. (2013) suggest practical activities for teaching students about the principles and purposes of remix – by, for example, re-subtitling film trailers using a site like Subtitle Horse (subtitle-horse.com) or creating their own LOLcats images (a popular meme) – as well as copyright issues. For the latter, they suggest incorporating a session on Creative Commons as part of a project which involves students selecting and using photos. Doing the selection first and then finding out how many of their photos they can actually use may jolt students into realising the ethical issues involved (pp. 109–14).

Conclusion

In this chapter, I've shown how empirical applied linguistics research into two very different online writing communities highlights the potential benefits of the web as a space for writers and writing. Despite concerns and misgivings, Wikipedia appears to be an example of effective collaboration, which is negotiated, managed and controlled through a dedicated community of editors. Meanwhile, fan fiction brings globally dispersed fans of a particular work or works together, and it allows them to do more than simply entertain themselves through their own stories but to develop a range of digital literacies in a supportive environment. In these virtual spaces, language – the written word – is a key resource not only in producing the finished texts but for establishing the collaborative networks that bring them into being. In Section C, Chapter 17, I look at the theories of literacy that underpin these emerging ideas about what constitutes effective, purposeful writing.

Task 11.1

Choose one of the following tasks.

1. Choose a topic, person or place on Wikipedia that interests you, and go to that article. Identify whether it is a Featured article or a controversial one, and try to get a general feel for the article. Then look at the Talk page (click on the tab in the top left hand corner) and choose two or three comment threads. Analyse the threads for the features discussed in this chapter:

   a. Authority claims, including references to norms and principles
   b. Use of hedges or features associated with spoken language
   c. Evidence of edits being made collaboratively.

   In what ways and to what extent do the Talk pages present a different approach to authorship from that presented by the articles themselves?

2. Choose a work of fiction that you like and are familiar with. (You may choose two and combine them.) Write the first chapter of a story that builds on the characters, plots or settings. Try to do so in a way that makes it relevant to you and to current issues in your life. Reflect on the difficulties in doing so, and the benefits it brings. How motivating is the activity? Does the process relieve 'the pressure of having to create a wholly new setting or cast of characters'? If you post the story online, how helpful is the feedback?

12 Using more than one language online

Introduction

Chapter 4 looked at the shift within applied linguistics from a concern with the distribution of languages online to an interest in how various languages are used in social media contexts. In Leppänen and Peuronen's (2012, p. 389) words:

> the focus is no longer on the measuring and surveying of the use of particular languages on the internet, but on the specific multilingual practices of internet users, the motivations behind their language choices and the functions and meanings these have for them in the specific internet contexts in which they operate.

The point is that when we actually look at how people communicate online, it is evident that they do not maintain strict boundaries between different languages but, as in spoken interactions, draw variously on whichever languages are in their repertoires and (as well as they can) whichever languages have currency in a particular digital situation. In this chapter, I explore some of the research into online code-switching – the practice of switching between languages while interacting online. What emerges from the research is that online (written) code-switching differs in important ways from spoken code-switching because of the affordances of digital contexts, including the networked audience, the availability of networked resources, and the graphic and visual resources available online (Androutsopoulos, forthcoming); and that ultimately the complexity of online multilingual practices challenges the usefulness of the term 'code-switching'. I start with an overview of how code-switching has been understood in relation to spoken interactions.

Traditional frameworks of code-switching

The study of code-switching developed around the empirical analysis of spoken data, and the emerging analytical frameworks are largely designed to explain face-to-face conversations between people from the same, bilingual, community (Gardner-Chloros, 2009). According to this body of research, code-switching can be divided into two types: code-switching and code-mixing. Code-switching can be seen as a 'contextualisation cue' (Auer, 1995; Gumperz, 1982) by which participants 'make relevant' certain aspects of context in a particular instance of talk. People achieve this through code-switching because the juxtaposition of different languages highlights the contrast between them in a meaningful way, drawing on the meanings that each language has for the participants. As Poplack (1980) explains, code-switches can operate intersententially (where each sentence is in a different language) or intrasententially (where clauses within sentences are in different languages), in order to fulfil discourse functions such as marking changes in topic or reporting speech; or participant-related functions such as addressing participants (Auer, 1984). In other words, each code-switch can be said to fulfil an immediate function in ongoing talk. In acts of code-mixing, on the other hand, participants pepper their talk with words and phrases from two or more languages and the individual switches 'do not carry meaning qua language choice for the bilingual participants' (Auer, 1998, p. 16): the motivation for code-mixing is therefore less functional and often more a display of shared identity.

It is to be expected that code-switching is shaped in part by the context in which it takes place. The contextual factors impacting on code-switching practices include a) the people involved, their relationships, social identities and educational background; b) the topic being discussed; and c) the setting where the interaction takes place (Cárdenas-Claros and Isharyanti, 2009). While the people and topic may vary across spoken and online contexts, the third factor predicts that code-switching will differ between the two modes, so that affordances of the internet will shape the code-switching that takes place online.

It is only recently that the practice of code-switching in written language has become a focus of attention in applied linguistics (Sebba, 2012), in part because of the increasing recognition of the opportunities provided by the internet for language contact and mixing on 'an unprecedented scale' (Androutsopoulos, 2013, p. 667; a point also made by Danet and Herring, 2007). Thus it is not surprising that internet researchers have drawn on models developed in relation to spoken interactions. The assumption that spoken code-switching is in some way the norm often means that online code-switching is evaluated in terms of its 'authenticity'; that is, its resemblance to spoken practices (Androutsopoulos, 2013). As we shall see in this chapter, however, the affordances and linguistic features of online contexts encourage us to question the suitability of existing models for online language, and to expand and redefine our understanding of what code-switching entails.

Similarities between online and spoken code-switching

Research into online code-switching has drawn parallels between the forms and functions of online and spoken practice. For example, multilingual features of digital communications often reflect mixed spoken codes (Deumert and Masinyana, 2008; Lexander, 2011). In his study of Senegalese text messaging, Lexander (2011) notes that a mixed code is often used to reflect the way in which young people talk to each other in Dakar. The language switches are not themselves functional, but the resulting mixed discourse serves to index a local, urban identity (following Lexander, French is in italics and Wolof underlined).

> Salut chou boy ci lo nek,namanala té a mbour walla, yangui noce mé dioxma ci affair yi,wagnil sa does,bonreveil matinal,bizu

> *Salut chou* boy, ci loo nekk? Namm naa la, *tu es* à *Mbour* walla? Yaa ngi *noce, mais* jox ma ci *affaires* yi. Wàññil sa *dose, bon réveil matinal, bisous*

> [*Hello dear friend, how are you? I miss you, are you in Mbour or what? You enjoy yourself, but give me my share* [of your wealth, etc.]. *Decrease your level of enjoyment, good morning-wake-up, kisses*]
> (Lexander, 2011, p. 439)

As Lexander (2011, p. 439) explains, texters' familiarity with this mixed code means that they do not always assign words to other languages. For example, the writer of the above message said in interview that 'chou boy' was part of urban Wolof rather than constituting a switch from French ('chou') to English ('boy'). This raises an important question as to whether such phrases constitute a switch between languages.

As the above examples suggest, code-switching in digital communication is functionally as well as formally similar to spoken interactions. People in digital contexts appear to draw on more than one language for much the same reasons as in spoken situations: to construct identity, express emotions, show alignments with other people and as a resource for structuring talk. For example, Fung and Carter (2007) show how, when Hong Kong students in the UK switched between Chinese and English in private chat conversations, Chinese discourse particles were used to display emotions that the interlocutors couldn't convey in English in a way that reflected spoken conversations as well as the local value placed on the two languages. In the following example, *ar* indicates a question in 'introduce ur brother to me ar' and acts to soften an assertion in 'bored ar … jane ho moon ar', while *lor* in 'watch your vcd lor' highlights the obviousness of the suggestion as well as suggesting resignation. The switch to Cantonese to express emotion ('jane ho moon') also reflects offline practices.

A: my brother is coming next weekend ... will you be here?
B: yes, why? introduce ur brother to me ar?
A: i thought you are going to somewhere ... i will of course introduce him to you la ... laa1
B: bored ar ... jane ho moon [*very bored*] ar ...
A: watch your vcd lor ... I have so much to revise ar .... =<
                              (Fung and Carter, 2007, pp. 251–2)

Digital media such as internet chat or instant messaging can be compared to spoken interactions in the sense that they are often dialogic, vernacular and multimodal (Androutsopoulos, 2010), and it may therefore be expected that code-switching in these contexts resembles that occurring in spoken interactions. As Leppänen and Peuronen (2012) point out, online genres which differ more sharply from spoken interactions may exhibit more differences with spoken code-switching and therefore: 'textual genres such as blogs, websites, webzines and fan fiction clearly require different methods of analysis from dialogic and interactive CMD modes and genres' (p. 398). In other words, code-switching is more likely to reflect spoken practices in channels used synchronously, than on asynchronous platforms. Androutsopoulos (2010) thus distinguishes between what he calls 'conversational' and 'non-conversational' code-switching online. One characteristic of non-conversational code-switching is that asynchronous modes afford time for planning, careful stylisation and structuring. Leppänen (2009), for example, analyses a fan fiction story in which code-switching acts as a narrative device, bringing together two different worlds (Finnish- and English-speaking) and also allowing a juxtaposition between the heroine's inner monologue and her dialogues in the fantasy world she inhabits. Leppänen and Peuronen (2012) also give the example of a Finnish traveller in Mexico, whose travel blogs use various languages for narrative effect and in consideration of his audience: he juxtaposes whole paragraphs in English (aimed at his wider audience) and Finnish (targeted more specifically at his close friends and family), with insertions in Spanish.

Differences between online and spoken code-switching

Androutsopoulos's (forthcoming) concept of 'networked multilingualism' identifies three affordances which shape multilingual users' practices: a) their orientation towards a networked audience; b) users' access to networked resources; and c) the physical constraints of the keyboard and screen.

a) The impact of networked audiences on code-switching

In early studies of online code-switching, the impact of the audience on switches tended to be considered in relation to differences between private and public channels, which were felt to correspond to informal and formal writing styles. For example, Androutsopoulos (2006) found that the dominant language used on public web-based forums among certain migrant groups in Germany (e.g. Persian, Indian and Greek) was not their heritage languages but German. This was probably influenced by the country in which the migrant communities were based, as well as the gradual loss of the heritage languages, particularly in younger generations. Given the growth of English as a global lingua franca since the mid-twentieth century, English is the choice of many online groups. For example, Durham's (2007) study of language choice on a Swiss medical association mailing list documented a shift towards what she refers to as 'Pan-Swiss English' between French-, German- and Italian-speaking Swiss participants. Durham argued that participants used English pragmatically to ensure everyone understood what was being discussed. Meanwhile, a number of studies have explored private means of online communication, including email (Tsiplakou, 2009), instant messaging (Fung and Carter, 2007) and SMS (Deumert and Masinyana, 2008; Morel et al., 2012) and found that people are building on intimate relationships in creative ways by drawing on their shared language histories and current repertoires. In many of these cases, people draw on languages not primarily for pragmatic reasons but as a 'semiotic strategy' in constructing identity online. For example, Tsiplakou (2009) documents how her circle of Greek friends playfully code-switch between English, standard Greek and regional varieties of Greek in their private email messages in order to create a group identity as highly literate, knowing and educated Greeks. In the following example, Andreas quotes from a piece of English-language literary criticism ('first self-conscious written narrative') and frames it deprecatingly with the informal discourse marker 'you know' and the switch at the end to Cypriot Greek, a variety of Greek which signals an uneducated, peasant identity. Thus the comment both signals his 'highly literate' identity whilst subverting it (Tsiplakou, 2009, pp. 385–6).

Opou, you know, first self-conscious written narrative, alla ullo logia, re koumbare

[*Where, you know, first self-conscious written narrative, but it's all words, mate*]

(Tsiplakou, 2009, p. 382)

On social network sites, users face an audience that cannot be categorised as public or private. Social network sites are often described as being 'semi-public', in the sense that the audience for any one status update or post is made up of a diverse range of people, all of whom the user has some connection with. Mixing in these cases appears to fulfil two functions: firstly, as an addressivity strategy for targeting individuals on the busy site; and, secondly, as an identity performance before a wider audience. These two functions are illustrated in the following status update posted by Dream, a Thai student in London.

> **Dream**   is thinking about buying a camera. She can't decide
> whether Nikon D90 or Canon 500D is better.
> นิคอนก็ดีมีตรรักแฟนเพลงเชียร์กันเยอะ
> แต่สีมันสู้ดสด ไม่รู้จะสดไปไหม
> แคนนอนตัวนี้ยังไม่เคยลองเล่น แต่สีธรรมชาติก็ชอบนะ
> T____T'
> (Nikon seems good and many people encourage me to
> buy one but the colours are very bright. I am not sure
> whether they are too bright. I haven't tried this Canon but
> I also like natural colours)
>
> (Seargeant et al., 2012)

The use of English in her status update reveals Dream's awareness of her wider audience, made up of people from a range of language backgrounds for whom English is a lingua franca. At the same time, the fact that she uses Thai to elaborate on her request suggests that she is targeting her Thai-speaking Friends because she either expects them to respond or is encouraging them to do so. The impact of the networked audience on language use, and implications for privacy, are explored in Chapters 6 and 14.

b) Language-related resources online

Access to 'networked resources' relating to language increases the possibilities for multilingualism, by making available to users such affordances as translation services and online dictionaries, enabling them to select from a greater range of languages online than they would be able to use in face-to-face spoken interactions. The ability to link to other sites, to embed photos and videos within posts, and to repost others' contributions also enables users to create a more highly multilingual discourse than they might otherwise construct. The ability to draw on these language resources may contribute in particular to the tendency for practices of 'minimal bilingualism' (Androutsopoulos, 2007), that is, the use of easily accessible, often formulaic phrases associated with a language not spoken to any high level of proficiency by a particular community. Morel et al. (2012, p. 283), for example, in their study of Swiss SMS text messages, found that most code-switching involved the insertion of highly formulaic greetings and expressions such as the English phrases 'What's up?' and 'You're welcome!'. Thus, what is encouraged by the availability of networked resources is a particular kind of code-switching which does not require full proficiency in the language. What this raises is the question of what it means to be a user of a language: is full proficiency a prerequisite?

c) Visual graphic resources

In relation to the last of Androutsopoulos's affordances, digital communication differs from spoken interaction in that users rely not on prosodic features and physical clues when expressing themselves, but on visual graphic resources (such as emoticons or emojis, punctuation and font) and on spelling. Androutsopoulos describes how people's 'digital literacy repertoires' include what he calls 'trans-scripting'. Trans-scripting can involve writing a language using the spelling conventions of another, as in <bizoo>, a spelling of French *bisou* ('kiss') according to English spelling conventions (Morel et al., 2012, p. 274); and <Doyc>, a spelling of German *Deutsch* ('German') which follows Greek spelling conventions (Hinnenkamp, 2008). Trans-scripting can also include writing a language in a script not normally associated with it. One example of an emergent online form is the writing of various languages in the Latin alphabet, including Arabic (known as Arabizi or Arabish), Greek (Greeklish), Chinese and Thai (known as 'karaoke language' because the script is often used to subtitle songs for karaoke). Although the online Romanisation of these languages was initially motivated by technological constraints (see Chapter 4), their continued use points to a greater social or personal significance.

The Roman letters are chosen either because their pronunciation corresponds with the target phoneme; because of a visual analogy with the corresponding letter; or because of their placement on the computer keyboard. For example, Greek η can be transliterated into:

- <i> (a phonetic transliteration),
- <n> (a visual transliteration) or
- <h> (a keyboard-based transliteration).

Numerals can be used alongside letters because of either their phonetic or visual similarity:

- in Greeklish, theta (θ) can be transliterated phonetically as <th> or visually as <8> (Androutsopoulos, 2009);
- in Arabizi, either <5> or <'7> can be used to represent the sound /x/ (similar to the final sound in Scottish *loch*): <5> because the word for 5 in Arabic begins with the sound /x/ and <'7> because of its visual similarity with the character (Palfreyman and Al Khalil, 2007).

As Androutsopoulos (2009) argues with respect to Greeklish, users tend to orient towards either a phonetic or an orthographic approach to transliteration (rather than mixing the two approaches), and their choice of approach is shaped not only by local group norms but also by individual ideological stances: the orthographic approach to Greeklish, for example, represents an attempt to retain the look of Greek orthography (Androutsopoulos, 2009). Androutsopoulos's (forthcoming) research centres on a group of seven students aged 16–18 at a Greek school in Northern Germany and involves the collection of online data as well as media diaries and interviews. He found that the use of Romanised Greek differed among participants, depending on their background: those such as Vee who had grown up in Germany spelt according to German spelling conventions, transliterating the Greek character <ξ> with the German spelling of the same sound <ks>, <θ> with <th> and <ω> with <o>. Meanwhile, those who had recently moved to Germany stuck to the visual transliterations typical in Greece. Agi, for example, captures the same Greek graphemes with <3>, <8> and <w>, respectively (Androutsopolous, forthcoming).

Creativity in transliteration is possible because of the lack of online regulation. In a study of Thai users online, Seargeant and Tagg (2011) describe their use of Arabic numerals 555 to indicate laughter (the number 5 in Thai is pronounced 'ha'). The following example took place in a conversation on MSN Messenger:

1	Dream:	I got a bar of white choc
2	Dream:	Someone put it in the envelope and wrote my name on it
3	Dream:	And put it in my flat postbox
4	Big:	555 Don't eat much na
5	Dream:	I ate it up laew lol
6	Dream:	Aroi duey [*It was delicious*]

(Seargeant and Tagg, 2011, pp. 508–9)

Su (2007) reports on a practice among Taiwanese internet users of what she calls Stylised English, in which Chinese characters are chosen because of their phonetic similarity to an English phrase. The following

Chinese characters are read as *ou mai ga* which corresponds to the English phrase, 'oh my god' (Su, 2007, p. 74):

As these examples illustrate, language contact online allows users to play with resources such as script, spelling and symbols that can only be appreciated visually, thus extending the practices associated with spoken multilingualism. As we go on to discuss, these examples also problematise the notion of 'switching' in favour of a more fluid mixing of language resources.

The value of a written form

In their study of literacy practices on Flickr, Barton and Lee (2012) show how the internet can enhance the social value placed on previously undervalued vernacular writing practices (Chapter 17). In several cases, the online use of a minority language serves to realign its relationship with local dominant languages. For example, Lexander (2011) argues that the use of Wolof and Pulaar alongside French in Senegalese text messages may raise the status of the somewhat marginalised African languages and challenge the functional separation otherwise maintained between them. For example, Pulaar and French are given an 'equal footing' (p. 437) in the following text message. Pulaar, in bold, is used for the formal greeting, but words in both languages have been playfully respelt to create an overall effect of intimacy and informality.

> Dioulmo wouri! Mi yarlima mi ané ada yarlo ada yaafo. È la féte ça s'est bien passé? Ça fé un bay
>
> **Juul mowuri. Mi yarlii ma mi yaafii ma anne ada yarloo ada yaafoo.** *Et la fête, ça s'est bien passé? Ça fait un bail.*
>
> [*Happy New Year! I have forgiven you, I ask you to forgive me. And the feast, was it good? It's been a while.*]
>
> (Lexander, 2011, p. 438)

The novelty of text messaging, argues Lexander, as well as increasing use and the value placed on it, mean that it is likely that writing practices originating in texted interactions will spread to other writing domains.

In other contexts, internet writing impacts on the linguistic status quo in different ways. For example, the social impact of Romanisation may vary across languages or regions. In Egypt, according to

Warschauer et al. (2007), the growing use of Arabizi online indicates a possible realignment of scripts and languages. They argue that the increasing use of the Romanised form of Egyptian Arabic online is contributing to a shift from traditional diglossia in Egypt to a more fluid multilingualism, with English and Egyptian Arabic challenging the dominance of Classical Arabic in written language contexts (Warschauer et al., 2007, p. 315). In contrast, Androutsopoulos (2009, p. 243) predicts a growing resistance to Greeklish from a majority of internet users, based in part on difficulties in reading Greeklish. However, he suggests some exceptions which may contribute to its continuing use in some online spaces: in Greek diasporic discussion forums, where a minority of users may not have access to the Greek script (p. 246); and among those who recognise the 'medium-related symbolic value' of Greeklish (that is, its value as a feature of computer-mediated language and its long association with the internet) (p. 244).

Conclusion

A growing body of research is beginning to document the ways in which people draw on various languages online, much as they have always done in contexts of face-to-face interaction across the world. In contrast to many spoken encounters, in online interactions users can draw easily on language-related networked resources, encouraging them to use 'bits' of languages in practices of 'minimal bilingualism'; and, given the fact that the digital communications we are looking at are written rather than spoken, people are also able to mix scripts in creative ways and to play with spelling. Thus studies of online code-switching problematise arguments about the dominance of English online, not only because of the opportunities afforded for other languages to be used alongside the 'global lingua franca', but because multilingual internet users emerge not as passive victims of globalising forces but as active agents able to draw on English and other languages for complex social purposes. This does not mean that non-English-speaking internet users necessarily have access to the information and services that are available to those who are able to read websites or interact using English, and this remains a matter for concern; but it does mean that English can be seen as a set of resources which form part of many users' language repertoires. The concept of the multilingual repertoire in turn challenges the traditional view that what people are doing is switching from one language to another, suggesting that people do not necessarily make such distinctions between the languages available to them. In Section C, Chapters 18 and 19, we explore the ideas behind this new way of understanding multilingual practices.

Task 12.1

Select a multilingual online text. The text could be (among others):

- an instant messaging or SMS text messaging exchange
- a status update and comments from Facebook
- comments generated on a post on Instagram, YouTube or other media-sharing sites
- Tweets using the same hashtag
- a blog post or fan fiction story using more than one language.

Then analyse the text:

- Label each turn as exhibiting code-switching or code-mixing;
- For each example of code-mixing, decide what effect the mixed discourse might have;
- For each code-switch, decide why the user switched language (their motivation) and what they hoped to achieve (the function).
- To what extent do you think the code-mixing or code-switching might resemble how the same people talk in face-to-face situations, and to what extent does it differ? Why? Think about the impact of the visual and networked resources, as well as the kind of audience addressed.

II

Social issues and social media

13 Performing identity online

Introduction

CB: Bentolunch for tomorrow (Friday)
Today my new bentobox arrived! It's a pretty bentobox
with a little bunny on the top. Of course I had to use it, so
I prepared my bento for tomorrow quickly. ^.^
(Sorry, I know my English is so so bad! I definitely have to
learn it better.. T.T

                                          (Barton and Lee 2013, p. 122)

The above photo caption, which accompanies an image of the user's new Japanese lunchbox posted on the photo-sharing site Flickr, highlights key findings from applied linguistics research regarding how users present themselves online. On the one hand, CB's comment makes evident the continuing importance of one's 'real' identity in online contexts – in this case, as a Japanese learner of English – in contrast to popular perceptions of the internet as a place to hide who you really are and construct yourself anew. On the other hand, the relatively disembodied nature of digital communication allows for careful selection in terms of what users reveal about themselves. In their online investigations of Flickr, David Barton and Carmen Lee (2013) noticed how frequently users commented on their own use of language, particularly English, and often in self-deprecatory ways, even when what they wrote in English suggested they commanded a great deal of communicative competence. The reason for doing this may be that comments such as 'Sorry, I know my English is so so bad!' serve to elicit empathy, to highlight the user's willingness to participate in the English-speaking forum despite their language difficulties, and to encourage other users to evaluate their contributions accordingly. When other users respond to such self-deprecatory comments, Barton and Lee noticed a different kind of positioning: as native speakers with the authority to evaluate CB's English:

Deebibi: Trust me, your English is a lot better than the English
of many native speakers. ^_~

                                          (Barton and Lee, 2013, p. 122)

By challenging CB's negative evaluation (as Barton and Lee point out), Deebibi is simultaneously praising CB's English and reinforcing CB's position as a non-native speaker unable to make such judgements herself: Deebibi is the native English-speaking expert.

Applied linguistics research has played an important role in shedding light on how identities are negotiated and managed in contexts of digital communication. Firstly, analysis of people's language use has revealed the importance of traditional social roles online, in the sense that gender and other differences are reproduced through language in digital contexts, challenging earlier assumptions that social distinctions would lose their significance online. Secondly, and often in response to this earlier research, language-related studies have detailed how offline social roles and identities can nonetheless be reconfigured and renegotiated in online contexts, given the lack of social cues and the novel set of resources available for identity work. This is not to say that 'offline' identities cease to have any relevance in online contexts, and it is evident from empirical research into attempted impersonations and spams that 'authenticity' – who you really are – remains crucial. In this chapter, I trace these developments in applied linguistics research and what they tell us about self-presentation online.

The reconstruction of traditional social roles online

An early contribution from applied linguistics research was to challenge prevailing assumptions that identities could be discarded at will in offline contexts. Prominent amongst this research is a series of investigations by Susan Herring into gender roles and identities online (Herring, 1993, 1998, 2000, 2003). In short, Herring's research showed that traditional gender roles were being replicated – or, to put it more accurately, reconstructed – in online contexts. In one study, Herring (1993) explored two academic bulletin boards (an early kind of online forum) using a mix of ethnographic observation, discourse analysis and participant surveys. The discourse analysis in particular confirmed significant differences in male and female participation: men participated more, received more responses and initiated more topics; they were more likely than women to contribute to 'issue'-related threads rather than personal discussions; and they adopted a style associated with men's talk in offline situations (making strong rather than attenuated assertions, asking rhetorical rather than real questions and challenging rather than supporting others) (Herring, 1993). Rather than liberating women, factors characterising digital communication – apparent anonymity, democracy and decontextualisation – seemed not to apply in these discussion lists: people usually knew who they were talking to and they 'simply transferred the conventions of academic discourse, as they might be observed for example in face-to-face interaction at a professional conference, to the electronic medium' (Herring, 1993). Herring's findings were reflected not only in other studies of academic lists (e.g. Savicki et al., 1996; Selfe and Meyer, 1991) but also in her own research into Internet Relay Chat (IRC), a form of chat popular in the 1990s. The latter research is particularly interesting, given the assumption that in casual synchronous contexts gender would be particularly invisible and often actively subverted; in contrast, Herring (1998) found that 89 per cent of all gendered behaviour across six IRC channels indexed stereotypical gendered behaviour, with users 'giving off' gender cues approximately every three to four lines of text. The following extracts illustrate differences in female style (including affectionate actions and expressions of support) and male style (in which actions are violent and language profane):

Exchange between female participants:

<KiKiDoe> *huggers* beff to her death hahaah
<Beth_> :)
<Beth_> you guys are so great! *happy sobs*

Exchange between male participants:

<wuzzy> any ladies wanna chat?
<[Snoopy]> fonz: she nice
<LiQuIdHeL> FUKCK YOU

(also reproduced in Herring, 2003)

However, subsequent language research has tended to problematise accounts of the straightforward replication of gender roles online (and offline). Studies point to other factors – such as online genre and national culture – which account for differences in male and female participation. In a study of blogs, for example, Herring and Paolillo (2006) found that so-called 'female' and 'male' language was accounted for less by the gender of the author and more by the subgenre of the blog – that is, whether it could be described as a filter blog or a personal diary (see Herring et al., 2005; and Chapter 11 of this book). The gender distinction lay in the fact that men were more likely to write the former kind of blog, and women the latter: Herring and Paolillo thus conclude that gender differences are less about 'gender-related' language items or styles and more about the different kinds of online texts that men and women write. In their study of teenage bloggers, Huffaker and Calvert (2005) found no difference between blogs written by girls and boys, although they confirm the importance of authenticity online (a point I return to later), describing the bloggers as maintaining a consistent self-presentation online. In their study of turn allocation in a Thai chat room, Panyametheekul and Herring (2007) found that female Thai participants were in fact empowered to break out of traditionally subservient cultural roles to dominate the online space. The researchers put this down in part to elements of Thai culture and in particular the valuing of 'politeness and civility' (p. 252) which had transferred online and which allowed women to participate more freely than western counterparts given the 'crude, aggressive' (p. 252) nature of many public sites. Such research highlights how gender roles are to some extent reconstructed through digital communication, but that their realisation may be shaped by various online factors including changes in technology and intergenerational differences (Androutsopoulos, 2006a, p. 428).

While this later research shifts the emphasis placed on gender as a motivating factor for language use online, other researchers go further to challenge the viability of gender itself as a pre-existing and language-external factor that shapes language use (Androutsopoulos, 2006a, p. 427). These researchers argue that gender is not biologically fixed or predetermined but interactively performed – that is, gender differences are created and reinforced *through* interaction. Crucially, while it is often likely that established social identities will be re-enacted, this view of gender as performance allows for the subversion and reconceptualisation of offline identities in new online spaces (Georgakopoulou, 1997; Rodino, 1997). In Chapter 20, I discuss the ideas underlying this conception of identity (e.g. Butler, 1990). In the rest of this chapter, I explore empirical studies detailing the ways in which identity is performed online.

Co-construction of identities online

Applied linguistics research reveals identity construction to be a process of active co-construction, in which users draw on potentially new resources for communicative purposes which relate to varying extents to their offline social roles and relationships. I illustrate these points in turn below, drawing on studies into various online contexts.

Firstly, constructing identity online is an interactive process of co-construction, reliant not only on how users wish to come across but also on how they are perceived and responded to by others. Newon (2011), for example, describes how members of a guild in an online game, *World of Warcraft*, position themselves as guild leaders in order to persuade others to follow them and to attain particular group goals – in this case, the successful raid of a dungeon. Newon was a participant in a 40-member strong guild and accompanied them on a number of raids. The leader of each raid was chosen from among the expert players, and their authority was based on their experience of the game and their perceived expertise, which they drew upon to maintain command and complete the task successfully. At the same time, their expression of authority was mitigated so as not to alienate the other players by the use of hedges such as 'I think' (which may also serve to mitigate the leader's responsibility if a raid did not work out); by the use of modals like 'should' and 'need' rather than 'must' to construct individual duty; and through the use of humour. It is interesting, however, to consider the extent to which offline roles and identities continue to be relevant in such imaginary worlds (particularly, perhaps, because the game was played using voice as well as text, meaning that social cues relating to gender or accent were difficult to hide). In the raids Newon observed, for example, the three female players never volunteered to be leader (Newon, 2011, p. 135). Perceived norms about the suitability of men and women to lead the group may have played a part in this.

Secondly, online users must portray themselves not through physical co-presence but through largely text-based visual resources, including written language, typography (Vaisman, 2011), orthography (Tagg, 2012) and the creative combining of different scripts (Palfreyman and Al Khalili, 2007; Su, 2007; Tagg and Seargeant, 2012), as well as photos, other images, videos and the embedding and sharing of hyperlinks to other sites (Kiernan, 2012). These resources allow users to position themselves in potentially new ways that reflect local and global changes in society. Peuronen (2011), for example, describes how a group of Christian Finns who practise extreme sports constructed an online community in part to perform in front of a wider audience, with their shared linguistic practices signalling their group membership to 'outsiders' who do not fully appreciate the references (Leppänen et al., 2014). They do so by adopting a shared communicative style, which combines different sets of resources. Firstly, their use of English alongside Finnish establishes them as modern, internationally oriented, English-speaking Finns; English is also drawn on as part of the informal and intimate register created, such as in the group's slogan 'Ride hard, live forever', which playfully exploits the expression 'Live fast, die young' (Peuronen, 2011, p. 155). Secondly, they also use English as part of their reference to products and practices related to extreme sports, and thus construct expertise in their knowledge of global, English-derived jargon and brand names ('USD UFS Throne Dominki Sagona boot', 'anti-rocker', 'KIZER Type "M" Chino Frame', pp. 168–9). Finally, English plays a part in their construction of a more formal Christian discourse, through which the group create a shared 'evangelical mission' (Peuronen, 2011, p. 173). Through these diverse orientations, the Christian Finns establish themselves as members of a 'community of practice', itself created through their particular linguistic choices – that is, the version of the community that presents itself online is forged through the affordances of written language. (The community also meets offline, which Peuronen draws upon to explain the cooperative and unconfrontational nature of the interactions.)

Users in various countries negotiate their identity as modern global players through the often playful Romanisation of languages not usually written in the Roman script – Hebrew (Vaisman, 2011), Chinese or Taiwanese (Su, 2007), Arabic (Haggan, 2007), Thai (Tagg and Seargeant, 2012) and Greek (Androutsopoulos, 2006b; Georgakopoulou, 1997; Tseliga, 2007). Vaisman (2011), for example, describes how an online community of female Israeli bloggers sought through creative linguistics practices to take back, or re-appropriate, their much maligned identity as *Fakatsa* (best described in English as 'bimbos' obsessed with celebrity and consumer fashion). These young girl bloggers created a form of typographic play, by which Hebrew characters were replaced by various ASCII characters (letters, numbers and punctuation), chiefly because they resembled the Hebrew characters visually but sometimes also because of phonological similarity. The resulting script relied on insider knowledge for decoding – most characters could be replaced by various ASCII characters – although the bloggers carefully ensured understanding by maintaining many of the original characters. As Vaisman (2011, p. 193) concludes, 'digital discourse is a powerful but also playful resource for (re)negotiating their stereotype as shallow, vain fashion victims and for reframing their social identities in a self-aware performance of a desirable, stylish girlhood'. Similarly, the use of English and a form of Romanised colloquial Arabic across Arab countries works as part of an identity display that contests traditional values and constructs the user as international, carefree and modern.

A: الأخت الفاضلة...الرجاء إحضار آراضر كتاب صقر معك غدا
[*virtuous sister, please bring Saqir's book with you tomorrow*]

B: ☺ this z the 1st time someone calls me "AL2O5T ALFADILAH"... ☺ lol. Anyway, don't worry, I wont 4get 2 bring the book 2mr. Take care.

(Jordanian texter, in Al-Khatib and Sabbah, 2008)

Thirdly, as the above examples begin to suggest, these selective displays of identity can be purposeful and highly relevant to the communicative demands of a particular online site. Camilla Vásquez's work on the user-generated review site, TripAdvisor, is a good illustration of this. The reviewers are largely unknown to each in the offline world and their own identity might at first glance seem irrelevant to the reviewing process – Vásquez finds that few populate their profile with personal information. In fact, however, elements of their identity are used in selective and purposeful ways, with many reviewers 'giving off' a lot about themselves. Such identity cues are used as a strategy of persuasion by people leaving reviews on the site, and in doing so making claims to authority as a reviewer based on 'authentic' experience. In the following hotel review, Vásquez explains how the user draws on various discursive strategies to add weight to her opinions: she constructs herself as a reasonable person [1] and a well-seasoned traveller [2], as well as someone familiar with hotel chains [3].

> [1] *I know $125 is not a great deal of money these days. I was not expecting a heck of a lot. However, I was expecting basic clean and comfortable accommodations.* [2] *I have traveled quite a bit.* [3] *and I have stayed in everything from Marriott Resort Hotels and Hyatt Resorts to Days Inns, Hampton Inns, Best Westerns, Residence Inns, La Quintas, and various Mom and Pop Motels to name a few. I have NEVER felt this ripped off. My stays have not always been perfect but I have always felt like I got what I paid for.*
> (Vásquez, 2014 [my annotation])

Importantly, whether users take heed of online reviewers seems to be explained by the extent to which they feel they are similar to the reviewer in question, and so their success as reviewers may ultimately depend on whether they can build solidarity with users. As Vásquez (2014, p. 85) suggests, this 'may also explain why users choose to more subtly interweave claims for credibility into reviews, as well as why they often downplay their complaints and set themselves up as "reasonable" people'. Similar identity constructions (and similar attempts to achieve solidarity) probably take place on shopping sites such as eBay, as initial research by Knight (2013) seems to suggest, with sellers apparently drawing on their personal lives to build trust with potential buyers.

As many of these examples suggest, offline identities are deeply relevant to, and embedded within, displays of identity online. Carmen Lee's research starts from the premise that people's technology use is deeply embedded in their everyday lives and, therefore, that their online language use must be understood within the wider context of their life experiences (Barton and Lee, 2012; Lee, 2014). Lee's approach also highlights the fact that online language use shifts throughout a person's life. The approach involves eliciting through interview what Lee calls 'techno-linguistic biographies', which constitute an individual's attempts to make sense of how technology shapes their linguistic practices. In one study, Lee (2014) explored the online writing practices of 20 Hong Kong university students, whom she interviewed for 30–50 minutes as well as recording for half-an-hour online. Despite similarities in their linguistic repertoires – the students spoke Cantonese as their primary language and English as a second language; wrote in standard written Cantonese; and code-switched online – differences emerged as they constructed their individual techno-linguistic biographies. History student Yan's record of online language use was oriented mainly around standard written Chinese, which she would sometimes mix with Cantonese and a creative use of the southern Chinese dialect, Hakka. The latter was possible because of Yan's Hakka background, but her insistence on standard Chinese (even when other forum participants would use English) is more likely explained by her personal feeling towards the language; as she puts it, 'I usually blog about in-depth feelings and I want to use a serious language to express myself' (Barton and Lee, 2012, p. 77). Both uses – the playful use of Hakka and the serious employment of standard Chinese – index her identity as a HongKonger with roots in a southern part of mainland China. In contrast, Tony, a HongKonger training to be an English teacher, had – since his online gaming experiences as a boy – always included English in his repertoire of online languages, even though he often chose for various reasons to use Chinese online. At the time of the study, Tony maintained two online personae: a largely Chinese-speaking, code-switching persona to address his friends; and an English-speaking formal persona for his students, known as Teaching Tony. His language use is vividly different across the two profiles. With his classmates on the teaching programme, he uses Cantonese for two reasons – for purposes of intimacy and marking his identity as a HongKonger; and because of a lack of confidence in his English. For his students, however, he uses English, the language of instruction, and a more 'academic' tone.

> Dear 4R students,
> I have put copies of three sets of reading practice paper in my cabinet outside staff room. Please come and get it yourself if you need them.
> (Teaching Tony)

> 收到了 Jim Scrivener 2010 的新作 <<Teaching English Grammar>>, 如果我TP之前就買左就好lah ......
>   [*Just received Jim Scrivener's new work in 2010* Teaching English Grammar. *I wish I had bought this before my teaching practice.*]
> (Student Tony)
> (Lee, 2014, pp. 106 and 105)

As the studies outlined in this chapter suggest, an apparent contradiction emerges from research into online identity. On the one hand, users are able to (re)construct themselves in discourse because of the relative anonymity afforded by digital communication, and foreground or reconfigure particular facets of their identities by utilising a range of graphic resources. At the same time, however, perceptions of authenticity – the ability to convince others that your experience and authority are genuine and based on real-life experiences – remain paramount. The perception that there should be a direct connection between the online persona and the offline self becomes very evident in the case of scams or online impersonations when people's sense of authenticity is violated. This is illustrated by Page (2014) in her analysis of Twitter spam such as the following direct message (DM) illegitimately sent from the Twitter account of a UK-based academic to all her followers:

I saw a real bad blog about you, you seen this? http://t.co/sgTbTcr

Whether her followers could determine the authenticity of the DM depended on the extent of their knowledge of the sender, one receiver commenting in an interview that 'luckily robots use bad grammar and the DM came from a senior lecturer in linguistics' while another 'clicked it would have been ~4am in UK'. Their evaluation also depended on their relationship with the sender, one receiver being: 'immediately wary of a DM from someone who's never DM'd me before'. Authenticity, then, is a negotiated process which plays an important role in the performance of credible online identity.

Conclusion

To sum up, applied linguistics research shows how social identity is actively negotiated by online participants in ongoing talk; and how ostensibly 'offline' identities can be ascribed, authenticated, negotiated and contested in 'online' situations. While offline identities continue to be held up as 'authentic', local purposes and communicative demands peculiar to the online contexts in which people are interacting can allow (or encourage) people to alter their presentations of identity through acts of expression – be it to take on a part in an online game, to project a group identity in a public space, to sound more convincing, to deflect criticism and so on. In Section C, Chapter 20, I look at the theory behind this view of identity. In Chapters 14 and 15 of this section, I look at how people's identity performances can be seen as attempts to address and align with others, and to form affiliations and a sense of community online.

Task 13.1

Investigate your own construction of identity on an online site or channel of communication which you use.

1. Start by identifying the different sections available for the expression of identity: e.g. on Facebook, the public areas would include your profile page, your status updates, and the comment function, as well as the private messaging facility.
2. For each section, identify the different resources that you use, and collect examples of each. What patterns (repeated usages) emerge?
3. Decide what kind of self-image or images you present, and how you use the various resources to do so. How authentic is your online image? (That is, do you present a coherent image which people may judge to relate to your offline self?)

If you are comfortable doing this, you might want to support this textual analysis with interviews with people in your Friends list. How do various Friends perceive your online identity and its authenticity?

14 Audience design on social media

Introduction

In Chapter 6, I discussed concerns surrounding the impact of social media on notions of privacy. With regard to social network sites, social researchers like danah boyd suggest that much of the problem lies in a combination of the following: a) the need for users to disclose a certain amount of personal information in order to gain social capital; b) the fact that such disclosures often take place in front of diverse audiences brought together from different parts of a user's life (so your boss or great aunt may read what is intended for friends); and c) the speed and ease with which such information can then be disseminated along online networks. The latter point means that a joke intended for close friends and family, such as Paul Chambers' tweet about 'blowing the airport sky high' if they didn't reopen in time for him to take his flight, can reach an unintended audience (the authorities) who treat Twitter as a public rather than a private space. The conclusion that social researchers reach is that people still care about privacy in the social media age, but that they define and manage it in new ways, relying not only on technical affordances but also using social and linguistic strategies to maintain their privacy whilst staying connected.

Applied linguistics research is ideally placed to explore these linguistic strategies for managing privacy. One relevant framework is 'audience design', as outlined by Bell (1984), which serves to explain speaker style; for example, how formal or elaborate any utterance is. Bell's framework is important not only because it takes into account the effect that a listener has on what a speaker says (or, at least, how he/she says it) but because it draws attention to the fact that different members of the same audience may encourage speakers towards different styles, and thus the framework highlights the complex ways in which speakers must sometimes vary their presentational strategies within one exchange or context. As such, the framework can be useful in exploring how online users manage the 'social convergence' that characterises social network sites (how they address their boss and their friends at the same time) and how they take into account the fact that a wider, unknown audience may also have access to their posts.

In this chapter, I outline Bell's model and then go on to suggest how it can be adapted to explain interactions on one online site, Facebook, including the particular audience roles that pertain on Facebook and the strategies available for addressing others. I then show how this comes together through examples from my own research into multilingual Facebook interactions (Tagg and Seargeant, 2014), which focuses on how language choice (the choice between one language or another) can be a resource for addressing certain members of the audience and excluding others.

Audience design

Bell's audience design framework constitutes an attempt to understand speakers' stylistic choices, that is, why a speaker says something *this* way on *this* occasion (to paraphrase Bell, 2001, p. 139). The framework originally emerged from research into how the same New Zealand newsreaders varied their pronunciation when reading the news on different radio stations, suggesting that they were imagining a different audience for each station and styling their utterances accordingly. Although Bell saw his framework as also applicable to face-to-face conversations where interlocutors are present and known, the underlying assumption is that people always construct an *idea* of their audience in order to give context to their utterances, and that these ideas shape what they say. The framework has immediate relevance for understanding language choice and privacy management on social network sites where a diverse and largely unseen audience must be constructed and targeted by the user (Litt, 2012).

According to Bell, audience roles are not predetermined but are allocated and reallocated throughout an interaction by the speaker. The three main audience roles in Bell's model are the *addressee* – the participant(s) 'oriented to by the speaker in a manner to suggest that his or her words are particularly for them, and that some answer is therefore anticipated from them' (Goffman, 1975, p. 260); the *auditor* – those who are not directly addressed but whose involvement is ratified by the speaker (that is, they are considered by the speaker to be taking part); and the *overhearer* – those whose involvement is not ratified but whose assumptions and hypotheses the speaker may wish to pre-empt (Clark and Carlson, 1982, p. 344). Normally, it can be assumed that addressees will have the most influence on a speaker's style and overhearers the least, although this may depend on the relationships between the people involved; for example, Yousseff (1993) describes how a child used more standard forms when their mother was present, regardless of whom they were addressing.

Bell (1999, 2001) recognised that speakers will also accommodate to non-present third parties – including groups to which the speaker belongs and those to which they do not – through what he called 'initiative style shift'. These shifts show the speaker to be taking the initiative because they are not responding to a perceived audience, but drawing on meanings from other contexts to shape the current situation. We may argue that in relatively novel online spaces, users may be more likely to take the initiative and to 'shape' rather than 'respond to' the online context, and that these decisions will feed into emerging norms. However, it should be reasserted that even so-called 'responsive' style shifts – where a speaker responds to a present audience – involve the imagining and active construction of an audience.

Audience design on Facebook

The fact that online writers must take into account large, diversified audiences is acknowledged in several studies looking at various digitally mediated contexts, including research into how scientists communicate science online (Luzón, 2013) and how Flickr users present their photography to both local and potentially global audiences (Barton and Lee, 2013). Other studies have directly applied Bell's framework to digital interactions on Facebook and Twitter. These include Page's (2014) analysis of violations on Facebook and scams on Twitter, both of which elicit different responses from different segments of a user's audience (see Chapter 13); Frobenius's (2014) analysis of how video bloggers on YouTube imagine and address an audience in an attempt to involve both new and returning viewers in their monologues; Johnson's (2013) investigation of how Welsh users on Twitter address different language groups; and my own investigation of multilingual interactions on Facebook (Tagg and Seargeant, 2014, a study I shall return to below). For the rest of this chapter, I focus mainly on Facebook, as it constitutes the focus of my study, although much of the discussion is applicable to other sites.

Although there are options for conducting one-to-one conversations on Facebook, the audience for most posts can be described as 'semi-public' in that, although a user decides who to friend, they cannot be entirely sure which of their Friends will read a post and respond. In this sense, as with the broadcast audiences explored in Bell's original research, the audience is largely invisible and unknown (boyd and Marwick, 2011). This is further complicated by the conflated nature of the audience, as boyd and Marwick point out, potentially comprising people from different parts of a user's life, and thus characterised by 'context collapse' (see Chapter 6). In our research, we explore the different segments of this audience, and their likely effects on users' posts, by adapting Bell's (1984) audience design model into the following five categories (Tagg and Seargeant, 2014). It should be noted that participants in any one Facebook interaction can be in different groups at the same time, or they can shift from one to another as the conversation unfolds. For example, the role of 'poster' applies not only to the user who initiates a conversation when they update their status, but also to anyone who responds to the initial post with a comment.

1 *Poster* of the status update or comment (corresponding to the 'speaker' in Bell's model)
2 *Addressee/s* (those to whom an update or comment is explicitly addressed)
3 *Active Friends* (the people whom a user usually interacts with on Facebook, who may in some cases pertain to Bell's 'auditors')
4 *Wider Friends* (the wider circle of social acquaintances, family and professional contacts, who might correspond to 'overhearers')
5 *The internet as a whole* (these might be termed 'eavesdroppers', following Bell's model, those whose presence can in some circumstances become suddenly known to the speaker with implications for their language style – seen in cases where posts are picked up on by the authorities or news media).

(Tagg and Seargeant, 2014, p. 172)

The main implications of this adapted model for understanding interactions on Facebook are as follows. Firstly, a user's awareness of their peripheral Friends (the overhearers) and, perhaps to a lesser extent, of the internet as a whole (the eavesdroppers) is likely to have some influence on what they say and how they say it even where they have closer friends in mind (addressees and auditors). Secondly, in posting a status update or comment, a user can draw on various audience design strategies to target and exclude particular parts of their imagined audience. I describe these in the next section.

Audience design strategies on Facebook

Speakers in face-to-face interactions can draw on various resources in assigning audience roles, including 'physical arrangement, conversational history, gestures, manner of speaking, and linguistic content' (Clark and Carlson, 1982, p. 346). For example, using their name, facing someone or gesturing towards them can signal the fact that a speaker intends to address them; more implicitly, alluding to a previous conversation or a shared experience can indicate who an utterance is primarily targeted at. While some of these resources – such as conversational history, manner of speaking and linguistic content – have parallels in digital communication, others are not available to online users. The resources which cannot be drawn upon are those which rely on the immediate physical space, such as the physical arrangement of the participants and the use of gestures. Different strategies are thus employed online. Gestures, for example, can be compensated for by graphic resources such as the '@' sign, which can be used to tag someone in a post or in a photo (often with the aim of drawing the attention of the individual, who is notified by Facebook, to the post or photo). In our study of an online Thai community, we explored their practice of 'photo tagging' (Tagg and Seargeant, 2012), by which they tagged each other in photos of what they were eating in order to elicit jealousy from each other. The practice was tied to their common interest in cooking, and the fact that they were geographically dispersed and trying out new experiences. In other words, photo tagging as an audience design strategy is augmented by the participants' shared interactional history, on- and offline.

The various strategies for audience design used on social network sites are likely to be as follows. The strategies range from the very explicit (direct address) to the implicit (style):

- Direct address strategies (use of the @ sign and, in some cases, the hashtag as a way of joining a particular conversation; photo- or post-tagging; use of groups or lists).
- Other structural affordances (e.g. dividing messages into separate posts).
- Content of post (topic; degree to which content can be described as public or private).
- Style (level of formality; degree of vagueness or explicitation) and language choice (including language, script and dialect choice; and switches between them).

(Tagg and Seargeant, 2014)

In the next section, I focus on language choice as an implicit addressivity strategy, drawing on examples from one participant in our study (Tagg and Seargeant, 2014).

Language choice as an addressivity strategy

I start this section by introducing Pauline, a multilingual Facebook user from France, before moving on to look at her addressivity strategies as reflective of those used by participants across our study (Tagg and Seargeant, 2014). The research study of which Pauline was a part had the broader aim of exploring how English as a lingua franca is used in online contexts to bring together and negotiate multinational communities across Europe. The study combined an analysis of interactional data – comprising exchanges which developed through the Comment function in response to status updates posted by participants – with written or spoken interviews with participants, in which they commented on their likely motivations for each language choice. Their explanations were taken as post hoc reflections, with all the caveats that attempts at self-rationalisation bring (Tagg and Seargeant, 2014).

Pauline, born in 1980, was at the time of the study a Master's student in Paris. Although she also speaks Danish and German, her preferred second language is English: she loved the language 'from the start' at school, took an undergraduate degree in English, and used it when spending time in the UK, Denmark and the Czech Republic. At the time of the study, she used Facebook 'almost every day, sometimes several times a day'; and she had 257 Friends, from countries including Brazil, the Czech Republic, Denmark, Germany, Japan, Nepal, the Netherlands, Togo and the UK. Of these, her active circle numbered around 30–40 from 'France and Europe, plus a few from the US'. She claims to use French and English 'fairly equally' on Facebook: 'French with my family and English with most of my friends'. According to Pauline, as well as consideration of audience, her language choice is also determined by factors such as her mood and the content of her posts, as well as a desire to play with words: 'sometimes I'll choose the language that allows me a pun'. These various factors intersect to explain her language choices on Facebook.

It's good to be from Deux-Sèvres!!

The chosen example is a conversational thread developing from Pauline's status update (included as turn 1 in the thread). It illustrates how people use complex strategies to simultaneously target different groups or individuals within a status update, and how language choice can mark an utterance as more or less private. The aim is not to generalise across social network site use, but to illustrate a framework with potential for a more general understanding of such interactions.

1	Pauline:	is enjoying the sun in Lille before going to Bressuire for the weekend. Deux-Sévrien, c'est trop bien!! :) [*It's good to be from Deux-Sèvres!!*]
2	Jens:	gotta love'em weekend trips. hvordan går det ven? [*How are you my friend?*]
3	Pauline:	det gaar fint, tak! havd med dig, ven? [*It's going well, thank you! How about you, my friend?*] hey, not everyone can take off to Costa Rica when they get itchy feet, so weekend trips it is for me...;-)
4	Carine:	trop mignon ta bébète!!! c'est celui de l'age de glace....:):):):) [*So cute the little animal! It's the one from Ice Age ...*]

| 5 | Elise: | bon retour au pays miss !;-) [*Enjoy going back home, miss!*] |
| 6 | Sophie: | ah ah! t'as kiffé le porte-clé, hein! [*Ah ah! You liked the key ring, didn't you!*] |

Status updates do not typically have a direct addressee, but addressing someone directly in a status update does occur, as this example illustrates. In the status update, Pauline announces her travel plans in English, before switching to French to recite a slogan about her home town. Pauline told us during interview that this was a 'hint' to Sophie, a friend from the same town who carried this slogan on a key ring. Following various comments from other people responding to Pauline's announcement (or, in the case of Carine, to her profile picture), Sophie notices the hint. In this case, language choice, the content of the post and interactional history serve to target Sophie as the intended recipient of the utterance. Interestingly, however, while on one level that particular utterance can be seen as a private message to Sophie, the post as a whole is also accessible on a different level to another, wider audience, presumably Pauline's active circle of Friends who use English as a lingua franca and who may have some knowledge of her travel plans, her home town and so on. At the same time, we might speculate that the highly contextualised language of the post and its lack of explicitation render it largely inaccessible to her wider circle of Friends – acquaintances and so on – who do not have such knowledge. They are nonetheless presented with a sunny, lighthearted picture of her life, described by McLaughlin and Vitak (2011) as an emergent norm on Facebook (see Chapter 13). In other words, through language choice and other strategies, one status update is targeted at three different segments of the audience, who can access it on different levels. This practice is paralleled in many of the status updates we explored, including the following.

Eva: is missing a certain man (hint: it is not Sinterklaas)
Pauline: Fac 'em all!

Different individuals or groups can understand Eva's status update on different levels: Eva's Dutch friends and those based in the Netherlands are likely to know the traditions surrounding Sinterklaas (or Santa Claus) and many respond to the cultural reference in the ensuing comments; but those close enough to Eva to interpret who 'a certain man' is will be able to respond even if they do not know who Sinterklaas is. A third addressee is probably the 'certain man' himself (who does not respond). The second example is clearly designed for English-speaking French nationals among Pauline's close friends in that it incorporates a multilingual English/French pun related to her own personal circumstances. As Pauline explained, the phrase is a play on the English expletive *fuck* and a reference to the university *faculté* ('faculty' or 'school') where she was having problems registering. Although any non-French-speaking English speaker might access the gist of her message, they are unlikely to access the nuances of meaning on the same level as English–French bilinguals.

The conversation between Jens and Pauline which then develops in the comments following on from the first post illustrates the way in which language choice can function to mark a topic or conversation thread as public or private. Jens responds to Pauline's status update in informal, playful English: 'gotta love'em weekend trips'. The content of this post shows that Jens is directly addressing Pauline (responding directly to her status update), but the engaging tone suggests his comment may also be intended for a wider audience, that of Pauline's other active Friends. He then switches to Danish to enquire how she is: 'hvordan går det ven?', and this distinction is maintained by Pauline who responds to his enquiry in Danish before continuing the banter in English: 'hey, not everyone can take off to Costa Rica when they get itchy feet, so weekend trips it is for me'. The language switch can be seen in two ways. On the one hand, Danish is not a lingua franca for Pauline's network and so it is likely that the switch to Danish renders that thread inaccessible to many of the people likely to be reading the posts, and would certainly not be immediately available to more casual readers (from among Pauline's Wider Friends). At the same time, this is not really the point – after all, if they wanted to, anyone could translate the post using online tools now embedded into the site itself. The main point is that the switch to Danish signals a change in purpose from light-hearted public banter to a private conversation not intended for a general audience.

The attempt to mark utterances as more private through switching from English (as a lingua franca) to a local language is evident elsewhere in our data. In the following exchange, for example, both Eva and Nina write in English until, in turn 5, Eva uses the acronym, BV, for *borstvoeding* ('breast-feeding') and they go on to discuss the issue in Dutch, in part because that is the language in which they had tended to discuss it in previous, face-to-face conversations (as Eva told us). Although many of Eva's Active Friends are Dutch-speaking, the switch also makes it clear that this is not a general conversation, and renders it largely inaccessible to passing Wider Friends who do not speak Dutch.

1   Eva: has found her mojo again!
             ...
4   Nina: enjoy it! Ive lost mine too.....

5   Eva: Is it hidden under BV-stress?

        ...

15   Nina: @ Eva: hidden onder slaapgebrek en fysieke uitputting
             en de vierde borstontsteking in 4.5 maanden. Heb nu
             besloten de 'dames' op early retirement te sturen. Kan
             me nu al verheugen op de grote hoevelheden alcohol
             die ik kan gan nuttigen;)
             [@*Eva: hidden under sleep deprivation and physical*
             exhaustion and the fourth mastitis in 4.5 months. Have
             decided to send the 'ladies' on early retirement. Already
             looking forward to the great amounts of alcohol I shall
             be consuming;)]

The impact of the last segment of the audience, 'the internet as a whole', is somewhat harder to identify through exploring people's interactions on Facebook. In part, this is because (following Bell's model) 'the internet' is likely to have much less impact on how a user posts than the other segments of the audience (the direct addressees and a user's Friends). Understanding what people do *not* post on Facebook because of their awareness of the potential public nature of Facebook – their knowledge that posts, for example, may be copied and pasted and reach a new audience beyond their Facebook Friends – is crucial to a full appreciation of the way in which privacy is managed online through linguistic strategies. The next step in applied linguistics research will be to combine interactional data analysis with interview data in order to fully explore this issue.

Conclusion

Social researchers address popular concerns about privacy online by reconceptualising privacy not as an absolute but as something that can be negotiated and managed through interaction. Through analysis of the language used in 'semi-public' sites, applied linguistics research reveals how users adopt often complex strategies to signal what is private and what is public, and to explicitly or implicitly target and exclude particular individuals. My own research suggests that language choice is a key resource in targeting particular language-speaking groups and excluding others, but choice of language intersects with a number of other strategies ranging from direct address (through, for example, the @ sign) and the use of contextualised and vague language (and, of course, language choice is also motivated by other factors such as personal preference or ability). Bell's framework for audience design has proved particularly fruitful for analysis of digital contexts, as it focuses attention on the way that an utterance can be shaped simultaneously for different members of an audience, often engaging with them on different levels. Through such addressivity strategies, users can self-disclose whilst retaining control over what they consider private; in boyd and Marwick's (2011, p. 24) words, they can learn to 'express themselves privately in situations where they assume that others are watching'.

Task 14.1

Collect your last five status updates from Facebook, and take notes on the following questions:

1. Which individuals or groups are you addressing in the update?
2. Who are you excluding?
3. How do you achieve this through language?

Consider any direct addressees, as well as groups from your active Friends and your Wider Friends (acquaintances, colleagues and so on).

15 Constructing virtual communities

Introduction

The idea of a community accessible only via my computer screen sounded cold to me at first, but I learned quickly that people can feel passionately about Email and computer conferences. I've become one of them. I care about these people I met through my computer ...

I'm not alone in this emotional attachment to an apparently bloodless technological ritual. Millions of people on every continent also participate in the computer-mediated social groups known as virtual communities.

(early internet adopter and scholar, Howard Rheingold, 1993)

As discussed in Chapter 7, popular concerns abound regarding the role that the internet plays in the breakdown of offline community relations, whilst high-profile cases of trolling and cyberbullying mean that many see the internet as a frightening, anti-social place (see Chapter 8). However, anecdotal and scholarly evidence exists to suggest that many people 'feel passionately' about the connections they form online, fuelling the argument that in some cases the internet may serve to offset the loneliness and isolation of contemporary urban life. As Herring (2008b) points out, there have been numerous attempts by social researchers to measure the extent to which an online site or group can be said to constitute a 'community', according to various criteria established in the light of offline communities: a shared space, common purpose, agreed norms, a sense of belonging and a regular pattern of interaction (Herring, 2008b; Rheingold, 1993). According to such criteria, however, online communities are often evaluated negatively in comparison to offline counterparts: people may never come together in a physical space; and interaction is often less regular or sustained (e.g. Parks, 2011).

Applied linguistics research has been important in focusing attention away from the structural elements of community formation and the extent to which online communities measure up to offline ones, to explore the ways in which online communities are imagined and discursively constructed by social media users: that is, to detail how people come together online, and to determine a) how they themselves perceive and evaluate the connections they form, and b) how their perceptions and evaluations impact on their behaviour (Fontaine, 2006; Tagg and Seargeant, 2014). Such research, which suggests that a sense of affiliation can emerge in a variety of online situations and that it can take various forms, serves to address popular concerns regarding the antisocial impact of the internet and to challenge existing definitions of community (explored further in Chapter 21).

One illustrative example of the power of online affiliations can be found in Page's (2012a) analysis of blogs written by people about their ongoing cancer treatment. The existence of what we might call a community can be ascertained in two main ways: firstly, through the links bloggers make to other personal blogs (Page found that women bloggers in particular were likely to link to other personal blogs with an average of around eight links in a sidebar per blog), suggesting that the bloggers identify with other bloggers; and secondly, through the interactions between the blogger and their readers. As Myers (2010) points out, bloggers often construct and respond to an audience within their posts by asking questions, giving directives and directly addressing their readers as 'you' (see Chapter 10). In the case of the people blogging about their experiences of cancer, it is evident from how they wrote their posts that the decision to keep their blog was driven by their desire to connect with an audience, and that this motivation subsequently shaped what and how they posted, as Sylvie's post illustrates:

> I decided to deliver my story in real time, as it happens, in this journal. This is my therapy, and my way of sharing the story in its raw, unedited form. It is my hope that other people who encounter difficulties can read this and gain strength from knowing that they are not alone.
>
> (Sylvie, 8 August 2006, in Page, 2012a, p. 54)

To some extent, one could argue that the *sense* of community constructed in blogs such as Sylvie's may provide some comfort, regardless of whether anyone responds. However, as Page (2012a, p. 56) suggests, the bloggers' accounts of their illnesses served to attract responses from people who had shared similar experiences around which they could bond. In other words, through their writing (and the affordances of the internet) they construct a community by bringing together like-minded individuals around a common concern. It is evident from their posts that the cancer patients found comfort from their readers, as illustrated by David's post:

A few of you wanted me to let you know how things went today, on my first day of chemo. I appreciate your support more than I can explain. I thought I'd let you know how things are going.

(David, 29 July 2005, in Page, 2012a, p. 55)

We might argue that blog readers comment only sporadically and that they may simultaneously align themselves with a number of online groups. However, the sense among participants that they are connected, and the value placed on this 'community', is important here, rather than any measurement of the persistence of their ties or the regularity of their interactions.

Types of virtual community

What brings individuals together online, and why? The cancer blogs explored by Page constitute a particular kind of online community, labelled a support group by Herring (2008b). Support groups can be seen as sitting within a wider taxonomy of online communities. Below I bring together two inventories (Herring, 2008b; Tagg and Seargeant, 2014) to detail different kinds of online affiliations that orient around:

1 *Shared interests*, including
   a *interest groups* (such as photography, Barton and Lee, 2012; Thurlow and Jaworski, 2011)
   b *support groups* (such as Page's 2012a bloggers)
   c *task-based groups* (such as Wikipedia or the Facebook translators community explored by Lenihan, 2014)
   d *transaction-based groups* (e.g. on commercial product-based sites such as Amazon or Ebay, see Knight, 2013).

   Overlapping with the notion of 'communities of interest' (Henri and Pudelko, 2003), groups that orient around the above shared interests have the potential to develop into communities of practice in the more traditional sense of the term (see Chapter 21), or to remain casual and diffuse.

2 *Shared social variables*, such as language and nationality, as in Androutsopoulos's (2006b) study of German-based diaspora forums or Caulfield's (2012) Irish language bloggers.
3 *Hashtag communities*, formed through 'ambient affiliation' (Zappavigna, 2011): fleeting communities formed when users of a site like Twitter use the transitory space opened up by a hashtag to rally around a topic (see also Zappavigna, 2012, 2014; and Knight, 2010).
4 The *extension of pre-existing offline social networks*, such as the geographically dispersed group of Thai friends explored by

Seargeant et al. (2012). It is worth noting in relation to these communities that they often share a sense of local knowledge, despite the varied geographical locations that participants currently have, but that new practices and reference points are likely to emerge from their interactions online.

5 *Node-oriented networks*, where individuals come together through their mutual friendship with a particular user (Tagg and Seargeant, 2014).

These are not exclusive or clearly defined categories, and many groupings will combine elements: for example, the online community of Finnish Christian extreme sports enthusiasts described by Leppänen et al. (2014) and Peuronen (2011) orient around their shared interest in sport, as well as their religious beliefs and national background; while the Irish Facebook translators explored by Lenihan (2014) bond through their shared task (of translating Facebook) as well as their language background. However, central to all these communities are, firstly, their basis in members' shared interests, values, goals and life experiences rather than geographical proximity or shared background; and, secondly, the way in which they extend the types of social organisation available to people in a pre-digital era, due to people's exploitation of the affordances of the technology.

In the rest of this chapter, I explore two examples of virtual communities and focus on the role played by language in their construction: the communicative patterns that result from node-oriented interactions on Facebook (Tagg and Seargeant, 2014); and the shared values expressed by viewers on TED.com (Drasovean and Tagg, in preparation).

'Let's not put spam on Eva's status': node-oriented networks on Facebook

It may seem evident that communities are likely to form on social network sites, given that such sites are 'predicated on notions of connectedness and the establishment of social networks' (Tagg and Seargeant, 2014, p. 9). Social network sites depend for their very existence on the relationships that people make, and ways to facilitate relationship-building are a part of the site infrastructure: the ability to search for and connect with another user's profile, the display of a user's Friends or followers, and the fact that people's posts are 'pushed' onto their Friends' or followers' homepages where they can comment on them. Social research into virtual communities has often focused on users' lists of Friends or followers, as well as factors such as how active they are on the site, and how they customise their profile page (e.g. Parks, 2011). However, as Vásquez (2014) points out in relation to profiles on TripAdvisor, it can be more fruitful to look beyond the more stable and consciously designed aspects of a person's social media account to focus on how they present themselves in interaction. In our own research, for example, we have explored the ways in which people imagine and respond to the 'community' that develops in the comments attached to a status update on Facebook (Seargeant et al., 2012; Tagg and Seargeant, 2014).

Our research focused initially on the use of English by speakers of other languages online, and how language choice – that is, switching between English as the site's lingua franca and other more localised languages – constituted an important resource in addressing particular individuals online and marking posts as more or less 'private' (see Chapter 14). Here I look again at the exchange explored in Chapter 14 (in relation to audience design), but this time focusing on the particular communicative dynamic that emerges within the unfolding interaction, and which to some extent explains their language choices.

1	Pauline:	is enjoying the sun in Lille before going to Bressuire for the weekend. Deux-Sévrien, c'est trop bien!! :) [*It's good to be from Deux-Sèvres!!*]
2	Jens:	gotta love'em weekend trips. hvordan går det ven? [*How are you my friend?*]
3	Pauline:	det gaar fint, tak! havd med dig, ven? [*It's going well, thank you! How about you, my friend?*] hey, not everyone can take off to Costa Rica when they get itchy feet, so weekend trips it is for me...;-)
4	Carine:	trop mignon ta bébète!!! c'est celui de l'age de glace....:):):):) [*So cute the little animal! It's the one from Ice Age ... :)*]
5	Elise:	bon retour au pays miss !;-) [*Enjoy going back home, miss!*]
6	Sophie:	ah ah! t'as kiffé le porte-clé, hein! [*Ah ah! You liked the key ring, didn't you!*]

Each participant in the 'conversation' addresses their comment directly to Pauline (with the exception of 'gotta love'em weekend trips' which could be intended for a more general audience), and there is no indication that the commenters are even reading each other's posts. They certainly do not explicitly engage with each other. In fact, the content of their posts differs – Jens and Elise respond to Pauline's travel plans (turns 2 and 5), while Carine focuses on Pauline's new profile picture ('trop mignon ta bébète!!!' in turn 4) and Sophie in turn 6 picks up on the reference to a local slogan in Pauline's status update ('Deux-Sévrien, c'est trop bien'). The bilingual status update appears to invite responses in any language, and language choice is probably motivated variously by individuals' personal preference and language ability, as well as accommodation to Pauline's language choices, their interactional history with Pauline and awareness of her language background.

In other examples, Pauline builds on this communicative dynamic by responding individually to different commenters. In the following thread (developing through responses to her status update in turn 1), she marks the different addressees through language choice (accommodating to the interlocutor's choices in turns 4 and 5), dividing her message into separate posts (turns 4 and 5), and a vocative in turn 5 ('Kate'), as well as style (turn 4 continues the playful elusive thread developed in turns 1 and 2).

1	Pauline:	is back. or is she?
2	David:	you never can tell
3	Kate:	tu es dispo vendredi à midi? [*Are you free on Friday at noon?*]
4	Pauline:	here and there at the same time...
5	Pauline:	Kate, la réponse est oui. je suis même dispo à 11h30 :) [*Kate, the answer is yes. I'm even free at 11.30 :)*]

Rather than describing this pattern as indicating a lack of connection between participants, we might instead identify the emerging norms for accepted behaviour on Facebook which are evident in the interactions. One such norm appears to expressly prohibit ostensibly 'private' interaction between users in the public space. McLaughlin and Vitak (2011, p. 306) report that American teenage users of Facebook felt it was 'courteous to utilize private messaging features for longer messages to an individual, or when they expected to exchange multiple messages with a contact, to avoid clogging Friends' News Feeds'. What happens when someone transgresses this norm is illustrated in another example from our data shown below. In this example, Julia and Josja start directing comments to each other in the space opened up by Eva's status update. The fact that this is transgressive is signalled, firstly, by Josja's warning 'let's not put spam on Eva's profile too' (turn 13) and, secondly, by Eva's response: she switches from English to Dutch and into her role as Julia and Josja's former teacher to admonish them: '@ Julia & Josja: het is net alsof jullie weer in mijn klas zitten :)' ('it is just like you are in my class again') (turn 18).

1	Eva:	has found her mojo again!
		...
6	Julia:	you gettin' married ? :D
7	Eva:	@Julia: got married in February :) See my photos!

8	Julia:	:D Niceee :D little late, but congrats !! Xx
9	Josja:	juuuuuuuuuules you didn't know Eva was married?
10	Julia:	No :$... I do now !! :D
11	Josja:	goh...
12	Julia:	pshhh xP
13	Josja:	let's not put spam on Eva's profile too.
14	Julia:	yeah.. I was thinking that too :P Sorry Eva :P ♥

...

| 18 | Eva: | @ Julia & Josja: het is net alsof jullie weer in mijn klas zitten :) [*@Julia & Josja: it is just like you are in my class again :)*] |

This communicative dynamic – whereby commenters tend not to interact with each other in the comment thread but with the initial poster – constitutes a realisation of what might be called 'node-oriented' networks oriented around a mutual Friend and characterised by a lack of direct interaction between all members.

'Very interesting talk, but I'm bothered about one thing': coming together around shared values on TED.com

If a sense of community is to be expected on a site like Facebook, which is designed to facilitate links between users, then how likely is it that sites with other purposes will similarly see the formation of affiliations between users? The question is an important one, given the increasing use of media-sharing or hosting sites such as Instagram, YouTube and TED.com. TED.com, for example, is a platform for the distribution of talks given at TED conferences, and the expressed goal of the site is that of 'spreading ideas'. Although it presents itself as a 'global community', there are few community-building resources – users cannot construct public profiles or link with other users. However, as with other sites, users can exploit the communicative space of the 'comments' section. Research suggests that they form transitory communities through their comments, by aligning themselves through shared values and appreciation of the talks.

Drasovean and Tagg's (in preparation) research into TED.com draws on Zappavigna's (2011) concept of 'ambient affiliation', which she developed in relation to Twitter. In Zappavigna's (2014, pp. 141–2) words:

> The affiliation in operation in microblogging may ... be seen as ambient in the sense that microbloggers as individuals do not necessarily have to interact directly in order to align around a common value. Instead they signal their alignments indirectly by displaying particular patterns of evaluation, or they can do so

directly through resources such as hashtags ... used to signal the evaluative target of a post.

The concept of ambient affiliation is grounded in a systemic functional linguistic (SFL) approach to language (Halliday, 1985) and in particular the 'Appraisal framework', a model for understanding how language is used to evaluate (Martin and White, 2005). The Appraisal framework divides people's attitudes into JUDGEMENTS (moral evaluations of people), AFFECT (emotional responses) and APPRECIATION (opinions about ideas or things),[1] and measures them in terms of how forceful or focused they are, and the extent to which they stand alone or respond to previous evaluations (whether they are 'monoglossic' or 'heteroglossic', to use the Appraisal terms). For example, the following Tweet from Zappavigna (2011, p. 797) can be analysed as follows (adapted from Zappavigna's analysis). The + sign is used to indicate positive rather than negative (-) attitude, and it is evident that punctuation can also increase the force of an utterance.

HOLY CRAP [FORCE]. OBAMA WON [JUDGEMENT+] HE WON [JUDGEMENT+]!!! [FORCE] IM SO [INCREASED FORCE] HAPPY [AFFECT+]!!! [FORCE]

What is important about Appraisal for our present purposes is that these ideational evaluations (various evaluations of people, objects and ideas) are seen to function as interpersonal resources in that users come together around shared values. This can be seen as taking place over time – such as when a traditional community comes to adopt a set of cultural values – or, in the case of Twitter, such affiliations can be seen as transitory and fragmented. As Knight (2010, p. 43) says, 'we discursively negotiate our communal identities through bonds that we can share, and these bonds make up the value sets of our communities and culture, but they are not stable and fixed'. According to Zappavigna, the use of the hashtag on Twitter means that users can affiliate around a topic or theme on a vast scale. For example, the following 'coffee addicts' can be seen as affiliating around the hashtag #needcoffee:

I hate waking up at 6am everyday. Ughh **#needcoffee**

I'm so out of it this morning. **#needcoffee** or **#moresleep**

I want to fast forward to 3:30, to where I'm laying in bed, taking a nap. **#needcoffee**

Getting out of bed can be so difficult some days...its one of those days. **#needcoffee**

I feel like a zombie. **#ineedcoffee**

Well that was a "fun" morning commute..gggrrrr. **#INeedCoffee**

The application of these observations to TED.com similarly worked from the premise that the site offered a virtual space within which users could comment on the videos and rally around their shared interest in the topic and (it turned out) shared values. Drasovean and Tagg (in preparation) explored a corpus of comments posted in response to videos categorised on the site as dealing with food. The users commenting on the site engaged predominantly in APPRECIATIONS of the ideas outlined in the videos – rather than JUDGEMENTS or AFFECT – and so on one level can be described as orienting towards ideas (rather than people). In doing so, however, they appeared to be actively attempting to interact and align with others in the following ways. Firstly, APPRECIATIONS were overwhelmingly positive and often used to frame and hedge subsequent criticisms (DISCLAIMS in the Appraisal framework):

> Interesting [APPRECIATION+], but [DISCLAIM] I would like to know more about the other types of feelings we get in our stomachs.

DISCLAIMS and ENTERTAINMENT, whereby users entertain other views, suggests a 'heteroglossic' orientation; that users are picking up on other users' ideas and thus constructing a dialogue with them. As Drasovean and Tagg point out, the interplay between DISCLAIM and ENTERTAINMENT also shows that group solidarity on such sites can be expressed through respect for others' opinions rather than simply through agreement (Martin and White, 2005).

> I don't think [DISCLAIM] that he tried to justify eating junk food so much as [ENTERTAIN] tried to make a joke about his own weight.

Positive APPRECIATIONS also preceded the telling of personal stories, a practice which suggests 'an intention to belong' (Drasovean and Tagg, in preparation):

> Wonderful! [APPRECIATION+] So inspiring [APPRECIATION+] and moving [APPRECIATION+]. I am a community worker, the coordinator of 37 community gardens in the city of Jerusalem (and a TEDtranslator too!) [personal story]

Finally, also indicative of a desire to connect is the high use of GRADUATION, of resources used to intensify or hedge the force of an utterance. The following example shows not only how FORCE is used to highlight the user's commitment to what they are saying, but how FOCUS can be used to avoid coming over as overly authoritative:

> To see what a <u>pure</u> [FOCUS]-herbivore dental structure looks like, look at a deer skull (gorilla doesn't come <u>anywhere near</u> [FORCE] that degree of adaptation to herbivorous diet), to see what a <u>pure</u> [FOCUS] carnivore looks like, look at a wolf's skull - both are <u>very</u> [FORCE] specific and practical designs, and don't look like ours <u>much</u> [FORCE]

In other words, the combined resources of force and focus suggest that users are engaged in trying to persuade others to accept ideas to which they express strong commitment, but that they are doing so in careful and sensitive ways that potentially show respect for differing views; thus bonding through their willingness to discuss and debate the ideas in the videos.

Ambient affiliation is less of a 'community' in the sense that levels of engagement and sustained interaction are likely to be lower than in traditional offline communities. But a sense of community – the feeling that users are talking to like-minded individuals – is clearly evident in the ways users attempt to reach and connect with each other.

Conclusion

Applied linguistics research highlights the key role that language plays as users establish and maintain relationships with each other in disembodied online contexts. Through looking at the language they use, it is possible to understand 'community' in much more fluid terms than is possible through focusing on structural criteria such as the duration or regularity of an online group's interactions. Instead, communities are identified in terms of how they are imagined or constructed by users as they direct their posts to what they perceive are like-minded others or mutual friends. With this much broader understanding of community, one that moves away from evaluating virtual communities in relation to the extent to which they measure up to 'real' communities offline, we can see how a sense of community is possible even in the most unlikely and transitory of online spaces – that is, in the Comments posted on sites such as Facebook and TED. com. In Section C, Chapter 21, I look at how online networks and spaces have been theorised in applied linguistics as part of a shifting conceptualisation of what it means to belong to a community.

Task 15.1

Draw a time-chart of all the online sites you have used. Think about each in terms of community. To what kind of community did you belong on each site? Which of the following defined it as a community?

- Affiliation around shared values or interests
- A sense of belonging
- Sustained and regular interactions
- Agreed norms and common purpose.

Are there any sites you have regularly used where you do not feel part of a community?

Note

1   I follow SFL conventions in the use of small caps for appraisal categories.

16 The linguistics of online aggression

Introduction

How can applied linguistics research help resolve instances of online aggression? Many of the issues discussed in Chapter 8 have serious consequences for people's health and well-being, and they can only be fully addressed with the expertise of therapists, police, youth workers and so on. However, in the fight against cyberbullying and online harassment, applied linguistics research can be useful not only in detailing the role played by language as part of any online aggressive encounter, but in revealing the way in which aggression is itself constructed, negotiated and challenged through language. Language is a key resource in the construction of social reality in offline encounters too, but it is particularly prominent in the disembodied situations in which online interactions take place. Online aggression (and other social acts) is performed through language and by rallying their linguistic and discursive resources victims can challenge, avoid or mitigate such behaviour.

In this chapter, I review some of these applied linguistics studies, drawing out the following main points in relation to language and aggression online. Firstly, linguistic analysis allows us to recognise and categorise aggressive behaviour, and awareness of the strategies that aggressors use can be a first step towards victim empowerment (Herring, 2002). Secondly, what is considered aggressive differs between contexts and can be explored by looking at how participants respond to potential aggressors. And, thirdly, certain forms of apparently antisocial behaviour may not always play a negative role in online situations but can at times be interpreted as playing a positive role in group bonding. Throughout the chapter I draw on various terms to describe similar behaviour: aggression, antagonism, antisocial behaviour and impoliteness: for the purpose of this chapter, these are used interchangeably, but see Culpeper (2011) for discussion of impoliteness as a linguistic term.

Identifying and categorising aggressive behaviours

Linguistic analysis has enabled researchers to begin describing and classifying aggressive behaviours in a way which could potentially empower victims. I illustrate this with reference to Susan Herring's work into male aggression towards females online. In what is probably the first language-related study of aggressive behaviour online, Herring et al. (1995) analysed, in their words, 'two unusual but revealing cases in which women spoke out from a female perspective in mixed-sex groups, and the reactions of male participants to this' (p. 70). The study was motivated in part by research showing that men dominate and often act aggressively in online situations (see Chapter 13). Their first finding was that the strategies used by men across two academic forums were strikingly similar, despite differences between the two channels. MBU was a small and friendly mailing list on which posts were usually short, informal and unmoderated; in contrast, Linguist was larger and messages tended to be longer, carefully crafted and subject to moderator approval. Both, however, were used to discuss academic topics and were frequented by academic, predominantly male participants (women made up 42 per cent and 36 per cent of the subscribers of MBU and Linguist, respectively) based in the United States. The incidents in question were similar on both sites – women either raised or expressed opinions on an issue and were met with hostile reactions from the men: on MBU, these opinions constituted objections to a proposed course on men's literature; on Linguist, a carefully researched argument that a local advertising sign ('If your date's a dog, get a vet') was demeaning to women.

The study showed how patterns of dominance and submission are 'actively constructed and enforced through everyday discursive interaction' (Herring et al., 1995, p. 92), underpinned by broader cultural expectations that, for example, women should not speak out at public events. Herring et al. (1995) traced the mechanisms used by men on both lists to silence women. In both cases, the interactions showed men progressing through the following strategies.

1 Avoidance
    a Lack of response (at first, men simply ignored the women's posts).
    b Diversion away from the main topic, either through:
       i Narrow or literal focus (that is, by focusing on one peripheral element of a post – such as a badly chosen quotation – to the neglect of the main point).
      ii Intellectualisation (a time-wasting strategy by which men reframe the women's points into theoretical, abstracted questions).

    c Dismissal of concerns as not worthy of discussion, either through:
       i Patronisation (in the discussion on the male literature module, one man wrote, 'Why are people [especially you ladies – oh God! – Women] so disturbed by studying the male?').
      ii Humour.
2 Confrontation: when women persisted, some men confronted the women with anger and with accusations of political correctness, lack of humour and taking over the list.
3 Co-optation: Herring et al. (1995, p. 86) call this the 'most pervasive and subtle silencing mechanism of all' which involves men adopting the women's ideas as their own, albeit twisting them slightly to fit their own agendas, and thus 'reclaiming control of the discourse' (p. 89).

Herring et al. (1995) also identified strategies used by women to challenge the men's attempts to silence them: persistence, consistency of focus, solidarity and 'metadiscursive commentary'. The last strategy points to an important resource which aided these particular women participants – their awareness as linguists of interactional patterns and feminist arguments about language. This enabled the women to label and critique the men's behaviour. For example, the following post by a female participant shows recognition of the men's 'literal focus' strategy:

> it's like ellen and many of us are trying to make some points about why this men's lit issue is going to the core and eating away, and the come back is not dealing with the issue but with the text used to make the example. it's frustrating. are you (in general) listening to what's being communicated?
>
> (Herring et al., 1995, p. 78)

One limitation of this 1995 study is its focus on academic forums, a relatively over-researched online site. In another study, Herring (1999) showed how a very different online channel – a chat room used for informal, synchronous conversation – followed similar patterns of abusive behaviour and rhetorical strategies to an academic discussion group also investigated in the study, suggesting (among other things) a general internet culture dominated by men. The stages through which abusive behaviour progressed were summarised as follows.

1 Initial situation.
2 Initiation of harassment.
3 Resistance to harassment.
4 Escalation of harassment.

5 Targeted participants accommodate to dominant group norms; and/or
6 Targeted participants fall silent.

(Herring, 1999, p. 156)

According to Herring's analysis, in neither case was there an obvious trigger for the abuse, except for a possible threat to the men's dominance of each site: on the academic list, men responded aggressively to a post by 'Mary Joos' outlining views seen as feminist; in the chat room, the women were talking and inadvertently excluding the men also in the room (1 and 2 in the list above). Women's initial resistance (3) eventually led to their acquiescence, either through silence or accommodation to the men's behaviour (5 and 6). In both cases, this seemed to be because the abuse escalated following their resistance (4), in different ways: the female chat participants were 'kicked' or ejected from the chat room by the male administrators, while men on the academic discussion list moved from specific objections to Mary's post to a 'full frontal attack on feminism' (p. 159) and on women's intellectual legitimacy. The women in the chat room then accommodated to the men's expectations by flirting with them; those on the academic discussion list similarly adopted male norms by utilising aggressive tactics, before falling silent – as Herring suggests, accommodating to another expectation that women do not have a public voice. Although the context, participants and purpose of the two channels were very different, the patterns of behaviour were markedly similar: 'women in each case are coerced into accommodation by being systematically presented with limited, undesirable choices: cease interacting with other women or be kicked/sexually degraded on #india [the chat room]; cease to express pro-female viewpoints or be vilified on Paglia-L [the academic discussion group]' (Herring, 1999, p. 160).

This early work by Susan Herring and colleagues is important in showing how the study of the language used by online abusers can help us understand the strategies used and why they might be successful, and to potentially indicate how victims might challenge their abusers. However, despite the potential of this research and despite some more recent work classifying antisocial behaviour on other sites (e.g. Haugh, 2010 on email; Luzon, 2011 on academic blogs; Pihlaja, 2011 on YouTube), more work is needed to understand the full range of aggressive acts currently taking place on contemporary new media sites, including social network sites and private messaging, as well as that taking place between children.

Importance of context and perception in identifying aggression

As suggested in Herring et al.'s (1995) study, linguistic analysis has also detailed how antisocial behaviour is shaped by the nature of the site, the demographic background of the participants, the topic and purpose of the site, and other variables or 'facets' shaping communication (Herring, 2007). What emerges across studies is the importance of local group norms, as co-constructed by the online community, in defining what constitutes antisocial behaviour. To turn that around, antagonism (and rapport) can be defined in terms of how individuals position themselves, and are positioned, in relation to the group's norms (Angouri and Tseliga, 2010; Graham, 2007; Luzon, 2011, p. 536; Nishimura, 2010). The recognition that what constitutes impoliteness is shaped by local norms has led researchers to focus on how behaviour is perceived, and reacted to, by other participants. To illustrate this work, I outline the work carried out by Claire Hardaker into how definitions of trolling are negotiated and co-constructed on online forums.

Hardaker starts from the assumption that a troller is difficult to identify, and thus research must start by identifying 'behaviours that are troll-like' (Hardaker, 2010, p. 227), before determining who uses them. She set about addressing this question by investigating how people identified and negotiated what constituted trollers and acts of trolling on a horse-related Usenet newsgroup, rec-equestrian (RE). The corpus includes nearly 200,000 posts spanning nine years, from 2001 to 2009. Using corpus software, Hardaker searched the data for words beginning with TROLL (eliciting *trolling, trollin, trollery, trollish* and so on), retrieving 3,727 hits which indicated instances where people were discussing trolling. These she explored in order to build up a definition of trolling (Hardaker, 2010; and see Chapter 8), and an inventory of trolling strategies, as perceived by participants (Hardaker, 2013).

Behaviours identified by participants as acts of trolling included the following. Each were identified by more than one participant, and occurred three or more times in the data set. The strategies show that trolling does not always constitute overt acts of aggression (only Aggress falls into this category), but also includes more covert, subtle attempts to deceive and manipulate (Hardaker, 2013, p. 80).

1 Digress ('straying from the purpose of the discussion of the forum', p. 69), often only considered trolling when other variables were taken into consideration, such as the status of the individual within the group and their interactional history.

2 (Hypo)criticise ('criticising someone for an offence of which the critic was also guilty', p. 71), usually applied to a troller's attempts to correct another participant's grammar.

3 Antipathise (when a post introduces a topic or viewpoint that is 'deliberately controversial or provocative', p. 73); for example, one perceived troller began by eliciting views on whether to buy their daughter a pony, and then expressed disgust and embarrassment at the idea that his/her daughter even wanted such an unfashionable pet (p. 73).

4 Endanger, by which the troll gives incorrect and thus potentially dangerous advice (aimed at newbies to the forum or to horses), which forces other users to engage with the troll in order to 'avoid leaving others with the impression that these activities aren't actually incredibly stupid', as one participant put it (p. 75).

5 Shock ('to be insensitive or explicit about a sensitive or taboo topic such as religion, death, politics, human rights, animal welfare and so forth' and, more broadly, 'an inappropriately thoughtless or hurtful response to any sensitive, upsetting, or emotional situation', p. 75).

6 Aggress (acts of deliberate aggression designed to antagonise and prompt response).

A user's intentions, however, are not always easy to gauge (by participants as well as researchers). Participants often had to debate whether an individual's behaviour constituted trolling, rather than indicating naivety, ignorance or an attempt to express a genuine, if misplaced, opinion. This was particularly true for the more 'off-record' strategies such as digress, antipathise and endanger. Similar negotiations have been noted by researchers investigating inappropriate behaviour on other sites: in their study of an asynchronous Greek student discussion forum, Angouri and Tseliga (2010) found that how participants on the forum respond to potentially impolite posts depends in part on their perceptions of the speaker. For example, user Dijhouse explains his decision to ignore Souel's post:

> Souel is not mature enough to be worth talking to; I wanted to teach him that he is not in his fiefdom here, and that we didn't come here to pick a fight, we just came to have a civilized <u>polite</u> [emphasis] discussion.
>   (Angouri and Tseliga, 2010, p. 70, author's annotation)

So, depending on participants' evaluation of an individual's intentions, the same behaviours (digressing, antipathising, endangering) may or may not be identified as trolling. Hardaker's research thus shows the importance of participants' responses and perceptions in identifying trollers and other online aggressors, and it highlights how what constitutes an act of trolling emerges from negotiation between participants and is therefore co-constructed and contextually dependent. In other words, behaviour is not always inherently antagonistic; how it is interpreted depends on participants' evaluation of the aggressor's intent and the way they interpret its effects. (Thus, someone with good intentions may be unfairly classified as antagonistic just as much as real trollers succeed in deceiving other users.) One implication of this for potentially more serious cases of cyberbullying is that attention needs to be paid to the surrounding online culture and norms in which the aggressive behaviour takes place, and the extent to which these might create an environment in which bullying is possible.

Linguistic items as resources available for aggression

The importance of context also means that a range of linguistic features from non-standard spelling to metaphor can in some cases function as resources with which to challenge or attack (Angouri and Tseliga, 2010; Pihlaja, 2011). In her study of academic blogs, Luzon (2011, p. 531) notes that typographical features can be used positively as a resource for expression as well as negatively, as with the exclamation marks in an utterance like 'SHUT UP!!!!', as can questions which, although not usually antagonistic in academic contexts, were used to challenge others online. Similarly, in her analysis of male aggression in a chat room, Herring (1999) shows how the use of asterisks in marking 'actions' was exploited by men to enact aggressive sexual acts, and that this use apparently discouraged women from drawing on this resource:

> ***Action: Aatank grabs st's butt and says "excuse me but is this seat taken"
>
> (Herring, 1999, p. 155)

As a final example, Pihlaja (2011) shows how metaphor can be taken up as a resource in acts of antagonism. In his study of two communities on YouTube, he shows that metaphors are not stable mappings, but emerge in the natural course of interaction and their use is highly contextualised. His focus is on the development of antagonism between two YouTube users: atheist 'fakesagan' and Christian 'jezuzfreek'. What begins as a debate around stem cell research quickly becomes personal and antagonistic as fakesagan refers to earlier behaviour of jezuzfreek's on the site (jezuzfreek had been critical about another user's video production) and then posts a two-part video entitled 'jezuzfreek thinks he's the pope of youtube' – a metaphor which might be glossed as 'YouTube user who appears to think he has some kind of moral authority on the site as leader of the Christian church'. Shortly before, jezuzfreek had referred to himself as a cop policing behaviour on YouTube, an analogy which may have primed the Pope metaphor. The Pope metaphor itself then became a resource for the expression of various opinions as it was taken up by other participants in ways that highlighted their different perspectives towards what constitutes appropriate interaction on YouTube. Users either play with the metaphor or take it literally, in some cases objecting to the comparison between jezuzfreek and the Pope. Thus, in this YouTube 'drama' (boyd and Marwick, 2011), metaphor emerges as a resource for expressing opinion and refuting others, as users 'extend, subvert and reappropriate the same metaphors with different meanings to suit their own purposes' (Pihlaja, 2011).

The constructed nature of aggression described here does not imply that some antisocial acts would not be universally condemned; rather, the recognition that what is aggressive depends on the immediate context encourages us to take a situated approach to its identification and resolution, and to take participant perspectives into account. Further research could explore the potential implications suggested here for teaching victims of bullying or harassment how to re-appropriate and exploit these linguistic resources in order to challenge or deflate the aggressor's own use of them.

Explaining online aggression

The final question addressed by applied linguists is why people act aggressively online. To some extent, however, people are antisocial online for much the same reasons as they are antisocial in offline contexts. As Herring et al. (1995, p. 92) conclude, the patterns of dominance and silencing evidenced in online interactions often appear to reproduce patterns familiar to face-to-face conversation, and they suggest that digital communication simply allows 'users (and investigators) to see ' more clearly the asymmetrical aspects of communication that would otherwise go by in speech too quickly to be noticed' (p. 92).

However, the ability of men to dominate women discursively online may be determined not only by wider cultural beliefs and practices, but by the male-oriented culture of the internet itself – stemming from hacker-culture and characterised by aggression and libertarianism – and the fact that group administrators and site designers (at least at the turn of the century) tended to be male (Herring, 1999, p. 163). An adherence to libertarian values and free expression of ideas appears to characterise a number of communities' responses to aggression. Herring et al. (2002, pp. 379–80) see a conflict between the decision by minority groups – including women – to seek their own space on the internet and their beliefs that censorship and exclusion are wrong. For example, beliefs in libertarianism are necessary to explain the women's hesitation on a feminist forum to eject a troller called Kent, even though he explicitly announced his intention to troll and refused to engage in meaningful discussion (Herring et al., 2002, discussed further below). Pihlaja (2011) notes that neither the Christian nor atheist YouTuber questioned the other's right to be on the site and to make and post videos, supporting Lange's (2007) claim that YouTube users share a belief in free speech. In other words, an underlying belief in the value of free speech and liberty on the web may have the unintended outcome of enabling a few to get away with aggressive acts.

In some cases, aggression can have the presumably unintended effect of increasing group solidarity, which has interesting implications for understanding why children may single out others for bullying. For example, much criticism on Luzon's academic blogs served simultaneously to construe conflict (with the author of the research) and to create consensus between the poster and other users (Luzon, 2011, p. 532) – illustrating the apparent truism that building group solidarity inevitably involves construing the exclusion of outsiders (p. 537). Angouri and Tseliga (2010, p. 76) describe 'solidarity' acts emerging in response to antagonistic behaviours on an academic forum (members would rally around in support of the victim), and argue that the core members of the forum defined antagonistic behaviours with reference to a strong 'we' identity. Herring et al. (2002) found that the feminists' eventual response to the troller, Kent, took the form of the formation of online regulations for dealing with future cases and thus the explicit setting out of community norms. Uncertainty about the procedures in place to deal with acts of trolling led to group discussion and negotiation which ultimately strengthened the group's identity as a community. As well as prompting discussion about what was appropriate and inappropriate on the site, Kent's trolls (his posts) also led to a new policy which stated that suspected trollers would be given three warnings before being ejected from the site.

In a final example of the role apparently antisocial behaviour may play in creating online solidarity, Page (2014) interviewed a group of young people about their experiences and perceptions of 'fraping' – a term they used to describe the act of hacking into someone else's Facebook account and posting obscene or untrue posts. Rather than being negatively evaluated by the young people, these violations were often viewed as a form of group bonding on the basis that reactions to the inappropriate post served to distinguish those close to the 'victim' from passing acquaintances or those not in the know – only the latter would be deceived by the 'frape'. In other words, the way in which Friends reacted served as a way of consolidating relationships within the noisy social network environment. The fact that someone had initially been able to hack the victim's account also indicated a degree of trust between them, as it was likely they would either need the password or to have access to their open laptop. The possible implication (which would need to be investigated) is that tackling cyberbullying amongst children may similarly require that we address the fact that apparent acts of exclusion (of a bully's victim) are simultaneously acts of inclusion, reinforcing the group to which the bully belongs.

Conclusion

Language-related research cannot prevent people from bullying or harassing others online, and nor can it fully explain why people do so. However, applied linguistics research into antisocial behaviour in various digital contexts provides an insight into how people enact aggression online, and the kinds of strategy that might be successful against such behaviour. The research also problematises straightforward definitions of aggression – what constitutes antisocial behaviour online is often determined by how other participants perceive it and how they react to it; and the impact of aggressive behaviour can be complex, with positive as well as negative outcomes for people involved. In each case, however, more research is needed to expand these initial forays and apply them to real-life cases of online abuse. As a final note of reassurance, applied linguistics research also suggests that aggression is not the norm online, despite the impression conveyed by the studies brought together in this chapter. Many more studies focus on collaboration, community and politeness online (see Chapter 14) than they do on impoliteness. In Luzon's (2011) study of aggression in comments posted on academic blogs, for example, expressions of conflict were much lower than positive expressions of bonding (105 occurrences of conflict compared to 1,594 indicators of positive social presence), and were only present in seven of the 11 blogs. Antisocial behaviour stands out and it needs to be addressed, but it is only one way of responding to the affordances of digital technology.

Task 16.1

Find an example of online aggression and analyse it in terms of:

- The stages that the aggressive behaviour goes through (see Herring et al., 1995 and Herring, 1999)
- The linguistic resources used
- The way in which 'victims' respond to the aggression
- Which factors contributed to and shaped the behaviour.

You may find the example of online aggression by:

a. Looking through your own email, text messaging or social network posts;
b. Selecting an online article and scrolling down the comments;
c. Finding examples of harassment on Twitter.

Section C

Theory

I

Digital language and literacy

17 Multiliteracies

Introduction

In August 2012, I made my first trip to Japan; on reflection, it was my first trip to a country whose national language is not traditionally written in the Roman script. There is a lot of English in the linguistic landscape of Japanese cities, as well as Japanese written in the Roman script, but if you come away from the main shopping malls and find yourself in the quieter part of town, all signage is in the traditional script, a combination largely of kanji (Chinese characters) and hiragana (used for loan words and grammatical items). What struck me most was my inability to recognise place names on signs or make out the very simple vocabulary I had learnt to repeat. The fact that I could not read the script (or even guess at it) was disorientating and odd, and for the first time I thought I knew what it might feel like to be illiterate in the midst of a modern society.

Nonetheless, it was reassuring to note how much I could infer from the context in which I came across the signage. Although I could not read a word, I knew that Japanese script was usually read from top to bottom. I could identify what purpose most of the writing had – giving directions or warnings, providing information, grabbing the attention of passers-by – through factors such as location and style. I could tell which writing had official status (such as the road signs), what was commercial (the shop signs) and what had been quickly scribbled by individuals (the odd bit of graffiti). I had an idea as to how these signs had been produced and how other people were likely to be using them. And the lack of any English or Romanised Japanese told me a lot about the neighbourhood and the people who were expected to pass through.

'Literacy' is a commonly used term and something that most people in developed countries can probably easily define as the ability to read and write – in linguistic terms, to 'decode' and 'encode' a text. This is the way in which I used the term 'literacy' in Chapter 9, focusing particularly on the mechanics of knowing how to spell. But being literate, as my experience in Japan shows, is not only about decoding and encoding language (although that is a significant part). When we learn to read and write, we do so in a particular place and time, and thus we learn the conventions of that place and time. We learn what is considered good writing (in that time and place) and what is not valued; we learn what we can do or achieve with writing; we learn what kinds of writing are appropriate when, where and with whom; and we come to know the power that written texts can have over our lives. To all intents and purposes, I was illiterate in the Japanese backstreets – but in other respects, what I had learnt about literacy in the UK allowed me to interpret some of what was meant by the writing I encountered there.

This book has until now focused on practical issues and data-based interventions. In this section of the book, I look at the theories and ideas behind the empirical studies. In this chapter, I focus on the way in which linguists since the 1970s have conceptualised 'literacy' not simply as a mechanical process of decoding and encoding but as a wider social practice or set of practices deeply embedded in particular contexts which enable us to do things, make relationships and take on particular roles within a literate society (Jones and Hafner, 2012, p. 12). This view of literacy is crucial to understanding the empirical observations about spelling made in Chapter 9, as well as the broader set of 'digital literacies' explored in Chapters 10 and 11. Although these chapters focus on the mechanics of literacy, a practices view of literacies allows us to reposition these concerns as foregrounding particular, highly visible and often valued aspects of literacy at the expense of other social issues involved in being literate.

Literacy, traditionally defined

Before the 1970s and 1980s, the dominant theoretical frameworks in literacy research tended to perceive literacy in fairly narrow terms and as a universal and largely predictable process. As the New London Group (a group of researchers bent on changing such conceptions) put it:

> What we might term 'mere literacy' remains centered on language only, and usually on a singular national form of language at that, which is conceived as a stable system based on rules such as mastering sound–letter correspondence. This is based on the assumption that we can discern and describe correct usage. Such a view of language will characteristically translate into a more or less authoritarian kind of pedagogy.
>
> (New London Group, 1996, p. 64)

Understood as the mastering of linguistic rules, literacy can be treated as a social variable that exists independently of any particular individual, society or cultural tradition (Street, 1984, p. 1) – people 'acquire' literacy or, perhaps more accurately, it is brought to them. Literacy introduced into a community can thus potentially transform it, again in predictable ways. Jack Goody and Ian Watt (1963), for example, extrapolate from their observations of the 'logical, specialized, and cumulative intellectual tradition' of sixth-century Ionia to argue that historical enquiry and scepticism was only made possible through the development of writing. The transformation is one-way, from literacy onto society – the ability to read and write alters how people think. Such accounts exclude the possibility that the apparent effects of literacy might emerge as part of a more dynamic and interactive process; in other words, that what it means to be literate can be contested and recreated as people exploit written texts to make meanings that have local relevance. Instead, literacy is seen as the agent for change and people are positioned as passive recipients.

If literacy is posited as an external and predictable variable, as Sebba (2007) points out, then the realisation of literacy in any one society can be identified, compared and evaluated according to objective benchmarks. There is, for example, a tendency within academia and popular opinion alike to assume that phonetic writing systems – in which letters represent sounds (or phonemes) – represent the culmination of historical progress from pictography (where symbols represent ideas or concepts) through logographic systems like Chinese (where characters represent words) and finally to the Roman alphabet (Sebba 2007, p. 15). In line with this perspective, the 'best' uses of the alphabet are seen as those which most perfectly achieve a one-to-one sound–symbol correspondence. Spanish would be a good example of such a 'transparent orthography'; English, in contrast, has an 'opaque orthography' with a highly irregular sound–symbol correspondence. The general assumption is that this disadvantages children learning to read in English (Hanley, 2010).

Although held up as self-evident facts, evaluative claims about literacy are in fact implicitly ideological – that is, they are embedded in and shaped by the assumptions, values and practices of the particular societies or cultures from which they emanate. Although English spelling is seen as being particularly problematic for learners, and studies such as Hanley's are important for identifying ways in which the teaching of English spelling can be improved, it is important to realise that they are focusing attention on the aspect of English spelling most valued in western society – the extent to which characters can be uniquely matched to a particular sound. In fact, as Hanley points out, English spelling also makes grammatical distinctions – the plural marker in English is always spelt the same (<s>) although in some words it is pronounced /s/ and in others /z/ (compare *cats* and *dogs*) and it distinguishes homophones (words that sound the same but have different meanings – compare *rose* and *rows*). In such cases, 'look is more important than sound' (Kress, 2000, p. 173). In his book on children's spelling, Gunther Kress shows how children learning to 'mean' through spelling engage in much more than simply learning to spell 'correctly' (Kress, 2000). In one example given by Kress (2000, p. 34), two children spell 'frogspawn' as 'frogs born' and 'frog's sporn', drawing respectively on their awareness of the world (frogs being born from frogspawn) and from their knowledge of English grammar (if the 'sporn' belongs to the frog, it must be 'frog's sporn').

Nor is it surprising that European missionaries perceived the phonetic alphabet – their writing system – as most 'natural' and 'efficient' (Barros, 1995, p. 282) and so proceeded to use it to produce written versions of indigenous languages in Asia, Africa and Latin America. As Maria Cándida Barros explains, these missionaries tended to overlook the possibility that the written language might be used differently by indigenous societies and in ways that challenged western assumptions about the purpose and nature of reading and writing. This potential clash is illustrated in the contrasting literacy strategies proposed by missionaries and an indigenist literacy group in Mexico, an observation also made by Sebba (2007, p. 24):

> The indigenists proposed the use of murals, whilst the missionaries preferred the book format. The mural was a Mexican cultural tradition utilised by important painters, such as Rivera, Siqueiro etc., after the revolution, and the indigenists suggested its extension to the teaching of writing. Their proposal was to produce wall-newspapers to be posted in public places, such as markets, which would deal with topics linked to the community or about the government. ... Muralism as a form of spreading literacy is related to a model of public reading which preserves features of orality through its collective use. In contrast, the reading material of the missionary was the book, associated with solitary reading.
>
> (Barros, 1995, p. 282)

Literacy as a social practice

The need to take contextual factors into account when discussing literacy is central to the 'new literacy' movement of the 1980s which, to use Brian Street's terms, sought to replace the traditional 'autonomous' model of literacy with an 'ideological' model (Street, 1984) which recognises the cultural basis of literacy (Sebba calls the latter the 'sociocultural model'). Researchers such as Street, David Barton, Michael Cole, James Gee, Mary Hamilton, Ron Scollon, Suzanne Scollon and Sylvia Scribner have reconceptualised literacy as a set of *practices* specific to particular societies (Barton, 1994; Barton and Hamilton, 1998; Gee, 1990; Scollon and Scollon, 1981; Scribner and Cole, 1981). 'Practices' in this model refers not simply to 'events' involving literacy (reading aloud a newspaper, signing a form, sending a text message) but to what can be inferred or theorised from observing these recurring events about 'broader patterns of social and cultural ways of doing writing' (Lillis, 2012, p. 85). These researchers were making the point that literacy varies according to the social context in which it takes place, in terms of how it is perceived, what form it takes and how it is valued, as well as the particular uses to which it is put. In a sense, the new literacy movement has extended already widely accepted ideas about the importance of context in understanding language use to the theorising of literacy.

This contextualised view of literacy has had a number of implications for how applied linguists approach the subject. Methodologically, if reading and writing practices vary according to social context, then investigating literacy requires a methodological approach that allows for a deep understanding of social context. Linguistic ethnography (Blommaert, 2007; Creese, 2008) has its roots in an approach which involves 'the researcher immersing him or herself totally in the culture under examination, living in the community and using this experience to provide very richly detailed data about how the members of the culture behave on a day-to-day basis' (Groom and Littlemore, 2010, p. 76). Such an approach requires a move from textual analysis to the use of an array of social research tools – observation and recordings, 'talk around texts', diaries and journals, questionnaires and interviews (Lillis, 2012, p. 81). Using these methods online – in what Androutsopoulos (2008) calls 'discourse-centred online ethnography' – raises various questions, not least the question of how context is defined online, and the extent to which it is necessary or possible to draw a line between people's offline practices, and those they engage in online. While some researchers situate ethnographic studies in the rich textual world which users co-construct online – thus excluding the offline from the relevant context – others explore how online practices are deeply embedded in people's offline lived experiences (e.g. Lee, 2014; Takahashi, 2014). (See Jurgenson, 2012 for further discussion of the online/offline divide – what he calls the 'IRL fetish' – and Chapter 20 for its implications for identity.)

A second implication is that if literacy is no longer seen as a stable, monolithic phenomenon, then it may be useful to talk not of 'literacy' but of 'literacies'. The pluralisation of the term is not simply a conceit, but a way of acknowledging the diversity subsumed under the term 'literacy' and the impact this may have on people's chances in life. The New London Group, who popularised the term 'multiliteracies', met in 1994 to discuss the role that literacy education could play in addressing the issue of social disadvantage (they met in New London, USA, hence the name). They identified what they saw as profound changes to public and private life over the twentieth century, charting a shift from national unity, shared values and cultural homogeneity towards an increasing acceptance and valuing of social and cultural diversity. These changes have implications for the demands that workers face – where once schools were required to produce a reliable and competent workforce which knew its place, contemporary workers require such qualities as flexibility, creativity and criticality. The New London Group argued that literacy education has an important role to play in 'creating access to the evolving language of work, power, and community, and fostering the critical engagement necessary for [young people] to design their social futures and achieve success through fulfilling employment' (p. 60).

As the New London Group also acknowledged, literacies do not vary only because of social and cultural differences (that is, because of differences in how people become and are literate). They also vary because being literate is never simply a matter of being able to decode and encode text, but also a matter of being able to interpret images, recognise and recreate genre conventions, take into account underlying agendas and so on (as I suggested in relation to my experiences in Japan). Digital technologies have seemingly added to the many ways in which people can communicate meaning, and to the different skills needed to do so: as the New London Group (1996, p. 64) points out, 'When technologies of meaning are changing so rapidly, there cannot be one set of standards or skills that constitute the ends of literacy learning, however taught.' In Section B, Chapter 10, I looked at the different ways in which these skills have been categorised. However, it is important to recognise that pre-digital practices are also multifaceted, in similar if more familiar ways. Goodman (2007), for example, suggests how 'visual literacy' and cultural knowledge might be necessary in decoding such everyday texts as toilet signs, wine bottle labels, posters, adverts and comics. It may be that digital technologies have through their relative novelty drawn attention to the variety of skills that writing and reading always entail, but which tend to be obscured by our familiarity with them.

Vernacular literacies

A final implication of literacy as social practice is that new literacy researchers are not solely, or even primarily, interested in literary or formal contexts but in ordinary people's everyday practices – that is, in 'vernacular literacies' (Barton, 1994), also known as 'local literacies' (Barton and Hamilton, 1998) and 'grassroots literacy' (Blommaert, 2008). Many literacy studies have focused on very ordinary or disadvantaged communities or groups, including Barton and Hamilton's (1998) study of a town in northern England; Wilson's

(2000) studies of literacy inside prisons; Mbodj-Pouje's (2010) research into farmers in Mali; Moje's (2000) study of 'gangsta adolescents'; and Heath's (1983) well-known comparison of three communities in the USA: the white middle class 'mainstream', the white working class community of 'Trackton', and the black working class, 'Roadville' (see Lillis, 2012, p. 79 for more examples). The kind of informal, private, non-prestigious, and largely unregulated practices documented in these studies ('vernacular literacies') contrast with the official, formal, regulated 'dominant literacies' associated with the public sphere (education, the law, the media and so on). Many practices, of course, combine dominant and vernacular texts (often subversively). When people scribble in the margins of their library books or start doodling on handouts in a meeting, they are effectively extending vernacular practices to dominant, official texts.

The concept of vernacular literacies is very useful in exploring what is happening when people interact online. In their exploration of the photo-hosting and sharing site, Flickr, David Barton and Carmen Lee (e.g. Barton and Lee, 2013) comment on how vernacular practices seem to have changed since Barton's (1994) study of pre-digital literacy practices in a community of northern England. They found that people often used the online space to do what they had always done (e.g. share photos), but that the technology allowed them to extend their practices (e.g. to annotate and tag their photos as a way of making them accessible and connecting them to similar photos). The potential for creativity was also enhanced, due to the resources and tools made available by digital photography and the space provided for experimentation and feedback. Perhaps most importantly, online vernacular practices appeared to be socially valued in a way that non-digital writing tends not to be – not only by the wider audiences that internet users are able to reach, but by public institutions:

> Flickr is regularly searched by publishers and journalists needing photos of specific topics for books, magazines and newspapers. Teachers and researchers are exploring its use in classrooms ... and extensive materials and advice on its educational potential are available on the internet.
>
> (Barton and Lee, 2013, p. 151)

In general, the internet appears to be having the effect of blurring the traditionally drawn line between the public and private spheres, meaning that once-localised activities and practices can potentially be widely circulated, with implications for identity construction as well as for people's ability to bring local issues to national or global attention. This is not to say that only with the internet can people achieve things through vernacular writing (see, for example,

Blommaert, 2008; Lyons, 2007), but that the internet has the potential to expand the reach and impact of people's everyday writing practices. The flipside of this is that literacy practices that once took place in private, locally owned spaces and without externally imposed regulation, are now taking place in spaces owned and controlled by corporations. For many users of Facebook, for example, the fact that their private writing takes place on the social network site becomes a problem when the company changes its privacy setting overnight and suddenly employers or parents can see posts or Friends lists once carefully hidden from them (see Chapter 6). For users needing to hide their activities from the authorities – particularly in countries like China, Russia or Iran – the changes in privacy can be devastating (MacKinnon, 2012). Political activists who want to exploit the affordances of sites like Facebook must contend with company policies that legislate against anonymity and pseudonymity on their sites.

Spelling as a social practice

In Chapter 2, I discussed the potential significance of textisms in digital communication, and suggested that spelling constituted a meaning-making resource. In this section, I explain some of the theory behind those ideas, drawing largely on the argument made by Mark Sebba that orthography itself is a social practice which carries social meaning.

For any language practice to have social meaning, argues Sebba, there must be choice involved – if a language user has made no choice, it is difficult to say that they mean anything by it. When we speak and write, we make myriad choices, from the channel of communication we decide to use (see the concept of 'polymedia' discussed in the Introduction) to the register we adopt and individual word choices – but spelling does not on the surface allow for much choice, if at all. The spelling of most languages now tends to be highly regulated with little room for what Sebba calls 'licensed' deviation, where more than one choice is acceptable. Exceptions indicate regional differences (British <colour> versus American <color>), words with foreign origins the spelling of which has yet to settle down (*hummus*, for example, can be spelt in various ways); as well as some less easily explained choices (such as <judgement> or <judgment>). In such a rigid system, it is difficult to imagine much potential for making-meaning. Even new literacy scholars have at times implied that spelling is simply part of the technology of producing literacy: 'we approach literacy as a set of socially organised practices which make use of a symbol system and a technology for producing and disseminating it' (Scribner and Cole, 1981, p. 236; cited in Sebba, 2007, p. 13).

However, while convention decrees that each word has one spelling, it is still possible to spell words in alternative ways, and here the potential for meaning emerges. Continuing with our example of English, which has a particularly varied sound–character correspondence, it is evident that words can be spelt in <u>unconventional</u> or 'unlicensed' ways without violating the underlying orthographic principles of English. To take one example from Sebba (2007, p. 28), in English the sound /uː/ (the default spelling of which is <oo> as in *too*) can also be spelt <o> as in *to*, <oe> as in *shoe*, <ue> as in *blue*, <ew> as in *flew*, or <ou> as in *group*. Even Spanish, where the sound–character correspondence is more unique (one sound tends to be represented by one character), permits some variation – for example, the sound /k/ can be represented by <c> (e.g. <u>c</u>oche, 'car') or <qu> (e.g. <u>qu</u>eso, 'cheese') or, with some words of foreign origin, <k> (e.g. <u>k</u>iosco, 'kiosk'). The use of <k> is familiar yet unusual in Spain and has therefore been adopted by anarchists and other subcultural groups to highlight their 'otherness' (Sebba, 2007, pp. 48–50).

It is convention, arising from social practice, which determines how particular words should be 'correctly' spelt from among possible sound–character correspondences. But it is the potential *choice* between these correspondences that allows us to make meaning. If somebody chooses to spell *what* unconventionally as <wot> (as in the text messages investigated in Chapter 9), the choice to do so implies that the user means something by it. In Britain, <wot> has a long and now fairly conventional association with graffiti – reaching back at least as far as the 'Wot no bananas?' campaign following the Second World War in Britain – indicating subversive humour. We might argue that the spelling of *you* as <u> is now conventional in many digital contexts. But the act of choosing between a licensed and an unlicensed form means something in terms of how an individual is positioning themselves and/or their texts within society. As Sebba (2007, p. 56) puts it, respelling can work either to construct identity, stance and opposition to the norms, or it can 'provide a way of contextualising the text (or parts of it) on the basis of whether it uses, or fails to use, possible variant spellings'.

Spelling, then, can be meaningful when people choose to deviate from standard, licensed conventions (and, because there is this choice, the decision to spell conventionally can also take on some meaning, particularly in unregulated digital spaces). However, at the same time, in order for deviation to be meaningful – indeed, in order for the act of deviation to be recognised – a word cannot be respelt in a way that strays too far from the licensed spelling but instead must honour the possible sound–character correspondences of a language. As Sebba (2007, p. 30) puts it, a respelling can only mean anything if it deviates 'in a way that allows the original meaning to be conveyed, along with additional social meaning which derives from defying the conventions'. As he goes on to explain:

> The variant spelling must be recognisable to readers as a variant spelling of a particular word; otherwise it is incomprehensible (the word cannot be recognised) and/or unable to bear social meaning (because it cannot be seen to be deviating from anything specific).
>
> (Sebba, 2007, p. 33)

The implications of this understanding of orthographic variation can be seen in my earlier discussion of text messaging (Chapter 9): firstly, 'textisms' must be seen not as random or chaotic but as drawing on a narrow range of possible choices; secondly, if these choices are determined by orthographic principles and by their closeness to the standard, then they presuppose some awareness of existing conventions (rather than ignorance of them); and, finally, textisms are not then an impediment to effective communication but another resource for making meaning.

Conclusion

In this chapter, I've outlined some of the ideas behind the empirical research described in Section B, particularly Chapters 9, 10 and 11 which explored spelling practices and other digital literacies. The work in those chapters must be understood as drawing on the concept of literacy as a complex social practice (or set of social practices), shaped through their use by a particular social group so as to fulfil immediate purposes and meet local expectations. In this sense, texters are not breaking rules, but rather exploiting and playing with conventions in order to make meaning in a locally relevant way. In many respects, digital literacy practices extend rather than break with existing practices (and thus textisms can be traced back to earlier pre-digital texts) but, at the same time, the internet is blurring the line between traditionally private and public spaces, providing a public place in which unregulated vernacular writing can reach a wider audience, make greater impact, and take on an enhanced social value (Barton and Lee, 2012). The pluralisation of literacies implies heterogeneity; in the next chapters, I look in turn at 'translanguaging' as a way of understanding how people draw on multilingual resources; and then at 'heteroglossia' as a broader means of capturing the multimodal, multilingual and intertextual practices that often characterise vernacular writing online, and the social tensions and conflicts between these and dominant or more established ways of writing.

18 Translanguaging via a superdiverse internet

Introduction

> I mix Chinese and English openly; have to, really. No secret about it. ... Why is it called code-mixing? Is it some secret message?
> (Chris, a 19-year-old British-born Chinese man in London, in Wei, 2011, p. 1229)

Chapter 12 explored the way in which internet users switch between different languages and showed that arguments about the online dominance of English are in fact more complex than they might initially appear. Linguistic description of actual practices reveals how people mix languages in various, intricate ways that defy easy categorisation into one or another language. As evident in Chapter 12, many of the studies into online multilingualism frame their accounts in terms of 'code-switching' and 'code-mixing', a long-established tradition of research within socio- and applied linguistics. However, as the quotation from a Chinese–English 'code-mixer' somewhat playfully suggests, the metaphors of mixing and switching between codes can be misleading, and are often challenged by the reality of multilingual practices in both spoken and online contexts. How, for example, can an utterance like 'ou mai ga' (a Chinese pronunciation of 'oh my god' which we looked at in Chapter 12) be described in terms of *switching* between Chinese and English? An emerging paradigm in sociolinguistics seeks to describe multilingual practices not in terms of switching but as a more fluid and complex process by which users draw on any and all of the languages in their repertoires, without necessarily making conscious distinctions between them: a process known as translanguaging. In the rest of this chapter, I outline the arguments made about translanguaging and its particular relevance in contemporary contexts, including online ones, which are defined by superdiversity. The chapter builds on the recognition of heterogeneity in people's practices discussed in Chapter 17 through the concept of 'multiliteracies', focusing particularly on the use of resources from more than one language.

Problems with the concept of 'code-switching'

Research into code-switching has tended to have as its aim the objective of countering popular opinion about language mixing and to paint a picture of code-switching as normal, motivated, generally interpersonal and often creative. The practice of switching between languages has tended to be negatively evaluated and considered deficient even by those who engage in it, although it can also be associated with covert prestige. In Gibbons' (1983) study, Cantonese and English code-switching by Hong Kong university students was viewed with hostility as showing arrogance; while in Chana and Romaine's (1984) study of Panjabi and English in the UK, members of the Panjabi community saw code-switching as broken-up and impure. Within the classroom, using a local language alongside an official language is rarely condoned, but is instead dismissed as bad practice or ignored (Creese and Blackledge, 2010). Research into code-switching has played a role in raising the profile of multilingual talk and challenging negative perceptions of the practice. However, the terms 'code-switching' and 'code-mixing' have been criticised recently on various grounds.

Firstly, the metaphor of switching assumes that what speakers are doing is moving back and forth between two separate languages, and that this is facilitated by flicking something in the brain. One problem with this is that we simply do not know if this kind of 'switching mechanism' actually exists, and the evidence often suggests that it does not (see Gardner-Chloros, 2009). Nor is there any evidence that speakers themselves experience their own multilingual practices in terms of switching (e.g. Sneddon, 2000); using more than one language is seemingly often not a conscious process, and speakers are in fact often unaware that they have been code-switching. Many bilingual speakers in bilingual communities appear to draw on resources from more than one language in the same way as a monolingual speaker operates in one language, drawing on different registers and styles. The question as to whether we can uphold a meaningful distinction between code-switching and monolingual practices of moving between registers and styles is returned to below.

Another problem is that the concepts of switching and mixing assume the unproblematic existence of separate, isolated languages. What we tend to experience as different languages (English, French, Chinese) are to some extent social constructs, often tied up with national identity: that is, the boundaries of these languages are defined and controlled for the purposes of nation-building and political security (Anderson, 1983/1991). The boundaries determining a particular language (what, for example, counts as 'English' and what counts as 'French') are not wholly natural phenomena but are laid down by people in their attempts to standardise and codify a nation's language use. However, given the shared histories of many languages, the constant contact between them and the increasing global circulation of bits of language, in reality these boundaries remain fuzzy. When I ask for a 'chai tea latte' in my local coffee shop, which language or languages am I using – and is that even a relevant question to be asking? The answer will have more to do with global power, consumerism and culture flows than it will with fixed sets of linguistic features. Perhaps the multinational coffee shop illustrates Lemke's (2002, p. 85) suggestion that 'It is not at all obvious that if they were not politically prevented from doing so, "languages" would not mix and dissolve into one another'.

Problems in assigning a word or phrase to one language or another (as in 'chai tea latte') are often exacerbated in written language, where words cannot be ascribed to a language through the pronunciation used by the speaker. Homographs and homophones used in SMS highlight the difficulties in ascribing one sign to a particular language when clues such as pronunciation are removed, as well as (in some cases) conventional spelling patterns. Morel et al. (2012) give the interesting example of *n8* which occurred in their corpus but which could be transcribed as German *nacht* or French *nuit* in SMS, such as 'bonne n8, spatzilein!' ('good night, little sparrow!') where both languages are mixed. In some cases, Morel et al. (2012) argue that texters may be playing with the ambiguity created in order to highlight a cosmopolitan, globalised identity. This is their reading of the following SMS, in which the English loan word, *w.e.*, apparently triggers a switch into English, followed by a switch to French for 'effort', a word spelt the same in both languages.

Ça va, le w.e. was worth l'effort

[*I'm ok, the weekend was worth the effort*]
(Morel et al., 2012, p. 271)

Although it is possible to argue that the construction and reification of national languages has never accurately reflected actual practices, it may be the case that at one time (between the eighteenth and twentieth centuries) the codification of discrete languages better matched a model of social organisation that no longer holds true in the twenty-first century, due to changes in social structures, power relationships, and the apparent emergence of 'superdiversity'.

Superdiversity

The concept of superdiversity was introduced by economist Steven Vertovec in 2007. Vertovec (2007) argued that diversity in Britain had changed since the 1990s such that established assumptions about where immigrants came from and who they were could no longer be relied upon by policy-makers and practitioners. In particular, Vertovec argued, immigrants could no longer be distinguished solely in terms of ethnic origin – and, in the case of Britain, specifically from places such as the Caribbean, India and other former British colonies – but also in terms of a range of variables including country of origin, legal status, access to employment and language which intersect in new ways and, importantly, operate on a larger scale than ever before (Vertovec, 2007, p. 1026). At the same time, the growth of the internet and digital communication technologies has meant that migrant communities can maintain links to their home countries in ways previously more difficult (Blommaert and Rampton, 2011). The implication for social policy – in Britain, other Western European countries and the United States – is that the promotion of collective identity and community-based measures may no longer be sufficient for tackling patterns of inequality and segregation.

The internet has been seen as playing an important role in fostering and extending superdiverse contexts (Varis and Wang, 2011). It does this by providing spaces which transcend geographical boundaries and distances (so that, for example, migrants can maintain links with home) and in which people who are based in various physical locales can come together around, for example, shared interests or shared pasts (see Chapter 15 for details on the different kinds of communities brought together online). For example, Varis and Wang (2011) document the role of the internet in facilitating 'subcultures' in China despite the complex system of censorship and governmental control. They focus on the Chinese hip-hop community as an example of a translocal community or 'supergroup' (Velghe, 2011) – a group of individuals from different backgrounds who develop their own social and linguistic conventions through sustained interaction – which is brought together with the help of the internet to 'engage with, circulate, appropriate and modify global hip-hop flows otherwise less visible and accessible for them' (Varis and Wang, 2011). As Varis and Wang (2011) point out, the internet also allows for the inclusion of remote or peripheral individuals such as a dialect rapper from Enshi (Varis et al., 2011; Wang, 2010). As such, the internet serves to further challenge assumptions that language use can be explained with reference to fairly stable and geographically bound social categories.

Language-related research has important implications for our understanding of superdiversity whilst, at the same time, superdiversity has helped linguists transform our understanding of multilingual practices. On the one hand, language can be seen as important in reproducing and interpreting superdiversity. Blommaert and Rampton (2011) make the point that language not only 'bears the traces' of superdiverse migration patterns and community dynamics, but that how and what people say or write is also constitutive of social reality; that is, language plays a part in producing and maintaining social relations and ideas about the world (as discussed in the Introduction). Thus language is central to an understanding of the way people are classified, managed and responded to in superdiverse (and other) contexts. For example:

> if one rejects an essentialist group description such as 'the Roma in Hungary', and instead seeks to understand how 'Roma' circulates as a representation in Hungarian discourse, how it settles on particular humans, how it comes to channel and constrain their position and activity, then it is vital to take a close look at language and discourse.
>
> (Blommaert and Rampton, 2011)

On the other hand, the concept of superdiversity has been useful in providing a descriptive account of social patterns with which to contextualise emerging views about language. One implication of superdiversity with relevance for ideas about language is that stable associations between a community or individual and a particular set of language resources can no longer be assumed (Blommaert and Backus, 2012). Blommaert and Backus (2012) argue for the replacement of 'community norms' with 'individual repertoires' which include all the 'bits' of language picked up by individuals as they move through contexts of superdiversity (see Chapter 20). An individual's repertoire will reflect to some extent that of their immediate community, but will also be shaped by their particular life trajectory. All of this suggests that, in superdiverse contexts, the linguistic categories traditionally used to describe social context – such as community and language variety – must be rethought.

New ways of looking at multilingual practices

Superdiversity, and the recognition that multilingual practices are more fluid than the concept of code-switching suggests, mean that linguistic analysis needs to avoid established analytical constructs and to proceed instead from a descriptive basis deeply embedded in actual usage (Blommaert and Rampton, 2011). As Jørgensen et al. (2011, pp. 28–9) point out, 'Speakers use features and not languages'. Analytical concepts such as translanguaging do not look at how different languages are used, but rather at how different features are taken up and exploited. As Blackledge and Creese (2014, p. 17) point out, the relevance of translanguaging for understanding and analysing language in use is that 'it becomes clear that the most important question is not about which language is mainly in use, but rather about what signs are in use and action, and what these signs point to'. This does not mean that the notion of languages is entirely irrelevant. Features are often associated with particular languages and come to take on the same values and meanings of these languages (Jørgensen et al., 2011, p. 30). As Jørgensen et al. (2011) point out, this association can be seen in stereotypes, whereby for example a Dane can adopt a Norwegian accent to suggest 'happy-go-lucky naivety' or 'Scandinavian brotherhood', depending on the context. This particular example illustrates the shifting nature of values, in the sense that different languages are likely to be evaluated differently in different places, at different times and by different people (Blommaert, 2010). On the other hand, however, their association with a language is not the only way in which linguistic features come to take on meaning or to be valued (Jørgensen et al., 2011, p. 28). Features can also carry meanings distinct from the languages with which they tend to be associated; or, rather, it can often make little sense to analyse one particular feature in relation to the language to which it might be said to 'belong'. For example, when a Senegalese texter greets a friend with 'Salut chou boy' (see Chapter 12), it is of some historical and social relevance that *salut* and *chou* are French and *boy* is English; but this was not relevant at the moment of texting to the composer of the message, who thought of the expression as part of his local, urban identity (Lexander, 2011, p. 439).

A number of terms have been suggested to capture the practice of drawing on features or resources associated with different 'languages', including polylingualism and metrolingualism, as well as trans-languaging. Metrolingualism, for example, focuses attention on the superdiverse urban spaces where heightened levels of diversity – and new kinds of diversity – are commonly felt to occur (Otsuji and Pennycook, 2011). The notion of metrolingualism captures the observation that, in contemporary superdiverse cities, connections between language use and traditional criteria such as ethnicity, nationality and geography cannot be assumed and instead users are seen as developing new repertoires in response to the urban situation. However, inherent in the term 'metrolingualism' – and in Vertovec's argument regarding superdiversity – is the assumption that such practices are both relatively new and predominantly urban. As Canagarajah (2011, p. 3) points out, however, this assumption is misleading. People are likely to have always drawn on multilingual repertoires in fluid ways, if not always so obviously in the west. Canagarajah cites examples from South Asia, ranging from rural villagers in present-day India (Khubchandani, 1997) to the combining of Tamil and Sanskrit in medieval *manipralava* writing (Viswanathan, 1989). The term 'translanguaging' avoids the explicit assumption that the practices it captures are solely a feature of post-modern, superdiverse cities.

Translanguaging

Translanguaging, which is probably the term that has been taken up most widely across linguistics and other disciplines, emerged as an analytical concept from research into educational contexts (Williams, 1996; Creese and Blackledge, 2010; García, 2009) in an attempt to normalise or place higher value on mixed language uses within pedagogical approaches. In other words, the aim of translanguaging researchers is to highlight the advantages of drawing on a child's full linguistic repertoire in helping him or her to learn: 'competence doesn't consist of separate competencies for each language, but a multicompetence that functions symbiotically for the different languages in one's repertoire' (Canagarajah, 2011, p. 1). A functional separation between different languages – that different languages are best suited for different educational purposes – should not be assumed. Instead, the languages that a child speaks can be drawn on in a 'dynamic and functionally integrated manner' (Blackledge and Creese, forthcoming). One language is not called upon to learn another; both are drawn on together. This view challenges the traditional pedagogic assumptions that in bilingual education, languages should be kept separate to avoid confusion and discourage bad practices.

The *transformative* potential of translanguaging is emphasised by researchers using the term. If we understand linguistic forms, as uttered on particular occasions, to be imbued with social and ideological meanings (see Chapter 19, which discusses Bakhtin's ideas about the heteroglossic nature of signs) then, in Wei's (2011, p. 1223) words, the act of translanguaging 'creates a social space for the multilingual user by bringing together different dimensions of their personal history, experience and environment'. The act of translanguaging can thus transform the status quo, creating new value systems and shifting world views. Wei's study of young Chinese men in London highlights the creativity and criticality of their multilingual practices: creative in the sense of pushing at social and linguistic norms; and critical in the sense of using the available evidence to question and challenge established views. The men Wei interviewed were very comfortable with their multilingual identities, moving between Mandarin, Cantonese and English to talk to different groups of friends and also drawing playfully on the three languages in nicknames, puns and creative mixes. What Wei stresses, however, is that the men could not be said to 'fully' know all the languages they used – Chris does not read and write in Chinese and Lawson was at the time attending Mandarin classes – and nor did they perceive themselves as English-speakers or Mandarin-speakers; rather, they saw themselves as multilingual speakers with access to a range of resources across the languages. Chris said:

> We are not completely Chinese anymore. We are British, if you see what I mean. I think mixing Chinese and English together is us, is what we do. If I speak Chinese only, I'm no different. You can see I'm Chinese. I look like Chinese. So if I speak English all the time, people will ask 'Why don't you speak Chinese?'. I do. I just want to speak both.
>
> (Wei, 2011, p. 1230)

Translanguaging allowed these young people to construct their own sense of identity within the transnational space in which they found themselves, rejecting traditional assumptions about their roles, creating social networks that cross language backgrounds, and constructing a vision of their futures as men of the world: as Chris said, 'When I finish uni, who knows? I could be anywhere' (Wei, 2011, p. 1233).

However, translanguaging does not mean that 'anything goes'. Language users are constrained not only by linguistic rules but by socially constructed rules and conventions. Firstly, as Jørgensen et al. (2011) point out, not all linguistic features are available to all speakers: in the case of English as a global language, for example, it is not possible for the marginalised in many English-speaking societies, such as in India, to gain access to English resources; in other cases, the resources may be available to a speaker who is denied legitimate access to, or ownership, of them – such as an upper-class pupil who hears urban slang every day at school but who is not seen by other pupils as a legitimate user of it. Secondly, how people use language is often tightly monitored. This also applies online, despite the fact that contexts of digital communication are often thought to be linguistically unregulated (Sebba, 2007). Varis and Wang (2011), for example, describe ways in which rules and regulations constrain online behaviour, ranging from government policy and censorship to the micro-level norms that emerge in particular sites or forums. The point is that, in superdiverse contexts online and off, the sources of authority may be emergent and multiple, including non-institutional conventions (such as those laid down by peers) alongside official regulations.

Limitations to the concept of translanguaging

For researchers of digital communication, and others, translanguaging overcomes some of the limitations of terms such as code-switching which fail to adequately account for the hybrid use of language resources in emerging multilingual, translocal contexts. However, the term brings its own limitations. Canagarajah (2011) points out that while translanguaging is used in part to avoid the binary distinctions held up by other approaches, its proponents to some extent continue to distinguish between 'multilingual' and 'monolingual' users and practices, usually romanticising the former: 'scholarship on translanguaging makes multilingual communication appear more diverse, dynamic and democratic than "monolingual" competence' (p. 3). Another implication of this view has been the exclusion of 'native speakers' from studies of multilingual or lingua franca contexts, on the basis that they approach such situations differently (a suggestion that Canagarajah challenges in his description of native English speakers' responses to a classmate's multilingual writing). This, he argues, is an 'artificial communicative context' (p. 6) which neglects consideration of the way in which multilinguals respond to people they perceive as native speakers in, for example, the classroom.

In actual fact, Canagarajah (2011) argues, it is difficult to uphold 'monolingual' as a valid construct with any objective reality. Firstly, most people do have resources from more than one language, even if they are very far from proficient in more than one of them; secondly, everyone moves between registers, styles and/or dialects in ways that reflect the repertoires of 'multilinguals'. This latter observation militates against an absolute distinction being made between monolingual and multilingual practice, in terms of the ways in which language resources are drawn on for pragmatic and interpersonal functions. A similar point is made in the code-switching literature where people have called for a broadening of the term 'code-switching' to include other kinds of switch, such as those between registers and styles within one language (Muysken, 2000). One argument behind this is that many of the functions carried out by language alternation can also be fulfilled through other shifts, thus raising the question of how a distinction between multilingual and monolingual practices can be justified. Morel et al. (2012) find evidence for this in their study of SMS text messaging and argue that code-switching is just one resource among many on which the texters draw. Their study is based on an SMS corpus of 27,000 text messages collected from texters across Switzerland and including Swiss German, standard German, French, Italian and Romansh. Morel et al. (2012) identify creative sign-offs within which shifts in style appear to carry out the same purposes as switches between languages. In 'Pas du soucis kiss' (Don't worry kiss) the switch to English demarcates the sign-off and heightens intimacy; but in 'Vivement ce soir … bisouilles' (Can't wait for tonight … kisses), the creative combining of 'bisou' with the suffix 'ouille' (all in French) serves a similar function (Morel et al., 2012, p. 267). In their study of Hong Kong users of the chat platform, ICQ, Fung and Carter (2007) similarly identify monolingual resources which appear to serve the same function as bilingual language play. For example, the users played with punctuation, typography and assonance, as well as switches to Cantonese, to indicate heightened emotion. In the following example, the users draw on Cantonese discourse particles, capitals and exclamation marks to indicate the urgency of the situation and their heightened emotions.

A: you forgot to bring the UID notes for me wor, please
        bring it bck to me tomorrow, VERY VERY URGENT !!!
B: I know r !! I reckon it in the CCN lect!!! sorry!! I 'll give it
        to u tom. !!! SORRY!!!!!!!!
                                            (Fung and Carter, 2007, p. 360)

In the next chapter, I look at another concept used in recent linguistic research, that of 'heteroglossia', which encompasses diversity in all its forms, including multilingual, multimodal and multi-authored practices; and which may therefore best capture the kind of hybrid language practices that take place in many digital contexts.

Conclusion

What translanguaging does do is to shift the norm from 'monolingual' to 'multilingual' practice and thus help to challenge 'dominant paradigms' (Canagarajah, 2011, p. 4). Canagarajah (2011, p. 4) concludes that the limitations to translanguaging may be resolved in time; that, once the previously dominant paradigms have been demolished, the binary oppositions can be further deconstructed. In the meantime, analyses of translanguaging practices often appear to struggle to describe language practices without recourse to notions of different 'languages'. In their discussion of polylanguaging, Jørgensen et al. (2011, p. 35) admit that they end up using 'cumbersome expressions' such as 'a word, which is generally taken to be English' rather than 'an English word'. Like other proponents of translanguaging, researchers using the term to explore digital communication may need to tread a careful line between promoting the recognition of the kinds of fluid language processes they identify on the one hand and, on the other, recognising and taking into account the power of languages both as social constructs and in the minds of individuals.

19 Heteroglossia

Introduction

Open almost any webpage and prepare to greet the sheer diversity of voices and modes that characterise the internet. YouTube, for example, like other media-sharing and social-network sites, is characterised by the convergence of various elements into one site. As Androutsopoulos (2010) explains, convergence can be seen not only as the *embedding* of multimedia content into a website (such as the video on a YouTube page) and the *integration* of different channels of communication onto one platform (such as wall posts, instant messaging, and private messages on Facebook), but by *modularity*: 'the way in which web pages are composed of a number of different elements – different in terms of origin, authorship, affordances, conditions of production and so on' (p. 208) (see the Introduction). YouTube's corporate owners design and populate much of the web interface – the banner, the search function, the sidebar are all institutionally created. The central element of any YouTube page – the video – is uploaded by a user (or group of users), who in some cases draws on the affordances of digital technology to remix or parody another video or other source. Such videos are instances of 'recontextualisation' (Androutsopoulos, 2010), in the sense that a text has been lifted from an original context ('decontextualised') and reworked for a new context ('entextualised'), with all the scope for critique and fresh interpretation that such a process brings (Leppänen et al., 2014). The video itself, then, embeds its own conversational history into the site; a conversation to which other users can then add their contribution, in the form of comments which may be composed in a range of written styles, registers, different languages, viewpoints, and from various geographical locations. Finally, the list of stills to the right of the main video which suggest similar videos is generated by the site but driven by the current viewer's past history, as are any advertisements – adding further trajectories to the mix. In sum, any one page may exhibit hybridity along a number of axes or dimensions: the composition of channels and modules, multi-authorship, multilingualism, multimodality and intertextuality. As Androutsopoulos (2011, pp. 279–80) argues, such hybridity cannot be captured by any one traditional linguistic approach (such as code-switching, translanguaging, multimodality or language variation) as these tend to prioritise one dimension of variation and to explain it in relation to contextual features which do not always find their parallels in digital contexts.

A number of language theorists and researchers of digital communication have therefore sought to describe and analyse online hybridity by adopting Bakhtin's concept of 'heteroglossia'. The advantage of heteroglossia over other terms used to describe variation is that the term encompasses all the dimensions of hybridity listed above and can be used, for example, to explain monolingual communication as much as multilingual (Bailey, 2007, p. 258); it emphasises user agency and social context; and it starts from the premise that all utterances are multi-authored and dialogic. In the rest of this chapter, I lay out the main tenets of heteroglossia, as understood in applied linguistics research, and show how it has been applied to digital communication.

Heteroglossia

Based on ideas he developed throughout the 1920s, the concept of heteroglossia was first introduced by Russian literary scholar and language philosopher Mikhail Bakhtin in his 1934 essay, 'Discourse in the Novel'. The term was part of Bakhtin's 'sociohistorical' theory of language, which challenged existing models of language by focusing on the social and ideological aspects of language use. In fact, heteroglossia can be seen as working on two levels: not only at a formal or textual level (in the hybrid combinations of features from across different languages, modes or voices), but also at the social level (the contrasts and tensions that accrue between different perspectives and positionings and which can lead to heteroglossic forms). As Bailey (2007) points out, Bakhtin's ideas were more in line with anthropological ideas about the social functions of language (Malinowski, 1965) than they were with formalist linguistics of the time which made a distinction between literary and everyday language, and which conceptualised language as abstracted from society and from people's intentions and desires. In contrast, as Ana Deumert puts it, heteroglossia:

> is not a feature of the 'system'. The diversity of language-in-use is actively created by speakers whose behaviour, although normative and habitual at times, is frequently unpredictable and innovative, often even artistic.
>
> (Deumert, 2014, p. 32)

This view has immediate relevance for digital communication, long seen as characterised by play and innovation (e.g. Danet et al., 1997; Tagg, 2013), as Deumert's own studies of digital communications in South Africa make clear (Deumert and Masinyana, 2008; Deumert, 2014). But furthermore, heteroglossia encourages us to conceive of linguistic hybridity as purposeful: it 'does not just *occur*, as one could say with regard to language variation, but it is *made*: it is fabricated by social actors who weave voices of society into their discourses' (Androutsopoulos, 2011, p. 282). In relation to new media, this has the advantage of avoiding technological determinism (as discussed in the Introduction), in that the technology can be posited as offering affordances which users can choose to exploit in particular (potentially heteroglossic) ways.

According to Bakhtin, the ways in which people use and exploit language are determined in part by their interpretation of, and their response to, the political and ideological connotations that linguistic forms accrue through repeated use. To break down that argument, the first point is that the meaning of words and phrases is shaped through the uses made of them; they carry with them myriad voices and evaluations associated with their history of use. These associations then shape what the word or phrase means in a subsequent use. Let's take an example, that of the term 'health and safety' in Britain, which was originally used to describe the official regulations and procedures put in place by state and corporate bodies to protect their employees and members of the public. For a large number of Brits, the term would now be intended or interpreted with an additional meaning involving over-officious and often ridiculous red-tape that stops anyone being able to get on with their work. The repeated use of that term to refer to what are seen as overbearing and pointless rules has imbued the term with a particular connotation.

At times, these past associations manifest themselves explicitly and it is possible to distinguish between the current speaker's voice and that of past users – for example, when people explicitly report what someone has said – and this Bakhtin calls 'double-voicing'. In the following text message exchange, for example, a South African couple draw on the language of Shakespeare to frame their own relationship, whilst simultaneously critiquing this portrayal through the written representation of a self-conscious *Ahem* and the use of digitalese (*u*, *luv*).

Wherefore out thou... Ahem... Where are u? (Zoleka)

Is this an sms from my oh-so-dear Julietta I see before me? I am here at last, my luv! What shalt thou cookest for thy sweet Romeo whenfore he visitest u? (Thami)

(Deumert and Masinyana, 2008, p. 128)

All communicative encounters embody the potential for such performances, but it may be that digital contexts such as text messaging are among those that particularly encourage such play, due not only to the close relations between participants and the informality of the situation (Carter, 2004) but the fact that people have time to craft their messages and the centrality, given the lack of paralinguistic features, of words for self-expression. In the following text message exchange from my own corpus, for example, the texters use a generally standard form of English to discuss what they might buy their brother for Christmas. However, in the fourth turn, Laura draws on an unconventional spelling of *what* (<wot>) to mark her response as playful and teasing, before answering Jo's question:

Jo: Do you have any ideas for David?
Laura: All he has said really is clothes.
Jo: Clothes?
Laura: You know, <u>wot</u> people wear. T shirts, hat, belt, is all we know.

(Tagg, 2012, p. 109)

<wot> stands out from the otherwise standard language and in doing so signals a change in how her utterances should be interpreted: 'wot people wear' is a joke that diverges from the main purpose of the exchange.

However, the argument is that all utterances, even those that do not explicitly highlight the tension between different voices, carry the connotations or 'taste' of previous uses. In Bakhtin's words:

> All words have the 'taste' of a profession, a genre, a tendency, a party, a particular work, a particular person, a generation, an age group, the day and hour. Each word tastes of the context and contexts in which it has lived its socially charged life; all words and forms are populated by intentions.

(Bakhtin, 1981, p. 293)

Thus the meaning of words shifts and changes as each successive use builds on or transforms previous uses. As suggested in the above quotation, while some uses may be idiosyncratic and individualistic, language also comes to be appropriated and organised into speech genres and other recurring patterns. Linguistic features are then interpreted through their association with a particular communicative purpose, context, or way of doing things: as Bakhtin (1981 [1935], p. 289) puts it, 'Certain features of language take on the specific flavor of a given genre: they knit together with specific points of view, specific approaches, forms of thinking, nuances and accents characteristic of the given genre'. With every fresh utterance, then, a user's linguistic choices are shaped by their awareness and exploitation of a variety of pre-existing types of language. These include:

> social dialects, characteristic group behaviour, professional jargons, generic language, languages of generations and age groups, tendentious languages, languages of the authorities, of various circles and passing fashions, language that serves the specific socio-political purposes of the day, even of the hour.
>
> (Bakhtin, 1981, p. 262)

Implied in much of the above is the importance of evaluation in heteroglossic language use. According to a Bakhtinian view, language cannot be considered neutral, for it is imbued with the evaluative meanings assigned through its use by socially and historically situated individuals in particular social contexts, from their own perspectives and with particular intentions. Thus, subsequent uses of language and texts will take on these previous evaluations, with meaning emerging through the way these users position themselves in relation to earlier stances, confirming or challenging them. Heteroglossia emerges from the tensions and contradictions that pertain to these competing voices and points of view, 'based on the sociohistorical associations they carry with them' (Bailey, 2007, p. 257) and in particular from:

> the co-existence of socio-ideological contradictions between the past and present, between differing epochs of the past, between different socio-ideological groups in the present, between tendencies, schools, circles and so forth.
>
> (Bakhtin, 1981, p. 291)

An example of the tensions from which heteroglossia emerges can be seen in a study by Lauren Squires into a 'text messaging scandal' that hit the US media in 2008. Text messages sent between two senior politicians who were accused of having an extramarital affair were crucial to the court case and frequently cited by the media. Squires (2011) drew on a dataset of 75 unique text messages, in three realisations – as originally recorded on the original court transcript; as they appeared on the television screen; and as they were read aloud by newsreaders – to explore the ways in which the text messages were recontextualised for the watching audience. As Squires points out, media representations of texting tend to focus on teenage texting practices and they do so by exaggerating what are seen as new or unique features of the language, such as the abbreviations and phonetic spellings (Thurlow, 2006). The tension in this case arose from the fact that these were adults, engaged, as Squires puts it, in very adult practices; and the dominant ideas cultivated in the media about how adults use language contrasted with the kind of language that these politicians were using (involving the use of capitals, repeated exclamation marks, and acronyms like LOL). As a result, the various omissions, additions and changes made to the text messages as they moved from transcript to the newsreaders' mouths worked mainly towards removing features of 'digitalese', standardising the language and rendering it mundane. At times, however, different versions competed with each other, as newsreaders through their readings tended to further standardise irregular spellings (such as 'sooooo') retained on the screen renderings.

Some caution, however, should be exercised in assuming that the existence of hybrid or heteroglossic forms necessarily entails ideological tensions or political stances, particularly in digital spaces such as websites:

> one aspect of web 2.0 heteroglossia is its dual nature as both intended and emergent process. In line with its traditional understanding, heteroglossic discourse is an outcome of intentional semiotic action, in which linguistic resources are juxtaposed in ways that index social, historical, ideological tensions and conflicts. However, web 2.0 heteroglossia also appears as a by-product, or side effect, of the composite structure of contemporary dynamic web pages which are not composed in their entirety by one single author.
>
> (Androutsopoulos, 2011, p. 294)

In other words, online heteroglossia may not always be politically charged but emerges from the inherent nature of webwriting – that is, the fact that any one webpage is often multi-authored and can be constituted through the recontextualisation of elements from elsewhere, whilst other elements, such as translations or advertisements, may be automatically generated.

Nevertheless, as the above begins to suggest, the Bakhtinian view of language posits language use as inherently dialogic, in the sense that any one particular use of language – including written works of literature as much as turns in a conversation – both responds to a previous utterance and anticipates future responses from a projected, or imagined, audience (see Chapter 14 for a discussion of imagined audiences). As Bailey (2007, p. 263) puts it, 'Talk and texts thus need to be understood in terms of past and ongoing social and political negotiations of which they are a part, not as forms in isolation'. Twitter offers a good illustration of the dialogic nature of language evinced by Bakhtin. As Gillen and Merchant (2013, p. 57) put it in their exploratory investigation of their own practices on the microblogging site: 'To participate in Twitter is to enter into a discursive relationship with others and to expect, to paraphrase Bakhtin, response, agreement, disagreement and more'. A Tweet sent today is clearly not, as Bakhtin might have put it, the first to break the eternal silence of the Twitterverse, but instead takes its place 'in a very complexly organised chain of other utterances' (Bakhtin, 1986, p. 69, cited in Gillen and Merchant, 2013, p. 57). What is particularly interesting is the way in which certain processes, such as dialogicality – which, as discussed above, are present in all language use – are embedded into the very infrastructure of a site like Twitter through the use of the @ and the hashtag to join a particular discourse and respond to (and challenge or contradict) previous Tweets. Thus, what is true but covert in most language situations becomes very visible and formalised online. In other words, the interactive and participatory nature of digital communication is neither new nor unique to the internet – in a Bakhtinian approach, all language is dialogic and multi-authored – but it may be that the internet foregrounds such features.

With its focus on the hybrid nature of all language use and on the social and ideological functions of hybridity, heteroglossia allows researchers to approach digital communications not as something completely different or new, but in the light of processes and practices that shape all language use. The term has seemingly great relevance for understanding digital communication. However, it is also, as a fluid, complex and socially embedded phenomenon, potentially very difficult to operationalise (Bailey, 2007, p. 263). In the final section of this chapter, I explore an attempt to apply it to digital contexts: an analysis by Jannis Androutsopoulos of 'vernacular spectacles' on YouTube.

Applying heteroglossia to digital contexts

In his study of videos posted on YouTube, Androutsopoulos (2011, p. 284) proposes the webpage as the unit of analysis, or 'anchor', within which he identifies three different levels of linguistic and textual organisation:

a   At the level of the single utterance (e.g. code-switches within a turn or contrasts between username and comment);
b   Relations between content and audience responses: for example, in comment threads where users converge or diverge linguistically from the language of the original post or video, in order to align with or challenge its stance;
c   Wider composition of the website including user interface, advertising space, and institutional and participatory content: 'user-contributed content may contrast to the linguistic design of the surrounding web interface' (Androutsopoulos, 2011, p. 285) and

'the linguistic choices of various components reflect and reinforce boundaries between actual user activity and its multiple corporate findings' (p. 286).

Androutsopoulos (2010) uses the concept of heteroglossia in his investigations of how globally circulating videos are localised by a particular dialect group, Bavarians in South Germany (that is, they make it relevant to a local community). In particular, he contrasts two localisations: one a cover version of Rihanna's hit song, 'Umbrella', rewritten in a Bavarian dialect around the theme of binge drinking and given as a title the phonetic pun, 'An Preller' (loosely glossed as 'being pissed' but sounding like 'Umbrella'); the other a translated version of a popular American YouTube rap about McDonald's. He describes as 'vernacular spectacles' such 'multimedia content that is produced outside media institutions and uploaded, displayed, and discussed on media-sharing websites such as YouTube' (Androutsopoulos, 2010, p. 203). His argument concerns the discursive and dialogic construction of local identity through vernacular spectacle, and the potential that such spectacles offer for the public performance of vernacular identities.

Heteroglossic tensions emerge from the contrast between original and localised versions; and from the dialogue between the spectacle itself and the user comments, but this happens in different ways in the two videos. 'An Preller' retains the music of Rihanna's song, along with conventions such as the song's structure, and overlays it with different lyrics which call on a Bavarian regional identity – it is written in 'a levelled, urban Bavarian' (p. 221) and lays claim to regional knowledge, including in its lyrics generalisations about the Bavarian community as well as specific cultural items such as the 'Mass' or Bavarian beer mug (p. 220). Although sung completely in Bavarian, there are written uses of English, including a comic strip reading 'pardy ends' (in which spelling is used to capture a Bavarian accent). One strength of heteroglossia is that it does not presuppose switches between languages as a whole, but between 'specifically contextualised instantiations thereof' (Androutsopoulos, 2011, p. 293). In other words, writers can be seen as drawing on what they know of a language to fulfil the purpose at hand, rather than having command (or not) of the language as a whole. I looked at this issue in Chapter 18 where the concept of 'translanguaging' is discussed.

As such, the video engages in the appropriation of globally circulating resources for local purposes, whilst simultaneously mocking and criticising the original version – an interpretation supported by user comments such as *so sehr wie ich das original hasse, liebe ich diese version* ('as much as I hate the original, so do I love this version') (Androutsopoulos, 2010, p. 222). Visually, 'An Preller' is a 'bricolage'

(Androutsopoulos, 2010, p. 220, drawing on Chandler, 1998), incorporating 'visual bits and pieces of very different origin, which gain new meaning in their dialogic relationship to the lyrics' (Androutsopoulos, 2010, p. 220). These 'bits and pieces' range from shots of the Bavarian flag and the 'Mass' to binge drinking and Mickey Mouse. In Bakhtinian terms, the video constitutes an act of *varidirectional* double-voicing – it challenges the original with its own, contrasting interpretation (Androutsopoulos, 2010, p. 225). In short, 'An Preller' can be seen as an act of 'local resistance' against the globally powerful corporate music industry.

In contrast, the lyrics of the Bavarian rap are faithful to the American version (albeit with some local flavour and some code-switching to English which resembles a typical practice of German rap), and can be seen as an appreciation (rather than critique) of the original video. The contrast lies mainly in the visual aspect of the video – rather than being set in the McDonald's drive-thru, the singing takes place in a living room, framed by stills at the beginning and end of the video which mark it as Bavarian – the flag and a local version of the restaurant's logo. Unlike An Preller, this video can be seen in terms of unidirectional voicing; 'it is a response that agrees and aligns with that of the original and uses it as a backdrop to demonstrate the actors' own creative skills' (Androutsopoulos, 2010, p. 225). Interestingly, however, this version invites comment more for the authenticity of the Bavarian dialect used than for its reworking of the original version, and debate as to whether or not the language is Bavarian or Franconian. Thus much of the tension is grounded in local antagonism between the two language communities and the working through of local language ideologies. The heteroglossic practices in the two recontextualised videos thus illustrate very different social processes – in the first, heteroglossia emerges from the tensions between the global and the local; in the second, it feeds into locally situated identity conflicts.

Conclusion

The concept of heteroglossia allows digital researchers to investigate hybridity in all its forms and in particular to consider the political and ideological functions, motivations and tensions that lie behind online diversity. Despite attempts to operationalise the term for the analysis of specific texts, heteroglossia is likely to remain a somewhat fluid analytical concept, lacking the precision of the categories and concepts it displaces: code-switching, multimodality, language variation. This may be its strength, shaking assumptions and freeing the researcher to explore various dimensions of hybridity and exploring various interpretations.

II

Social issues and social media

20 Identities in interaction

Introduction

In Section A, Chapter 5, I looked at the popular concerns arising from people's abilities to hide or distort their identities online. This affordance may be taken up for various reasons, ranging from criminal and immoral actions to people's attempts to foreground the unrealistically sunny side of their lives on social network sites. These concerns were addressed in Section B, Chapter 13, where I explored the findings of empirical language-related research into the ways in which offline identities and relationships are reconstructed online (rather than discarded). In this chapter, I look at the theoretical ideas about identity which underlie this empirical research. According to the contemporary discursive turn in social research, identity is not a predetermined, stable property of an individual, but a set of resources on which people draw in presenting and expressing themselves through interaction with others. People actively co-construct and negotiate 'who they are', and present themselves in different ways depending on the contextual circumstances in which they are interacting. Central to these identity performances and underpinning them is the need for 'authenticity', reconceptualised as an interactional process of negotiation and validation. In these respects, although the novelty and distinctiveness of online interaction may bring to the fore the constructivist nature of identity, social media encounters are no different from our everyday interactions offline: an important point in rationalising our fears about anonymity and self-promotion.

The rest of this chapter is structured around the five principles which Bucholtz and Hall (2005) identify as central to social and linguistic accounts of identity: emergence, positionality, indexicality, relationality (including the positioning of someone as 'authentic' rather than contrived) and partialness.

The emergent nature of identity

The first two principles identified by Bucholtz and Hall (2005) – emergence and positionality – are concerned with the way in which identity comes into being. The principle of emergence suggests that identity should not be treated as something that exists prior to, or separate from, an individual's social interactions. Identity is not a property of the self which is reflected in a person's linguistic and discursive practices; rather, identity is a construct that emerges in the process of social encounters. The emergent, or constructive, concept of identity is particularly evident in cases where people transgress expected identity assignments (to give Bucholtz and Hall's example, where transgender people reject labels and features associated with the gender to which others assign them). However, the important point is that such identity assignment is *always* a process of negotiation, even where the identity labels ascribed and the performances given correspond to wider social expectations and social structures; that is, where they draw on previously established resources (Bucholtz and Hall, 2005, p. 588). This notion of 'performing' identity (rather than 'having' or 'being' a particular identity) owes much to the 'dramaturgic' model of the self, popularised by Erving Goffman in the mid- to late-twentieth century. As Goffman (1959, p. 245) puts it, a person's identity:

> is a product of a scene that comes off, and is not a cause of it. The self, then, as a performed character, is not an organic thing that has a specific location, whose fundamental fate is to be born, to mature, and to die; it is a dramatic effect arising diffusely from a scene that is presented.

Goffman argued that people in everyday interactions work together in 'teams' to put on theatrical performances for audiences (and that they take on the role of audience for others' performances). Team members co-operate in maintaining a particular 'interpretation of the situation' and in presenting a united front before the audience. Teachers, for example, may avoid contradicting each other in front of their pupils: as one teacher put it, 'Just let another teacher raise her eyebrow funny, just so they [the children] know, and they don't miss a thing, and their respect for you goes right away' (cited in Goffman, 1959, p. 95). Team members also share a 'backstage' relationship that they perform when the stage curtains come down and they relax into informal roles; for example, when teachers have a break in the staff room they adopt different roles from those they take on during supervision in the playground or when teaching in class. Admittedly, Goffman's work focused on public arenas (which he could observe) and less on our performances 'backstage'. However, we can take from his work the argument that some interactions are not more or less contrived than others, but rather that people's social lives comprise a complex show of constructed fronts as they collude in different teams – on stage or backstage – to present versions of themselves.

One limitation of Goffman's work is that the roles he envisages for team members do not emerge during interaction but have an existence beyond their immediate performances (Davies and Harré, 1990). In other words, although people can adopt different roles and move in flexible ways between them, the roles themselves are to some extent predetermined and static. This limitation is addressed by Rom Harré with the concept of 'positioning'.

The principle of positionality

In a series of papers, Harré and colleagues challenge the popular idea that interlocutors take on fixed or *a priori* 'roles' in conversation, arguing instead for the validity of the 'conversational phenomenon' of positioning (Smith, 1988) – 'the discursive process whereby selves are located in conversation as observably and subjectively coherent participants in jointly produced story lines' (Davies and Harré, 1990, p. 48; see also Harré and Langenhove, 1999; Harré and Moghaddam, 2003) – as a way of understanding identity construction. That is, rather than adopting or moving between predetermined roles, we constantly position and reposition ourselves and each other within any one interaction, in line with broader narratives and frameworks of understanding, and drawing on our beliefs about ourselves, past experiences, knowledge of conventions and rules, and ideas about interlocutors' beliefs and expectations. The way in which speakers are positioned at any one point is not predetermined and nor does it have independent existence beyond the dynamics of the unfolding interaction. The ways in which we position and are positioned are not necessarily conscious or deliberate, and they draw on socially established roles and conventions, but the term implies agency, in the sense that subject positions are determined by the experiences and interpretations of the individuals involved:

> the concept of a person that we bring to any action includes not only that knowledge of external structures and expectations but also the idea that we are not only responsible for our own lines but that there are multiple choices in relation not only to the possible lines that we can produce but to the form of the play itself.
> (Davies and Harré, 1990, p. 52)

At around the same time, philosopher and feminist Judith Butler showed how gender is constructed and reaffirmed through discourse; that is, the roles which we associate with men and women are the result of their repeatedly being performed in interaction with others (Butler, 1990). This insight highlights the fact that people are active producers of feminine and masculine roles, rather than having them passively assigned at birth, and it also explains variability in how gender is constructed. Linguist Deborah Cameron (1997, p. 60) argues that '[e]ven the individual who is most unambiguously committed to traditional notions of gender has a range of possible gender identities to draw on', explaining that:

> [p]erforming masculinity or femininity 'appropriately' cannot mean giving exactly the same performance regardless of the circumstances. It may involve different strategies in mixed and single-sex company, in private and in public settings, in the various social positions (parent, lover, professional, friend) that someone might regularly occupy in the course of everyday life.

However, the principle of positionality also expands the notion of performative identity from macro-social categories such as gender to include performances of localised identities (Bucholtz and Hall, 2005, pp. 591–3). These local identity categories range from positions or orientations taken within one interaction (including the temporary adoption of particular participant roles, such as joke-teller or engaged listener) to expressions of alignment with local cultural groups which often intersect with broader social categories. The argument is that people simultaneously position themselves in terms of macro-social categories, other localised groupings and participant roles.

The principle of indexicality

The principle of indexicality serves to explain *how* identities are brought into being through people's discursive practices (Bucholtz and Hall, 2005, pp. 593–8). Indexicality refers to the way in which particular linguistic choices are implicitly linked to features of the social world; they *index* (or 'point to') social rather than referential meanings. 'Hence two or more phonological variants of the same word may share the identical reference but convey different meanings, e.g. differences in social class or ethnicity of speakers, differences in social distance, differences in affect' (Ochs, 1992, p. 338). Indexicality works on all linguistic levels – not solely on individual sounds, words and structures that come to be ideologically imbued with social meaning, but also at the level of a dialect or language. If you dropped some French into a conversation with British friends, this choice might index for your friends various things about you – that you were glamorous and chic, perhaps; or being pretentious. The point is that this is not inherent to the French language, but emerges from the connotations that the particular variable (French rather than English) may have among some British people.

It is through repetition and habitual practice that identities come to be tied to particular linguistic repertoires. According to Blommaert and Varis (2013, p. 146), 'Identity discourses and practices can be described as discursive orientations towards sets of features that are seen (or can be seen) as emblematic of particular identities'. As Ochs (1992) points out (and as we saw in Chapter 13 with Herring's work into male and female language), a linguistic feature and a particular social identity might be indirectly linked by means of an interactional stance. That is, a linguistic feature becomes associated with a particular stance – say, aggression or sympathy – which then becomes associated with a particular social category (e.g. man or woman) (Bucholtz and Hall, 2005, pp. 595–6). In other cases, a linguistic feature may come to be associated with an interactional stance through its use by a particular group.

Studies by sociolinguist Penelope Eckert elaborate on how, in their performances of identity, people draw on and adapt various linguistic resources, alongside other aspects of their manner or appearance, to position themselves in locally meaningful ways. Eckert focuses on the orientations of high school students in California towards alternative social roles – burnouts or jocks. Burnouts hang out in the downtown area where they eventually find jobs, while jocks are school-oriented, involved in athletics or school politics. Although jocks and burnouts account for only half the high school students researched, the salience of their roles is such that others define themselves as 'in-betweeners', in relation to the two groups. And although the two social groups are strongly class-related – few jocks are working class and few burnouts middle class – the exceptions suggest that allegiance to one or other of the social groups is more important in determining linguistic choices than social class. This suggests that although, in Eckert's (2007, p. 125) words, 'the basic features of our dialect are set in place by the environment in which we grow up, the actual deployment of those dialect features – as well as of many linguistic features that are not part of regional dialects – is left to individual agency'. In other words, people can pick and choose from an existing array of available linguistic features in constructing their own style; in turn, people's stylistic practice aligns them with the social group, or social identity, associated with that style.

The principle of relationality and the need for authenticity

The final principles – of relationality and partialness – refer to the situated nature of identity. Bucholtz and Hall's relationality principle (pp. 598–605) highlights the way in which an identity performance is understood, by participants, in relation to other possible identity performances. One frequently researched relation is that of similarity and difference or, in Bucholtz and Hall's terms, adequation and distinction. For example, Cameron (1997) describes how a group of male college students in the USA engaged in a seemingly feminine practice of 'gossiping' about gay men they knew whilst watching soccer on the television. Cameron explains this as an attempt by the men to position themselves in relation to the homosexual men as 'red-blooded heterosexual males' (1997, p. 62). In mixed-sex interactions, these men may avoid gossiping, in order to distance themselves linguistically from 'women' and define themselves as being not feminine. What is important here is the way in which people highlight an individual's or group's characteristics in order to position them as alike or different, downplaying those features that do not support this process of adequation or distinction – thus similarity and difference are themselves socially constructed and emergent. However, sameness and difference are not the only relations within which identities are evaluated. Other relations include authorisation and illegitimation (the way in which identities are affirmed or rejected by institutionalised power or local processes of evaluation), and by authentication and denaturalisation.

Most people can empathise with the need to be judged 'authentic': '[b]eing qualified by others as a "wannabe", "a fake" or some other dismissive category is one of many people's greatest anxieties' (Blommaert and Varis, 2013, p. 148), yet it is more difficult to explain why we value authenticity and the term defies straightforward definition. In lay terms, authenticity is often seen as a superordinate term for 'criteria of "truthfulness", "reality", "consistency", "coherence" and so on' (Coupland, 2003, p. 417). Coupland (2003) attempts to pinpoint the criteria which underlie these lay definitions (and see Van Leeuwen, 2001): to be authentic, something must have a real existence, a degree of longevity, a place within a wider context, social acceptance or authorisation, and a social value: what is authentic is generally valued for being so (although why we value these criteria remains unknown, as Van Leeuwen, 2001, points out). Applying this to the evaluation of identities online, we might posit that an online participant would be deemed authentic by interlocutors if their online behaviour was seen to consistently relate to an online persona (over time and, in any one interaction, through the use of a coherent set of stylistic features) which in turn was seen to have parallels with who they are offline (Gill, 2010; Page, 2014, p. 49). 'Passing' as authentic, as Blommaert and Varis (2013) put it, to an online audience on a social network site can gain an individual important social capital (Ellison et al., 2011); as can the ability to detect inauthenticity (Page, 2014, p. 50 and see Chapters 13 and 14).

As this suggests, contemporary accounts of authenticity do not describe it as an inherent quality residing in an individual but as a process of authentication or validation by which interlocutors negotiate what is to be considered authentic. We need, argues Van Leeuwen (2001, p. 396), '[t]o ask, not "How authentic is this?", but "Who takes this as authentic and who does not?", and "On the basis of which visible or audible cues are these judgements made?"' According to Blommaert and Varis (2013), whether something or someone can be deemed 'authentic' depends on their being judged as 'having enough' of the features associated with the identity they are trying to convey. 'If, for instance, we use too wide a pitch range and too much dynamic variation in our speech, this may be seen as excessive ... On the other hand, if there is too much restraint, the performance will come across as learned by rote, and hence also as inauthentic and insincere' (Van Leeuwen, 2001, p. 394). 'Enoughness' is itself determined locally, judged by category members deemed to be 'competent' (the 'expert authenticators' mentioned by Coupland, 2003). What is considered authentic is thus highly contextual (Page, 2014, p. 50) and culturally specific (Van Leeuwen, 2001, p. 394), so that what is authentic in one context would not be considered so in another. The criteria of 'enoughness' is important to the present investigation of digital communication, because it is within the kinds of transient, disembodied, playful contexts that we see on social media that (just) 'enoughness' becomes increasingly relevant. For example, token uses of English on an international site might be 'enough' to qualify a user as authentically cosmopolitan and worldly.

Coupland (2003) argues for the continuing importance – in fact, the possibly increased importance – of authenticity for individuals in late modernity, as well as for sociolinguistic investigation of language use (Blommaert and Varis, 2013; Coupland, 2003; Van Leeuwen, 2001, p. 397). Rather than seeing authenticity as less relevant to complex, fragmented, superdiverse urban societies, Coupland argues that the current fragmentation in fact increases our need to seek value in the authentic: 'People and groups will perhaps need to be more active in creating and refashioning senses of personal authenticity, salvaging the real from the considerably less orderly semiotic conditions of late-modernity' (Coupland, 2003, p. 427). Tagg and Seargeant (2014) argue that authenticity acts as an anchor for online communication, in the sense that it provides a baseline from which to judge the reliability of an interlocutor. Importantly, however, 'the real' is increasingly not seen to lie in stable demographic categories – in the circumstances surrounding an individual's birth – but in the extent to which an individual is able to enact authenticity and to be accepted as authentic by a particular community. In Coupland's (2003, p. 417) words, '[s]pecific ways of speaking and patterns of discursive representation can achieve the quality of experience that we define as authentic'. Coupland (2003) describes the gap that often exists between traditionally conceived communities and categories, and who an individual really feels they are, as a 'performance space' (p. 428). As such he challenges traditional sociolinguistic accounts of authentic language as the attested, naturally occurring, unmediated and 'true' utterances of a traditional rural community (the kind of speaker often prioritised by sociolinguists) in favour of the individual who constructs identities seen as authentic in his or her social encounters – someone who *earns* their authenticity (Coupland, 2003, p. 428).

The principle of partialness

Finally, the principles of emergence and relationality – the idea that identities are constructed in relation to immediate interactional contexts and demands – lead to the principle of partialness (Bucholtz and Hall, 2005, pp. 605–7); that identities are always partial, shaped not only by a person's sense of self (deliberately or unconsciously performed) but by ideological and social constraints imposed by a particular situation. In Bucholtz and Hall's (2005, p. 606) words, identity performance is:

> in part an outcome of interactional negotiation and contestation, in part an outcome of others' perceptions and representations, and in part an effect of larger ideological processes and material structures.

Partiality does not imply a lack of sincerity. Instead, the complexity of contemporary life means that an individual's choices may be guided by a disparate, dynamic cluster of different sources of authority or influence – what Blommaert and Varis (2013) call 'micro-hegemonies' – which together make up what constitutes that person's social identity (or identities). Blommaert and Varis (2013) suggest, for example, that someone's political party preferences may not match their lifestyle choices – a Green Party supporter may drive a gas-guzzling car – but that both choices find validation in a different set of community values.

The partiality principle also provides a reworked definition of agency – not as the ability to independently and rationally construct one's self, but as the ability to work within social and ideological constraints to achieve relational identity work: the 'accomplishment of social action' (Ahearn, 2001; Bucholtz and Hall, 2005, p. 606). This definition of agency encompasses both deliberate intentions and unconscious actions, seeing both as playing a role in constructing identity; and allows for 'distributed agency', through the co-construction of particular identity positions.

Conclusion

A number of online affordances come together in encouraging or enabling people to present themselves in ways that sometimes depart from how they might be perceived in other situations: the potential for anonymity; asynchronicity or time lag; the physical distance between interlocutors; the largely text-based channels; the availability of networked resources such as dictionaries and other reference works, translations, and photos; and the graphic resources of script, spelling, font and layout. However, while the circumstances may be novel and thus attention-grabbing, the process of identity construction is not. Contemporary accounts of identity as emergent, relational and partial show how individuals actively (if subconsciously) work to (re)position themselves and others in the course of unfolding interactions, drawing on linguistic features to index particular social identities. This is not to say that people cannot exploit this process to dangerous or undesirable ends online; but that attempts to counter such activities can usefully take into account the dynamic and selective ways in which online actors reconfigure their offline identities to perform themselves in new ways online.

21 Sociolinguistic communities

Introduction

The sociolinguistic concept of 'community' has undergone profound changes since it was first introduced in the middle of the twentieth century. Originally conceived to describe groups of individuals and families with shared traditions and a long history of living and working closely together (think of a village or an urban neighbourhood), the concept has now expanded to include a variety of ways in which people can connect with each other: attachments which are often long-distance, transitory, mobile, multiple. As we shall see, developments in sociolinguistic ideas about community to some extent parallel perceived changes in the real world, given the quickening pace of globalisation, the shake-up of traditional structures and sources of authority, the greater possibility for mobility, and people's increasing ability to use digital communications to establish networks beyond their immediate vicinity. If we look at how people come together through digital communications, we can make two observations. On the one hand, we can see virtual networks as an exemplification *par excellence* of the way in which sociolinguists now conceive of 'community' (as detailed below); on the other hand, virtual networks serve to further challenge and extend our understanding of the myriad ways in which people can construct relationships and feel connected.

In this chapter, I outline the move from the traditional concept of community to the more flexible, transitory communities that characterise contemporary sociolinguistic conceptions. I then look particularly at how virtual communities – as conceived by different internet researchers – fit into this new way of understanding how people come together and make connections.

From the speech community to social networks and communities of practice

The concept of the speech community was developed in the 1960s, at a time when the world was only beginning to see the effects of globalisation. The sociolinguistic notion of the 'speech community' built upon the assumption that people tend to form homogeneous, immobile, stable groupings based on a shared history, a common 'native' language, and geographical proximity. This allowed sociolinguists such as William Labov (e.g. Labov, 1972) to contextualise language features by linking them to social structures and uses; in other words, to show how language was shaped by society and, in particular, how an individual's language use could be explained by their belonging to a particular social category (age, gender, class and so on). This research challenged the then prominent decontextualised Chomskyan focus on 'competence' (the abstracted and idealised capacity of an individual for producing language) over 'performance' (actual language use as shaped by social and cognitive factors and including variety and disfluency). Recognition of the explanatory power of the speech community led, among other things, to the establishment of sociolinguistics as a legitimate field of enquiry.

However, the notion of the community in sociolinguistics has undergone substantial developments since it was taken up by sociolinguists in the 1960s. In the late twentieth century, two concepts, those of social networks and communities of practice, were particularly important in developing the idea of the speech community. In their different ways, both were attempts to empirically link patterns of language use to social structures; that is, to base conclusions on 'observed exchanges among actors' (Haythornthwaite et al., 1998, p. 214) rather than on assumed correlations between one's social roles and status and one's language use.

Social network theory offered more nuanced ways of understanding how relationships within and across communities shape language patterns. Social networks are the patterns of relationships that people construct through interaction, be that when socialising, communicating for work purposes or through shared interests or experiences (Meyerhoff, 2006). These patterns vary according to the frequency and nature of the interaction (stronger or weaker links), the extent to which everyone within a network knows each other or not (the extent to which networks are 'dense' or 'loose'), and whether the ties are specialised or multiplex (that is, focused on a single interest or a range of concerns). Such groupings are of interest to sociolinguists due to the fact that patterns of language use have been found to correlate to social networks, and because language change especially happens swiftly and effectively *within* age groups and social cohorts (i.e. social networks), but not *across* them (Meyerhoff, 2006). The foundational work of James and Lesley Milroy in Northern Ireland showed how language change correlates with the patterns of social connections which make up social networks, and they thus argued that these networks are as important as larger social variables, such as class or gender, for explaining how variation occurs within a community (Milroy, 1987).

While social network theory constituted a new way of understanding how relationships within and across speech communities shape language patterns, the concept of the community of practice (Lave and Wenger, 1991; Wenger, 1998) showed how people's allegiances are also shaped by shared professional or personal interests. That is, the notion explains to some extent how people can belong simultaneously to different groups which are characterised not only by geographical proximity or shared histories, but by the mutually structured and goal-oriented endeavours of their members. Communities of practice can be defined as groups which are bound together by common purposes and practices, and which entail an amount of shared specialised knowledge and mutual engagement. They can be considered a particular type of social network, characterised by sustained, regular interaction and the mutually structured endeavour of its members who interact in the service of a joint goal. Again, communities of practice are important for sociolinguistics because they develop a shared culture (based on their specialist interests), and this is manifest, in one way, by the discourse they use (including a shared jargon and set of genres) (Barton and Tusting, 2005; Eckert, 2006). Within professional, educational or interest-based contexts, shared language practices are an important part of the broader range of shared social practices which comprise group membership. The related notion of the 'discourse community' – communities which may never meet but which share similar language and communication practices – has similarly been useful in foregrounding the role of shared language conventions within geographically dispersed groups driven by mutual goals and activities (Swales, 1990).

However, the use of the term 'community' to describe such networks is in some cases problematic. As Gee (2005, p. 214) suggests, the sense of belonging and of membership associated with the term, which was central to the original conception of speech communities, is not always present in professional- or education-based communities of practice. More recent work has attempted to account for the more fluid networks that appear to characterise modern life.

Community as the product of networked connections

While social networks, communities of practice and discourse communities have a stronger empirical basis than that of the speech community, they do not go far enough in explaining the diversity and mobility documented in modern societies. Some sociolinguists have begun to call for, and adopt, an approach which rejects any assumption about the link between particular 'languages' or linguistic features with someone's origins or affiliations (Blommaert, 2010). For some researchers, the idea of community-based patterns of language use has been replaced entirely by the notion of individual linguistic repertoires, each person's 'very variable (and often rather fragmentary) grasp of a plurality of differentially shared styles, registers and genres, which are picked up (and maybe then partially forgotten) within biographical trajectories that develop in actual histories' (Blommaert and Rampton, 2011, p. 6; and see Blommaert and Backus, 2012). The implication of this view is that sociolinguistics need to explain how people move between groups and the extent to which they adopt (or choose not to adopt) a group's shared language practices, and why they might feel strong allegiances to certain groups, regardless of the depth or duration of their interactions with other 'members' (Blommaert and Rampton, 2011).

This shift in sociolinguistic thinking comes at a time when social diversity seems particularly prevalent. On the one hand, the shift comes as migration and increased mobility appear to be challenging any assumption of shared values and practices within local communities. Modern society in the twenty-first century appears to be characterised by 'superdiversity', a term coined by Vertovec (2007) to capture increasingly complex patterns of migration; in Britain, for example, the predictable swathes of adult worker immigrants from the Indian subcontinent and from the Caribbean have given way to smaller groups of migrants entering the country from various routes and with varying social demographics, skill sets and linguistic knowledge (see Chapter 18). At the same time, in modern society, it is increasingly acceptable for people to align with a variety of potentially conflicting interests and concerns in different parts of their lives, and therefore to orient around various 'micro-hegemonies', to use Blommaert and Varis's (2013) term (see Chapter 20). One stark example of this from Britain might be the shifting fortunes of the two main parties (Labour and Conservative) now that voters tend to choose on the basis of single issues (pensions, green policy, university fees) rather than a lifelong commitment emerging from their social class background. On the other hand, as well as this increasingly diverse (or 'superdiverse') society, communications technology allows both migrants and those embedded in a local community to build global or translocal ties which extend beyond – and may be seen as more significant than – the immediate community.

Contemporary conceptions of community – as the product of networked connections, and as flexible, shifting and interactively constructed – are confirmed and extended through consideration of social media alignments. Communities in this sense should not be seen as restricted to either an offline or an online environment. Instead, they should be viewed as complex networks which are often grounded in local contexts but which extend with the use of digital technology across geographical locations in virtual space (Haythornthwaite and

Kendall, 2010; and see articles in the special issue of *American Behaviourist Scientist* 58/3 (2010)). The concept of 'translocality' (Blommaert, 2010) is useful in this respect to describe the linking together of various localities without assuming that this makes any of these localities somehow 'global'; instead, individuals retain their local values and practices within the culturally diverse space. An illustration of this would be a discussion of the World Cup on an online football forum, to which football fans from various countries will bring their own interpretations of teams' performances and the likely outcomes of each match for evaluation and debate. As Blommaert (2010, p. 79) puts it, '[c]ommunication, thus, always involves issues of transporting the signs or objects of one place into those of other places, where they can be re-interpreted otherwise'.

The theorising of virtual communities can be divided into two main approaches, both of which shift the focus away from the idea of community in terms of groups of people and move it, on the one hand, towards the reconceptualisation of community in terms of space; and, on the other, towards a focus on the various networks to which an individual belongs.

Virtual communities as online affinity spaces

For some potential 'communities' based online, the notion of space – albeit virtual rather than physical or geographical – has been re-appropriated from traditional definitions and reworked to better explain what goes on within digitally mediated contexts. The concept of 'affinity space', for example, emerged from James Paul Gee's attempt to replace the criterion of community membership with the notion of a space in which people interact and which may (or may not) lead to the kind of strong, lasting connections which typically define more traditionally conceived communities (Gee, 2005). In other words, an affinity space does not involve identifying people's roles and status within a group or measuring their commitment to other members or to group goals. Gee instead focuses on social space and the extent to which its design (and the way its design is understood and can be exploited by users) facilitates shared practices and goals. Gee is particularly interested in looking at affinity spaces as opportunities for learning, and it is interesting to note how the characteristics he identifies as defining an affinity space contrast with those of the typical school classroom:

a 'Common endeavour' rather than social categories such as age or gender;
b Common space, in the sense that the social space accommodates everyone without segregating ('from new to experienced, from

unskilled to highly skilled, from minorly interested to addicted, and everything in-between' (Gee, 2005, p. 225);

c Co-construction, in the sense that people using the space are able to change it through their interactions and actions;

d Distributed knowledge, in that people are encouraged to 'connect or "network" their own individual knowledge' (Gee, 2005, p. 227);

e Flexibility, in terms of the forms of participation and routes to achieving status;

f Democratic structures, without rigid hierarchies.

（adapted from the 11 characteristics listed by Gee, 2005）

While Gee's focus is on learning, the concept of affinity space is a useful one for understanding the way in which people can move between online groupings in an often transitory and casual fashion not accounted for by notions of community and belonging (Herring, 2008b; Parks, 2011). The concept can also be used to describe and explain the formation of a more traditional community of practice within an online context, in cases where the use of a shared space leads to the development of shared language practices, conventions and norms, as well as a sense of group identity (Baym, 2010). Online affinity spaces include the fan fiction sites discussed in Chapter 11, where writers learn informally from other users, all of whom (newbies and experienced) participate and present their work in the same space; as well as online games, such as that discussed in Chapter 13 (Newon, 2011), where raid leaders are self-selected from groups of players. Gee's concept is also useful in explaining how multiple groups – in the sense of shared practices and regular interaction – can emerge from within any one online space. A superficial yet popularly salient view is that users of one site or platform share community features: for example, we talk of the Blogosphere, the Twittersphere or the virtual world of Second Life as distinct communities of users. To an extent, these users are bound by adherence to shared practices, conventions and principles: Baym (2010, p. 78), for example, suggests that the character constraint on Twitter encourages shared language usages that suggest community practices. Nonetheless, within the one social space, smaller groupings can emerge, which draw on more widely shared conventions but which also develop local features.

However, given the growth of social networking, the concept of an affinity space cannot be used to fully describe an individual's networks when they extend beyond one easily definable online space (site, forum, channel), as Baym (2010, p. 90) points out, or when groups themselves begin to form networks across online spaces in a process Baym (2010, p. 91) calls 'networked collectivism': think of any institution or association with a range of social media profiles across different sites. Such connections emerge from the *sense* of belonging or affiliation that many users report, in a way that is not fully captured by the notion of 'space'. Rather than shared space, what is important to the formation of these networks is the fact that users' behaviour is shaped by perceived ties and attempts to affiliate with other people (Drasovean and Tagg, in preparation; Zappavigna, 2014).

Virtual communities as personalised networks

Despite Gee's focus away from people as a defining characteristic of 'community', social network sites (SNSs) in particular open up a space in which connections between users can be expressed and deeper personal affiliations can potentially be forged. This is because SNS communities tend to orient not around shared interests, but mutual friends. In Chapter 15, I described our finding that exchanges on SNSs appear to orient around particular individuals or 'nodes' (Tagg and Seargeant, 2014). In our data, this materialised in a communicative dynamic by which users would direct their comments back towards the status updater, often without acknowledging other commenters and giving no outward sign of having read their posts. The increasing importance of people – rather than interests – as nodes in online social networks is noted by other researchers (boyd, 2006; Jones and Hafner, 2012; Papacharissi, 2011). Jones and Hafner (2012), for example, contrast earlier forms of digital communication such as Usenet with contemporary SNSs in terms of the way in which people are networked: the former required people to be placed into different groups while the latter allow for fluid and complex relationships:

> previously people were organized into interest groups like files in folders, whereas now people are linked to other people in complex networks based not on interests but on relationships ... We are like nodes in a vast network of relationships that allows us to be connected to a whole lot of people whom before we might never have shared a folder with.
>
> (Jones and Hafner, 2012, pp. 145–6)

As Jones and Hafner (2012, pp. 146–7) point out, social media enables people to strengthen their weak ties – in other words, to make the weak links we have with acquaintances and contacts more visible and durable. As Granovetter (1973) explained in a pre-digital age, 'strong weak ties' can be very useful as sources of information and support. The strength of social media is not that it enhances our close friendships, but that it consolidates our wider, 'weaker' networks (Jones and Hafner, 2012, p. 147). In cases where individuals use their networks as a means to learn and share knowledge, we might describe such networks in terms of communities of practice, in the sense that individuals are able to develop 'a personal learning network' (Hanson-Smith, 2013). However, seeing community in terms of personal networks also means that the make-up of the 'community' that each user experiences will be unique: 'no two SNS users will have access to the same set of people or messages, giving them each an experience of the site that is individualized yet overlapping with others' (Baym, 2010, p. 90). This has led researchers to move away from the idea of the group towards the notion of the 'networked individual' (Papacharissi, 2011), 'networked individualism' (Baym, 2010, p. 90) and 'egocentric communities' (boyd, 2006).

The more diffuse the online networks, the more they depend on how individuals themselves perceive and construct a sense of community, rather than their actual interactions or any structural group boundaries. The notion of the 'imagined community' can be traced back to the work of Benedict Anderson, who argued that the connections between any large, dispersed group of people should always be thought of as constructed rather than 'real' (Anderson, 1983/1991). In other words, while the connections people experience may feel very real, they are based less on actual ties (created through interactions) than on the construction and projection of shared values and goals. While Anderson was interested in the nation state as an imagined community, his ideas are particularly relevant to the globally dispersed networks possible through digital communications. In social researcher danah boyd's words, for example, SNSs allow people to 'write community into being' (boyd, 2006, also cited in the Introduction). What is important to boyd is a user's list of Friends or followers, which 'defines the context' or 'provides individuals with a contextual frame through which they can properly socialise with other participants'; in other words, how any one user experiences an SNS depends on the networks they have established and through which information will be filtered. boyd terms these 'imagined egocentric communities', communities of like-minded friends or followers who are linked by their mutual affiliation to the user who imagines them into being and who determine the information flow. On the basis of our research (Tagg and Seargeant, 2014), we would argue for a more intricate and dynamic re-conceptualisation of the egocentric community whereby a distinct context is created afresh with each posting, as a user imagines and addresses a particular group or individual from within their Friends list; or, indeed, simultaneously addresses various individuals or groups in different ways within the one post (see Chapter 14). Regardless of the degree of complexity, the sociolinguistic relevance of the individualised network lies in the fact that an individual's language use is not shaped by a pre-existing community, but rather their language choices are shaped by their perception of and response to an imagined community's practices, which in turn play an active role in the interactive construction of community.

Conclusion

Throughout the history of sociolinguistics and beyond, the idea of 'community' has remained a somewhat nebulous, highly subjective and often idealistic notion. Nonetheless, as Baym points out, researchers continue to find it useful as they seek to identify and understand the ways in which people make connections with others. To some extent, the ways in which people form communities have been transformed by the availability of digital technology, given the new resources and affordances at people's disposal and, in particular, the fact that the internet allows people to connect regardless of time, geography or social background (assuming that they have an internet connection). At its heart, however, online community is about what community has always been about – seeking people out, making connections and showing allegiances. It is also important to note that online communities do not form in isolation from the offline world, and nor should they be seen as replacing people's offline connections. They should instead be seen against a backdrop of wider changes to local communities, both shaping and being shaped by offline social trends and practices.

Glossary

affordances
features and potential functionalities which users perceive a technology to have. These perceptions then shape how people utilise the technology and for what purposes. Affordances are shaped by people's past experience with technology as well as their social assumptions and beliefs.

ambient affiliation
a term used by Zappavigna (2011, 2012, 2014) to refer to the way in which Twitter users can affiliate on a transient basis around a **hashtag** topic and thus around the assumptions and values associated with it.

analogue
see **digital**

anonymous
a loosely affiliated group of *hacktivists* – people who use the **internet** for political activities (the term is a portmanteau of *hacking* and *activist*) – which formed on the anonymous imageboard 4chan in the early twenty-first century. Perhaps best known for the Guy Fawkes masks worn by members at public events and demonstrations.

appraisal
a model for understanding how writers and speakers align themselves with other people, things and ideas and express evaluative stances, developed by Martin and White (2005) within a **systemic functional linguistics** approach.

apps
'application software' or computer program installed on the operating system of computers and **smartphones** or in a web browser (web app) to carry out a specific function. Popular communication apps include WhatsApp (USA) and WeChat (China). Apps can be free or incur a purchase fee.

ASCII
the 'American Standard Code for Information Interchange', a system for encoding characters based on the English language and the basis for most character-encoding schemes, including **Unicode**.

asynchronous
typically used to refer to online communication that does not take place in real time (in contrast to speech and to **synchronous** online interactions like chat) and where

responses may be delayed. Such sites include bulletin boards, email and the comment function on websites.

authenticity
the process of **positioning** oneself in interaction in a way that convinces others that your projected persona is at any one time a true and coherent reflection of your identity. Also an ideal or principle which guides our evaluation of ourselves and of others.

blogs
websites which comprise regular entries or posts displayed in reverse chronological order, so that the most recent post appears at the top – used to provide links to interesting or relevant websites but now tend more to function for personal or political opinion.

bricolage
used by linguists to refer to the way in which speakers and writers can draw on a range of sources in constructing their spoken styles and written texts, recombining available resources to create something new. See Hebdige (1984).

code-mixing
see **code-switching**

code-switching
moving between more than one language within a conversation or other text. Often distinguished from **code-mixing** on the grounds that code-switches have immediate communicative functions, while code-mixes involve more indiscriminate, unmotivated switches creating a mixed discourse with its own communicative impact.

colloquial contractions
reduced or contracted written forms which reflect informal or regional pronunciation as well as suggesting emotions of anger or affection.

community of interest
a *community of interest* forms when users come together around a shared interest. Such communities are usually characterised by a weak affiliation between members who identify with the topic of interest rather than with other users and are not generally motivated by a common goal (Henri and Pudelko, 2003).

community of practice
used by Jean Lave and Etienne Wenger (1991) to refer to groups of people who affiliate around a shared profession or craft, and thus engage in common practices and language uses.

context collapse
initially coined by Michael Wesch (2009) to explain the difficulties of self-presentation people experience as they make YouTube videos, given the vast, diverse potential audience they face. Also applied to 'semi-public' social network sites by social researchers such as danah boyd to capture the way in which status updaters must simultaneously address people they know from different offline contexts.

contextualisation cue
introduced by John Gumperz (e.g. 1982) to describe the use of linguistic or other features by users to make relevant particular contextual features. For example, the switch from English to a local language in a Facebook post might signal a change in the level of **privacy** assumed.

convergence
a generic term used to describe the ways in which various distinctions are being eroded by developments in digital media, ranging from the embedding of different voices and elements from different sources on the same webpage, through the bringing together of different media onto one device, such as the **smartphone**, to the levelling effect of digital technology on commercial and professional producers and everyday users (see **convergence culture**).

convergence culture
used by Henry Jenkins (2006) to refer to the way in which contemporary media productions and ordinary users alike draw on (and move between) a variety of media platforms in creating and accessing content. One illustration of this is transmedia storytelling, by which a story (such as Buffy the Vampire Slayer or Doctor Who) is told and accessed in various ways: television, websites, online forums, video games, comic books and so on. This example also highlights the role that ordinary users play in creating content, so that commercial and professional organisations now occupy the same spaces and engage in similar activities as grassroots organisations and users.

corpus
a digitally stored collection of texts, which are selected according to external criteria (such as text type) and which are accessed non-linearly; that is, linguists search for key terms which are displayed in short extracts of texts or concordances; or they generate word frequency lists. Language corpora are exploited by linguists for language description and other research purposes.

Creative Commons Licence
a software licence which gives producers some flexibility in how they would like their creations to be used (for example, producers can choose to allow users to use their work only if it is attributed and/or only for non-commercial purposes).

cyberbullying
the repeated online targeting of a particular institution or individual in a hostile, aggressive or unwanted way which is intended to cause harm or upset.

digital
the terms analogue and *digital* refer to different ways of storing, transmitting and processing data. Most electronic gadgets are now driven by digital technology: watches, cameras and washing machines as well as computers and mobile phones. In this book, *digital communication* is used to describe the interactions people have with each other through the **internet** or similar networks, such as those used by mobile phones.

digital divide
used to refer to the increasing gulf between those with **internet** access and **digital literacies**, and those without. Although it has been criticised as overly simplistic,

the term serves as a useful reminder that not everyone has access to the internet, and that those without access do not have the same opportunities to obtain information or to stay connected.

digital literacy
coined by Paul Gilster in 1997 to refer to the skills and knowledge required to participate online (to read texts, contribute to them and to interact with other users). Digital literacy is generally broken down into a range of different areas, including language-related skills and knowledge, familiarity with the technology and critical skills. For this reason, some researchers pluralise the term. Digital literacies incorporate the skills needed to read and write printed texts, as well as requiring some new skills, such as that of remixing or conducting and filtering online searches.

digitalese
used in this book to refer to the language of text messaging and other forms of digital communication which is characterised by spelling variants or **respelt** forms. It is a version of the more commonly used *textese* which draws attention to the use of variant spelling in domains other than **SMS text messaging**.

disembodiment
the increasing use of photos and videos online means that digital communication is not 'disembodied' in the sense that it was in the 1990s, when interaction was almost solely text-based. However, in contrast to face-to-face conversations, digital technology allows for text to be consumed in contexts which are removed (spatially and temporally) from the (offline) contexts in which they are produced (see Scollon and Scollon, 2002).

drama
internet drama connotes exaggerated or attention-grabbing performances that are played out in front of an audience on social media. According to Marwick and boyd (2011), internet drama is used by teenagers to capture 'a host of activities and practices ranging from gossip, flirting, arguing and joking to more serious issues of jealousy, ostracization, and name-calling'.

emergent
social or linguistic practices, features or phenomena which are not prescribed or brought to a particular interaction from elsewhere by the participant, but which emerge in the course of the immediate interactions. **Respellings** in text messages are thought to be emergent to some extent, in that they are often created spontaneously and picked up on by interlocutors; however, popular respellings are also circulated online and in media discourses, and become a part of people's repertoires that way.

emoticon
a representation of a face with various expressions, formed using punctuation marks and used in digital communication to indicate the tone in which a message should be read. There are two styles of emoticon: western emoticons tend to be read sideways and focus on the mouth to express emotion, while Japanese style emoticons are positioned upright and emotion is found in the eyes.

eye dialect
variation in spelling which involves a word being **respelt** according to the default (most typical) spelling of the constituent sounds as pronounced in the local standard. For example, in British English, an eye dialect spelling of *what* is {lthan}wot{gthan}. Eye dialect tends to suggest (or **index**) a lack of education or refinedness.

fan fiction
stories which draw on the plot, characters and scenarios of existing fiction, written by fans of the original fiction. Fan fiction writing pre-dates the **internet**, but the internet has allowed writers to come more easily together and to publish their stories online.

flaming
hostile, obscene or aggressive behaviour occurring online (see O'Sullivan and Flanagin, 2003; Thurlow et al., 2004).

folksonomies
taxonomies created by users in the process of tagging photos and posts and in this way organising web content.

fraping
a portmanteau of *Facebook* and *rape* used by young people to refer to the act of hacking into someone else's Facebook account and posting obscene or untrue posts. These acts can be viewed negatively or positively by the people involved.

genre
used in linguistics to refer to socially recognised text types characterised by shared contextual features external to the text, particularly common purposes. Typical genres include recipes, business letters, lectures and emails.

globalisation
a complex interplay of technological, social, economic and political processes which are serving to interconnect the world. Language both facilitates *globalisation* (such as when English or Arabic are used as lingua franca languages) and is shaped by it (such as when new regional or global forms of English emerge).

GNU (General Public Licence)
a very widely used software licence which grants people the right to freely use, modify and add to a piece of software and derived works.

hashtag
the hashtag (#) was adopted by Twitter users to indicate the topic of their Tweet, as in #worldcup2014. By searching for a hashtag string, users can generate all the Tweets posted on the same topic.

homepages
a homepage is now usually the main page of a website, which automatically loads when you type in a web address. In the 1990s and early 2000s, *personal homepages* also meant something different; the term referred to personal websites run by individual users and can be seen to some extent as a precursor of the personal **blog**.

homographs
words that share the same written form (they are spelt the same) but are pronounced differently. Examples in English include *close* (meaning 'shut' and 'near') and *bear* (meaning 'carry' and the animal). In digital communications, homographs are unlikely to cause confusion because users can determine the word that is meant from the context; however, in multilingual messages it may be difficult to assign words that are written the same across languages to a particular language without using pronunciation as a clue.

homophones
words or other linguistic items that sound the same but differ in meaning and in spelling, such as *rows* and *rose* in English.

hyperlinks
electronic links between webpages or elements within a webpage (such as an image) which are usually highlighted in blue and underlined, either in a menu at the side of a webpage or as part of the running text.

hypertext
text that is structured by **hyperlinks** and which forms the underlying infrastructure of the **world wide web**.

indexicality
the way in which language use points to features of the social context. Linguistic features become associated (through repeated use) with particular social groups and are thus made available to the same processes of evaluation which are targeted towards the particular individuals or communities involved. Hence, a linguistic feature such as h-dropping can come to suggest (to *index*) such social characteristics as level of education and social class.

information overload
the problem perceived to be caused by too much information being available to or pushed upon individuals in contemporary society, accessed through the **internet** as well as the television, radio and print texts.

internet
a global system or network of connected computers. The term is often used in social and linguistic research to refer generally to virtual space.

Internet Protocol (IP) address
a number assigned to networked devices which includes information about where the address was assigned and thus points to the likely geographical location of the user.

Internet Relay Chat (IRC)
an early popular form of online communication, involving group discussions in forums.

IRL
'in real life', a term used in chatrooms and by gamers and Second Lifers (users of the virtual world, Second Life) to refer to their offline contexts.

linguistic ethnography
a methodological approach to linguistic study which builds on traditional ethnography methods and foregrounds the role that language plays in people's social activities. Ethnography involves researchers immersing themselves in their participants' lives, drawing on methods such as observation, recordings, diaries and interviews. Many of these methods can be transferred to digital communications, with researchers participating or lurking in online forums and other **internet** communities, although this can raise ethical issues and problems such as defining the boundaries of the site under investigation. See Androutsopoulos (2008) for his version of *discourse-centred online ethnography*.

literacy
popularly defined as the ability to read and write, the term literacy is used more widely in applied linguistics to refer to a range of skills and cultural awareness needed to be literate in a particular society. See **digital literacy**.

location-based social network site
a kind of social network site with GPS-based **affordances** which enable users to exploit their current physical location to, for example, tell other users where they are, locate nearby users, and check in to restaurants and bars.

lolcats
an early **internet** phenomenon, featuring images of cats with grammatically incorrect captions usually purporting to come from the featured cat, such as 'I can has cheezburger?' http://icanhas.cheezburger.com/lolcats

mashups
videos created through combining two different, often incongruous or contrasting, sources for humorous or ironic effect. For example, Dubisar and Palmeri (2010) discuss how professional and amateur composers expressed their political allegiances or views in the 2008 US presidential election through *mashed* videos, including one transforming Barak Obama's 'Yes we can' slogan into a catchy hip-hop song and one depicting his Republican opponent John McCain singing an old rap song.

media
used in this book to refer to online platforms or channels such as Facebook, Twitter, Skype and Snapchat.

memes
in Davison's (2012, p. 122) words, 'a piece of culture, typically a joke, which gains influence through online transmission'. *Memes* often take the form of an image and caption, which occur in modified iterations. One classic is the *fail meme* (Zappavigna, 2012) where the word 'Fail' is placed over the image of an unsuccessful or unintended incident.

microblogging
the act of sharing short messages through online media such as Twitter or Tumblr. The word derives from **blogging** because of the shared focus on disseminating news and opinion, but *microbloggers* face a restricted character allowance.

minority languages
languages spoken by a minority of speakers within a particular territory.

mode
or *semiotic mode*, can be described as a system for making meaning or a way of representing a message. Modes include image, colour, sound, typography and format as well as language. Many texts combine various modes and can be said to display **multimodality**.

multimodality
the use of more than one **mode** of communication to convey meaning in a text.

networked multilingualism
used by Androutsopoulos (forthcoming) to explain the features that characterise multilingual practices in digital communication.

networked resources
defined by Jannis Androutsopoulos (forthcoming) as 'all the semiotic resources the global computer network has to offer', the term draws attention to the ease with which such resources can be accessed and appropriated into a text.

node-oriented network
used by Tagg and Seargeant (2014) to describe the kind of affiliations seen on **social network sites** which are based on mutual friendships. Interactions on social network sites may also be characterised by *node-orientation*, in the sense that commenters on a status update tend to direct their comments directly back to the status updater (the node) without necessarily engaging the other participants.

orthography
as Sebba (2007) explains, *orthography* differs from *spelling* in that it refers to the principles of a language's writing system which determine which spellings are possible. So, English orthography allows {lthan}gh{gthan} to occur together to convey the sound /g/, which occurs in the spelling of *ghost* but not in the spelling of *goat*.

performance
the term *performance* has been extended within language-related research (and others) from its conventional meaning of theatrical display to refer to the ways in which people routinely enact various identities in their everyday interactions. A distinction can still be made in this research between the use of 'performance' to refer to something that is said for effect and held up for evaluation by others, and performance as referring to practices enacted every time individuals engage in interaction with others (Swann, 2006, pp. 21–2, for example, compares *joke-telling* – where jokes are prefaced by 'performance markers' and thus made to stand out from the general conversation – with *conversational joking* which is embedded within the wider talk). The latter focus is adopted by sociolinguistics looking at speaking style (stylistic choices involving dialect, slang and register that speakers make in their routine conversations). The term 'performance' is useful in highlighting the fact that speakers (and writers) have agency in foregrounding aspects of their identity and choosing how to present themselves in different contexts.

phishing
the act of sending messages to large numbers of users which purport to be from a legitimate user or corporation in order to trick users into clicking on a link or entering sensitive personal details which can then be used by the *phishers* to gain access to bank accounts and so on.

photo-sharing sites
sites whose main purpose is to facilitate the uploading and online sharing of photos, such as Flickr and Instagram. Users can usually tag their photos, enabling other users to find them, and to make personal links with other users.

polymedia
used by Daniel Miller (Madianou and Miller, 2012) to refer to the contemporary 'mediascape' (that is, the range of media that are now widely available, generally at no extra cost). Looking at people's use of online media must now involve consideration of the choices people make between different media; and, where these decisions are not made on the basis of access or cost, their choices must be seen as open to social and moral evaluation.

positioning
the ways in which individuals align themselves with various discourses or values in interaction, as well as with (or in opposition to) their interlocutor. Thus, interactional roles and evaluative stances are not seen as fixed or predetermined but as constructed (or co-constructed) and reconstructed throughout an interaction.

practices
social activities which tend to be culturally contingent and embedded in a particular context. Researchers adopting a *practices* approach to language look less at finished texts as a unit of analysis and rather towards how, why, where and when people produce such texts; that is, they prioritise process over product. As Lillis (2013, p. 78) points out, in practice this requires an empirical methodology that focuses on exploring the context in which people speak and write and which explores their own understanding of what they are doing; and a focus on issues of power, agency and cultural norms.

privacy
in social research, *privacy* is not seen as an absolute condition but a social construct that is negotiated and contested. Privacy involves managing access to the self, and balancing personal disclosure with the ability to withhold sensitive information.

reading strategies
purposeful actions taken by readers to help them construct meaning as they interact with a text. Presupposes a view of reading as an active process of co-construction between reader, writer and text.

recontextualisation
the process of removing a text from one context and embedding it in a new context. This happens most obviously with, for example, reported speech, where an utterance is freed from its original context and often held up for evaluation and negotiation in a new context.

remixes
the result of re-engineering or otherwise changing a work to create a new artefact.

repertoire
the full range of language **resources** available to either a community or an individual, and from which they can select according to their social purpose and context. Given increasing mobility and the recognition that many people belong to multiple social groups (and will thus have access to resources from various contexts and communities), the notion of the individual *repertoire* may be more useful in capturing social reality than that of the community repertoire (Blommaert and Backus, 2011).

resources
in sociolinguistics, used to refer to the communication features and strategies available to a community or individual. *Resources* can be linguistic and paralinguistic, including gestures in speech and punctuation in writing. These resources can be said to make up a community or individual **repertoire**.

respelling
a word that is spelt in a non-standard way in order to convey social meaning. Used by Sebba (2007) to avoid the evaluative connotations of words like *misspelling*. Respellings are not motivated by ignorance and are not mistakes. Instead, they carry meaning because they depart from the legitimised norm in principled ways.

robots
(or *bots*) are programs which automatically upload posts onto social media sites, usually to **spam** or **phish** other users.

Romanisation
the practice by which languages traditionally written in another script are transliterated into the Roman (or Latin) script. The transliteration is usually either *phonetic* (Roman characters are chosen because their typical pronunciation resembles that of the sound being conveyed), or *orthographic* (in the sense that the Roman character visually resembles its counterpart in the other script).

scambaiting
scambaiters aim to engage an online scammer for as long as possible in order to waste their time and resources, and often to get as much information from them as possible to pass on to the authorities.

selfie
short for *self-portrait*, a selfie is usually taken using a mobile phone and is thus characterised by an outstretched arm (holding the phone) and an awkward angle. The popularity of the practice and the term has recently inspired the coining of *otherie*, meaning a photo of somebody other than yourself.

smartphones
mobile phones with wireless internet access and web-browsing functionalities, which also support **apps** and have a touch screen.

SMS text messaging
the sending of short, typed messages, usually between mobile phones, over the Short Message Service (SMS). Users either pay per message, or have a certain

number of messages included in their monthly contract. On contemporary **smartphones**, SMS text messaging sits alongside other web-based messaging services, such as WhatsApp or Facebook Messenger.

social capital
is defined by Ellison et al. (2011, p. 873) in their study of Facebook as, 'the benefits individuals derive from their social relationships and interactions: resources such as emotional support, exposure to diverse ideas, and access to redundant information'. Can be traced back to work by French sociologist Pierre Bourdieu (1986).

social media
a term used broadly by many researchers to refer to all digital media which facilitate interaction, ranging from instant messaging channels to the comment function on websites.

social network sites
sites such as Facebook whose main purpose is to establish and maintain links between users based on social and friendship ties. According to boyd and Ellison (2008), *social network sites* are characterised by three main features: a member profile; a network of links with other members; and the ability to view and search those links. The use of *network* rather than *networking* is deliberate, as it reflects the fact that the networks usually comprise people a user already knows, rather than involving the formation of new links.

spamming
the act of automatically sending an online message randomly to a large number of users with the view of trying to sell them something.

status update
a short and generally untargeted announcement posted on Facebook in response to a set, site-generated question prompt ('What's on your mind?' at the time of writing). A user's status updates appear in their Friends' News Feeds and other users can comment on them or 'Like' them (click on a button that then indicates that the user likes the update). Comments appear below a status update, resembling a thread of written conversation. 'Likes' are counted and this is noted below the update.

synchronous
traditionally used in linguistics to refer to spoken interactions that take place in real time, and often applied in studies of new media to refer to the fast-paced interactions that typically take place through instant messaging and online, to distinguish them from more **asynchronous** forms of online communication. As Garcia and Jacob (1999) point out, the term is somewhat misleading, given that online posts (however quickly exchanged) are produced out of sight of the receiver, who must wait until the composer hits send. Thus the production circumstances are very different to speech. Garcia and Jacob suggest the alternative term *quasi-synchronous*.

Systemic functional linguistics
a linguistics approach which regards language as a 'system of meanings' (Halliday, 1985, p. xiv) and posits users as making choices from the available meanings. Systemic functionalists hold that language emerged from the human need to make meaning and is thus driven by various functions or metafunctions: the *ideational* (the

expression of experience and ideas), *interpersonal* (the mediation of human relationships), and *textual* (the organisation of language into a coherent whole).

technological determinism
the assumption that our behaviour is controlled or 'determined' by technology, a view which ignores human agency in shaping how the technology is developed and what it is used for.

technologisation of practice
a term used by Rodney Jones (2002) to refer to the way in which a technology becomes associated with a particular way of doing something, so that it becomes difficult to imagine using the technology for another purpose, or using a different technology for the same purpose. The shift from paper and printed texts to the **internet** may be a good example of this, as many people feel that reading online can offer only an inferior experience to that of a book – probably in part because the connection between reading and paper is so entrenched.

text
in linguistics, a text is a unit of analysis, hierarchically placed above the word and sentence, and defined not only by form but by meaning and context. For example, a conversation would be considered a text, defined by structural features such as opening and closing sequences and **synchronous** turn-taking, as well as contextual features such as the relationship between participants, their purpose in interacting, and the level of formality. David Crystal (2011) argues that texts are harder to delineate online, because of **hypertext** and the shifting nature of online texts.

textisms
commonly used in the academic literature to refer to spelling variants or **respellings** which have been seen to occur in **SMS text messaging** and other forms of digital communication.

trolling
a particular kind of anti-social behaviour online, which involves a *troller* trying to disrupt an online discussion by posting aggressive, provocative or unwelcome messages (known as *trolls*). Trollers are not always overt about their intentions, but often attempt to deceive other users into believing they are sincere (that they are naive, don't know the local norms, or that they genuinely hold the controversial or unpopular views they espouse).

typography
features of a printed or online text relevant to its style and appearance, such as punctuation, colour, font type and size, and layout.

Unicode
a widely used industry standard for encoding text maintained by the Unicode Consortium, developed in the 1980s and 1990s to enable multilingual computer processing by unifying the various encodings for different scripts.

Urban Dictionary
an online slang dictionary, compiled by users. Various definitions are listed under each entry, and ranked according to user ratings. See: www.urbandictionary.com.

Usenet
an internet discussion system, organised into *newsgroups*, established in 1980 and popular in the 1980s and 1990s (used, for example, by Tim Berners-Lee to introduce the **world wide web**). It is still in use, although user numbers have dramatically declined. **Spam** and online porn might be said to have originated with Usenet, and to have contributed to its decline.

vernacular spectacles
used by Androutsopoulos (2010) to describe the activities that surround the embedding of a video on a media-sharing site like YouTube. The action of uploading the video and subsequently discussing it in comments is *vernacular* in the sense of being local and at grassroots level, standing outside the commercial or professional media world.

walled gardens
closed platforms which limit information and applications to those available internally. They are often depicted as attempts by **internet** site developers to manipulate and control users' experience of the wider web by limiting their access and functionalities. Apple, for example, limits users to their products and services or to approved external **apps**.

webcam
online communication via a video camera, such as that embedded in *voice-over-Internet protocol (VoIP)* technologies such as Skype.

wiki
an online site which allows users to add, modify or delete content and thus to collaboratively create a document. The online encyclopaedia *Wikipedia* is probably the best-known example of a wiki.

world wide web (www)
a network of interlinking websites or webpages (documents containing information) which are carried on the **internet** and accessed either through search engines such as Google, or by navigating from one webpage to the next via **hyperlinks**.

Bibliography

Abrahams, M. (2011) 'Don't let the trolls get you down' the *Guardian* 13 June. Available: http://www.theguardian.com/education/2011/jun/13/internet-trolls-improbable-research?commentpage=1. Accessed: 17 February 2014.

Acquisti, A. and R. Gross (2006) 'Imagined communities: awareness, information sharing, and privacy on the facebook' in *Privacy Enhancing Technologies: 6th International Workshop*, PET 2006, Cambridge: Springer, pp. 36–58.

Adewunmi, B. (2013) 'The rise and rise of the "selfie"' the *Guardian* 2 April. Available: http://www.theguardian.com/artanddesign/2013/apr/02/rise-and-rise-of-the-selfie. Accessed: 10 February 2014.

Adler, D. (2013) 'How a digital "bullying button" can help social workers tackle cyber-bullying' the *Guardian Social Care Network* 9 August. Available: http://www.theguardian.com/social-care-network/2013/aug/09/digital-button-help-manage-cyber-bullying. Accessed: 17 February 2014.

Aflerbach, P. and B.-Y. Cho (2009) 'Identifying and describing constructively responsive comprehension strategies in new and traditional forms of reading' in Israel, S.E. and G.G. Duffy (eds) *Handbook of Research on Reading Comprehension*. New York: Routledge, pp. 69–90.

Ahearn, L. (2001) 'Language and agency' *Annual Review of Anthropology* 30: 109–37.

Al-Issa, A. and L.S. Dahan (eds) (2011) *Global English and Arabic: issues of language, culture and identity*. Berne: Peter Lang.

Al-Khatib, M. and E.H. Sabbah (2008) 'Language choice in mobile text messages among Jordanian university students' *Sky Journal of Linguistics* 21: 37–65.

Alloca, K. (2012) '"Gangnam Style" is your international hit of the month' *YouTube Trends*. Available: http://youtube-trends.blogspot.jp/2012/08/gangnam-style-is-your-international-hit.html. Accessed: 21 February 2013.

Altman, I. (1975) *The Environment and Social Behaviour: privacy, personal space, territory, crowding*. Monterey, CA: Brooks/Cole.

Anderson, B. (1983/1991) *Imagined Communities: reflections on the origin and spread of nationalism*. London: Verso.

Anderson, D. (2005) 'Global linguistic diversity for the internet' *Communications of the ACM* 48/1: 27–8.

Androutsopoulos, J. (2000) 'Non-standard spellings in media texts: the case of German fanzines' *Journal of Sociolinguistics* 4/4: 514–33.

—— (2006a) 'Introduction: sociolinguistics and computer-mediated communication' *Journal of Sociolinguistics* 10/4: 419–38.

—— (2006b) 'Multilingualism, diaspora, and the internet: codes and identities on German-based diaspora websites' *Journal of Sociolinguistics* 10/4: 520–47.

—— (2007) 'Bilingualism in the mass media and on the Internet' in Heller, M. (ed.) *Bilingualism: a social approach*. New York: Palgrave Macmillan, pp. 207–30.

—— (2008) 'Potentials and limitations of discourse-centred online ethnography' *Language@Internet* 5, article 9.

—— (2009) '"Greeklish": transliteration practice and discourse in the context of computer-mediated digraphia' in Georgakopoulou, A. and M. Silk (eds) *Standard Languages and Language Standards: Greek, past and present*. Aldershot: Ashgate Publishing, pp. 221–49.

—— (2010) 'Localising the global on the participatory web' in Coupland, N. (ed.) *The Handbook of Language and Globalisation*. Oxford: Wiley-Blackwell, pp. 203–31.

—— (2011) 'From variation to heteroglossia in the study of computer-mediated discourse' in Thurlow, C. and K. Mroczek (eds) *Digital Discourse: language in the new media*. Oxford: Oxford University Press, pp. 277–98.

—— (2013) 'Code-switching in computer-mediated communication' in Herring, S.C., D. Stein and T. Virtanen (eds) *Pragmatics of Computer-Mediated Communication*. Berlin and New York: Mouton de Gruyter, pp. 659–86.

—— (forthcoming) 'Networked multilingualism: some language practices on Facebook and their implications' *International Journal of Bilingualism*.

Angouri, J. and T. Tseliga (2010) '"you HAVE NO IDEA WHAT YOU ARE TALKING ABOUT!" From e-disagreement to e-impoliteness in two online fora' *Journal of Politeness Research* 6: 57–82.

Anis, J. (2007) 'Neography: unconventional spelling in French SMS text messages' in Danet, B. and S.C. Herring (eds), *The Multilingual Internet: language, culture and communication Online*. Oxford: Oxford University Press, pp. 87–116.

Atkinson, R.C. (1968) 'A reply to Professor Spache's article, "A reaction to computer-assisted instruction in initial reading: the Stanford Project"' *Reading Research Quarterly* 3/3: 418–20.

Atkinson, R.C. and D.N. Hansen (1966) 'Computer-assisted instruction in initial reading: the Stanford Project' *Reading Research Quarterly* 2/1: 5–25.

Auer, P. (1984) *Bilingual Conversation*. Philadelphia and Amsterdam: John Benjamins.

—— (1995) 'The pragmatics of code-switching: a sequential approach' in Milroy, L. and P. Muysken (eds) *One Speaker, Two Languages: cross-disciplinary perspectives on code-switching*. Cambridge: Cambridge University Press, pp. 115–35.

—— (ed.) (1998) *Code-Switching in Conversation: language, interaction and identity*. New York and London: Routledge.

—— (2000) 'Why should we and how can we determine the "base language" of a bilingual conversation?' *Estudios de Sociolingüística* 1/1: 129–44.

Austin, J.L. (1962) *How to Do Things with Words*. Cambridge, MA: Harvard University Press.

Bailey, B. (2007) 'Heteroglossia and boundaries' in Heller, M. (ed.) *Bilingualism: a social approach*. New York: Palgrave Macmillan, pp. 257–74.

Bakhtin, M. (1981) (transl. Emerson, C. and M. Holquist) *The Dialogic Imagination*. Austin: University of Texas Press.

—— (1986) (ed. Holquist, M.; transl. Emerson, C. and M. Holquist) *Speech Genres and Other Late Essays*. Austin: University of Texas Press.

Barak, A., M. Boniel-Nissim and J. Suler (2008) 'Fostering empowerment in online support groups' *Computers in Human Behaviour* 24/5: 1867–83.

Baron, A., C. Tagg, P. Rayson, P. Greenwood, J. Walkerdine and A. Rashid (2011) 'Using verifiable author data: gender and spelling differences in Twitter and SMS' Talk given at ICAME 32, University of Oslo.

Baron, N. (1998) 'Letters by phone or speech by other means: the linguistics of email' *Language and Communication* 18: 133–70.

—— (2000) *Alphabet to Email: how written English evolved and where it's heading*. Abingdon: Routledge.

—— (2008) *Always On: language in an online and mobile world*. Oxford: Oxford University Press.

—— (2009) 'The myth of impoverished signal: dispelling the spoken-language fallacy for emoticons in online communication' in Vincent, J. and L. Fortunati (eds) *Electronic Emotion: the mediation of emotion via information and communication technologies*. London: Peter Lang, pp. 107–36.

—— (2010) 'Discourse structures in instant messaging: the case of utterance breaks' *Language@Internet* 7. Available: http://www.languageatinternet.org/articles/2010/2651. Accessed: 11 October 2014.

Barros, C.D.M. (1995) 'The missionary presence in literacy campaigns in the indigenous languages of Latin America' *International Journal of Educational Development* 15/3: 277–87.

Barton, D. (1994) *Literacy: an introduction to the ecology of written language*. Oxford: Blackwell.

Barton, D. and M. Hamilton (1998) *Local Literacies: reading and writing in one community*. London: Routledge.

Barton, D. and C. Lee (2012) 'Redefining vernacular literacies in the age of Web 2.0' *Applied Linguistics* 33/3: 282–98.

—— (2013) *Language online: investigating digital texts and practices*. Abingdon: Routledge.

Barton, D. and K. Tusting (eds) (2005) *Beyond Communities of Practice: language power and social context*. Cambridge: Cambridge University Press.

Baym, N. (1998) 'The emergence of online community' in Jones, S.G. (ed.) *Cybersociety 2.0: revisiting computer-mediated communication and community*. Thousand Oaks, CA: Sage, pp. 35–68.

—— (2010) *Personal Connections in the Digital Age*. Cambridge: Polity Press.

BBC (2001) 'Campaign to keep Greek pure' *BBC News* 11 January. Available: http://news.bbc.co.uk/1/hi/world/europe/1111635.stm.   Accessed: 21 November 2013.

Bechar-Israeli, H. (1995) 'From bonehead to clonehead: nicknames, play, and identity on internet relay chat' *Journal of Computer-Mediated Communication* 1/2. DOI: 10.1111/j.1083-6101.1995.tb00325.x.

Bell, A. (1984) 'Language style as audience design' *Language in Society* 13/2: 145–204.

—— (1999) 'Styling the other to design the self: a study in New Zealand identity making' *Journal of Sociolinguistics* 3/4: 523–41.

—— (2001) 'Back in style: reworking audience design' in Eckert, P. and J.R. Rickford (eds) *Style and Sociolinguistic Variation*. Cambridge: Cambridge University Press, pp. 139–69.

Bender, E.M., J.T. Morgan, M. Oxley, M. Zachry, B. Hutchinson, A. Marin, B. Zhang and M. Ostendorf (2011) 'Annotating social acts: authority claims and alignment moves in Wikipedia Talk Pages' *Proceedings of the Workshop on Language in Social Media* (LSM 2011), pp. 48–57.

Benkler, Y. (2006) *The Wealth of Networks: how social production transforms markets and freedom*. New Haven, CT: Yale University Press.

Bergholz, A., J. De Beer, S. Glahn, M.-F. Moens, G. Paax and S. Strobel (2010) 'New filtering approaches for phishing email' *Journal of Computer Security* 18/1: 7–35.

Berners-Lee, T. and M. Fischetti (1999) *Weaving the Web: the past, present and future of the World Wide Web by its inventor*. London: Orion Business.

Bernicot, J., O. Volckaert-Legrier, A. Goumi and A. Bert-Erboul (2012) 'Forms and functions of SMS messages: a study of variations in a corpus written by adolescents' *Journal of Pragmatics* 44: 1701–1715.

Biber, D. and S. Conrad (2009) *Register, Genre, and Style*. Cambridge: Cambridge University Press.

Biddle, S. (2011) 'How the hashtag is ruining the English language' *Gizmodo* 28 December. Available: http://gizmodo.com/5869538/how-the-hashtag-is-ruining-the-english-language. Accessed: 21 November 2013.

Black, R.W. (2006) 'Language, culture, and identity in online fanfiction' *E-Learning* 3/2: 170–84.

—— (2007a) 'Fanfiction writing and the construction of space' *E-Learning and Digital Media* 4/4: 384–97.

—— (2007b) 'Digital design: English language learners and reader feedback in online fiction' in Knobel, M. and C. Lankshear (eds) *A New Literacies Sampler*. New York: Peter Lang, pp. 115–36.

—— (2009) 'English language learners, fan communities, and twenty-first century skills' *Journal of Adolescent and Adult Literacy* 52/8: 688–97.

Blackledge, A. and A. Creese (2014) 'Heteroglossia as practice and pedagogy' in Blackledge, A. and A. Creese (eds) *Heteroglossia as Practice and Pedagogy*. New York: Springer.

Blanchard, B. (2010) 'China's minority languages face threat of extinction' *Reuters* 11 March. Available: http://www.reuters.com/article/2010/03/12/us-china-languages-idUSTRE62B0EW20100312. Accessed: 18 February 2014.

Blommaert, J. (2007) 'On scope and depth in linguistic ethnography' *Journal of Sociolinguistics* 11/5: 682–8.

—— (2008) *Grassroots Literacy*. London: Routledge.

—— (2010) *The Sociolinguistics of Globalisation*. Cambridge: Cambridge University Press.

Blommaert, J. and A. Backus (2011) 'Superdiverse repertoires and the individual' in de Saint-Georges, I. and J.-J. Weber (eds) *Multilingualism and Multimodality: current challenges for educational studies*. Rotterdam: Sense Publishers, pp. 11–32.

Blommaert, J. and B. Rampton (2011) 'Language and superdiversity' *Diversities* 13/2: 1–21.

Blommaert, J. and P. Varis (2013) 'Enough is enough: the heretics of authenticity in superdiversity' in Duarte, J. and I. Gogolin (eds) *Linguistic Superdiversity in Urban Areas: research approaches*. Amsterdam: John Benjamins, pp. 143–59.

Blommaert, J. and F. Velghe (2014) 'Learning a supervernacular: textspeak in a South African township' in Blackledge, A. and A. Creese (eds) *Heteroglossia as Practice and Pedagogy*. New York: Springer, pp. 137–55.

Blood, R. (2002) *The Weblog Handbook: practical advice on creating and maintaining your blog*. Cambridge, MA: Perseus Publishing.

Boardman, M. (2004) *The Language of Websites*. Abingdon: Routledge.

Bohn, R. and J. Short (2012) 'Measuring consumer information' *International Journal of Communication* 6: 980–1000.

Bolinger, D. (1946) 'Visual morphemes' *Language* 22: 333–40.

Borochovsky-Bar-Aba, E. and Y. Kedmi (2010) 'The nature of SMS discourse: the case of Hebrew' *Folia Linguistica* 44/1: 1–30.

Bourdieu, P. (1986) 'The forms of capital' in Richardson, J.G. (ed.) *Handbook of Theory and Research for the Sociology of Education*. New York: Greenwood, pp. 241–58.

boyd, d. (2001) 'Taken out of context: American teen sociality in networked publics'. Unpublished PhD thesis, University of California, Berkeley.

—— (2006) 'Friends, friendsters, and MySpace Top 8: writing community into being on social network sites' *First Monday* 11/12. Available: http://firstmonday.org/article/view/1418/1336. Accessed: 6 October 2014.

—— (2008) 'Facebook's privacy trainwreck: exposure, invasion, and social convergence' *The International Journal of Research into New Media Technologies* 14/1: 13–20.

—— (2010) 'Making sense of privacy and publicity' *SXSW–Interactive* (Austin, Texas, 13 March). Available: http://www.danah.org/papers/talks/2010/SXSW2010.html. Accessed: 9 July 2010.

—— (2012a) 'Participating in the always-on lifestyle' in Mandiberg, M. (ed.) *The Social Media Reader*. New York: New York University Press, pp. 71–6.

—— (2012b) 'Networked privacy' *Surveillance & Society*, 10/3, 4: 348–9.

—— (2014) 'Why Snapchat is valuable: it's all about attention'. Available: http://www.zephoria.org/thoughts/archives/2014/03/21/snapchat-attention.html. Accessed: 15 April 2014.

boyd, d. and N. Ellison (2008) 'Social network sites: definition, history, and scholarship' *Journal of Computer-Mediated Communication* 13: 210–30.

boyd, d. and E. Hargittai (2010) 'Facebook privacy settings: who cares?' *First Monday* 15/8. Available: http://firstmonday.org/article/view/3086/2589. Accessed: 6 October 2014.

boyd, d. and A. Marwick (2011) 'Social privacy in networked publics: teens' attitudes, practices and strategies'. Talk given at Oxford Institute's 'A Decade in Internet Time: Symposium on the Dynamics of the Internet and Society' 22 September.

boyd, d., E. Hargittai, J. Schulz and J. Palfrey (2011) 'Why parents help their children lie to Facebook about age: unintended consequences of the "Children's Online Privacy Protection Act"' *First Monday* 16/11. Available: http://firstmonday.org/ojs/index.php/fm/article/view/3850. Accessed: 6 October 2014.

Brumfit, C. (1995) 'How applied linguistics is the same as any other science' *International Journal of Applied Linguistics* 7/1: 86–94.

Bruns, A. (2008) *Blogs, Wikipedia, Second Life, and Beyond*. New York: Peter Lang.

Bryant, S., A. Forte and A. Bruckman (2005) 'Becoming Wikipedian: transformation of a participation in a collaborative online encyclopedia'. Proceedings, Group '05, Sanibel Island, Florida, 6–9 November.

Bucholtz, M. and K. Hall (2005) 'Identity and interaction: a sociocultural linguistic approach' *Discourse Studies* 7/4–5: 585–614.

Buckingham, D. (2007) *Beyond Technology: children's learning in the age of digital media*. Cambridge: Polity.

Bunn, A. (2012) 'Do you ever conduct searches in another language? 76% of people search in two or more' *Greenlight blog* 29 March. Available: http://www.greenlightdigital.com/gossip/blog/do-you-ever-conduct-searches-in-another-language-76-of-people-search-in-two-or-more/. Accessed: 18 February 2014.

Bushell, C., N. Kemp and F.H. Martin (2011) 'Text-messaging practices and links to general spelling skill: a study of Australian children' *Australian Journal of Educational and Development Psychology* 11: 27–38.

Buszard-Welcher, L. (2001) 'Can the web help save my language?' in Hinton, L. and K.L. Hale (eds) *The Green Book of Language Revitalisation in Practice*. San Diego: Academic Press, pp. 331–45.

Butler, J. (1990) *Gender Trouble: Feminism and the subversion of identity*. New York: Routledge.

Calvani, A., A. Fini and M. Ranieri (2009) 'Assessing digital competences in secondary education – issues, model and instruments' in Learning, M. (ed.) *Issues in Information and Media Literacy: education, practice and pedagogy*. Santa Rosa, CA: information Science Press, pp. 153–72.

Cameron, D. (1995/2012) *Verbal Hygiene*. Oxford: Oxford University Press.

—— (1997) 'Performing gender identity: young men's talk and the construction of heterosexual masculinity' in Johnson, S. and U.H. Meinhof (eds) *Language and Masculinity*. Oxford: Blackwell, pp. 47–64.

Campbell, A. (2013) 'Time to empower parents to take on the cyberbullies' *The Herald Scotland* 10 August. Available: http://www.heraldscotland.com/comment/columnists/time-to-empower-parents-to-take-on-the-cyberbullies.21835442. Accessed: 17 February 2014.

Canagarajah, S. (2011) 'Translanguaging in the classroom: emerging issues for research and pedagogy' *Applied Linguistics Review* 2: 1–28.

Cárdenas-Claros, M.S. and N. Isharyanti (2009) 'Code switching and code mixing in internet chatting: between "yes", "ya", and "si" a case study' *Jalt Call Journal* 5/3: 67–78.

Carney, E. (1994) *A Survey of English Spelling*. London: Routledge.

Carr, N. (2011) *The Shallows: what the internet is doing to our brains*. New York: W.W. Norton.

Carter, R. (2004) *Language and Creativity: the art of common talk*. Abingdon: Routledge.

Castellá, V.O., A.M.Z. Zornosa, F.P. Alonso and J.M.P. Silla (2000) 'The influence of familiarity among group members, group atmosphere and assertiveness on uninhibited behaviour through three different communication media' *Computers in Human Behavior* 16/2: 141–59.

Caulfield, J. (2012) 'Communities in clusters: a case study of Irish language bloggers and Twitter users and their place in the multilingual web'. Paper given at *Language and New Media: New Challenges for Research and Teaching Linguistics*, 26–7 April, University of Leicester.

Chalabi, M. (2013) 'How prevalent is online abuse?' the *Guardian Reality Check* 29 July. Available: http://www.theguardian.com/politics/reality-check/2013/jul/29/online-abuse-twitter-social-media. Accessed: 17 February 2014.

Chana, U. and S. Romaine (1984) 'Evaluative reactions to Panjabi/English code-switching' *Journal of Multilingual and Multicultural Development* 5/6: 447–73.

Chandler, D. (1998) 'Personal home pages and the construction of identities on the web'. Available: http://www.aber.ac.uk/media/Documents/short/webident.html. Accessed: 29 November 2013.

Cheng, J. (2009) 'Baiting Nigerian scammers for fun (not so much for profit)' *ars technica* 12 May. Available: http://arstechnica.com/tech-policy/2009/05/baiting-nigerian-scammers-for-fun-not-so-much-for-profit/. Accessed: 23 January 2014.

Chiluwa, I. (2008) 'Assessing the Nigerianness of SMS text-messages in English' *English Today* 24/1: 51–6.

Cho, R.-Y. (2013) 'Adolescents' constructively responsive reading strategy use in a critical internet reading task' *Reading Research Quarterly* 48/4: 329–32.

Clark, H.H. and T.B. Carlson (1982) 'Hearers and speech acts' *Language* 58/2: 332–73.

Cohen, S. (1973) *Folk Devils and Moral Panics*. St Albans: Paladin.

Coiro, J. and E. Dobler (2007) 'Exploring the online reading comprehension strategies used by sixth-grade skilled readers to search for and locate information on the Internet' *Reading Research Quarterly* 42/4: 214–57.

Coiro, J., M. Knobel, C. Lankshear and D.J. Leu (eds) (2008) *The Handbook of Research on New Literacies*. Abingdon: Routledge.

Coleman, E.G. (2012) 'Phreaks, hackers and trolls' in Mandiberg, M. (ed.) *The Social Media Reader*. New York: New York University Press, pp. 99–119.

Collot, M. and N. Belmore (1996) 'Electronic language: a new variety of English' in Herring, S.C. (ed.) *Computer-Mediated Communication*. Amsterdam: John Benjamins, pp. 13–28.

Cook, G. (2003) *Applied Linguistics*. Oxford: Oxford University Press.

Cormack, M. (2013) 'Concluding remarks: towards an understanding of media impact on minority language use' in Jones, E.H.G. and E. Uribe-Jongbloed (eds) *Social Media and Minority Languages: convergence and the creative industries*. Bristol: Multilingual Matters, pp. 255–65.

—— (no date) 'Gaelic and new media'. Available: http://www.gla.ac.uk/media/media_278830_en.pdf. Accessed: 18 February 2014.

Cottingham, R. (2007) 'Cartoon: on Facebook, nobody knows ...' *Social Signal* 23 June. Available: http://www.socialsignal.com/blog/rob-cottingham/on-facebook-nobody-knows. Accessed: 10 February 2014.

Coulthard, C. (2013) 'Self-portraits and social media: the rise of the "selfie"' *BBC News Magazine* 7 June. Available: http://www.bbc.co.uk/news/magazine-22511650. Accessed: 10 February 2014.

Coupland, N. (2003) 'Sociolinguistic authenticities' *Journal of Sociolinguistics* 7/3: 417–31.

Cramb, A. (2003) 'Girl writes English essay in phone text shorthand' *The Telegraph*, 3 March.

Creese, A. (2008) 'Linguistic ethnography' in King, K.A. and N.H. Hornberger (eds) *Encyclopedia of Language and Education* (vol. 10: *Research methods in language and education*). New York: Springer, pp. 229–41.

Creese, A. and Blackledge, A. (2010) 'Translanguaging in the bilingual classroom: a pedagogy for learning and teaching' *Modern Language Journal* 94, 103–15

Cronin, M. (2013) *Translation in the Digital Age*. Abingdon: Routledge.

Crowston, K. and M. Williams (2000) 'Reproduced and emergent genres of communication on the World-Wide Web' *The Information Society* 16/3: 201–16.

Crystal, D. (2000) *Language Death*. Cambridge: Cambridge University Press.

—— (2003a) *A Dictionary of Linguistics and Phonetics*. Oxford: Blackwell Publishing.

—— (2003b) *The Cambridge Encyclopedia of the English Language*. Cambridge: Cambridge University Press.

—— (2008) *Txtng: the Gr8 Db8*. Oxford: Oxford University Press.

—— (2011a) '"O brave new world, that has such corpora in it!" New trends and traditions on the internet'. Plenary paper given to ICAME 32, University of Oslo, 1 June.

—— (2011b) *Internet Linguistics*. Abingdon: Routledge.

—— (2012) 'A global language' in Seargeant, P. and J. Swann (eds) *English in the World: history, diversity, change*. Cambridge: Cambridge University Press, pp. 151–96.

Culpeper, J. (2011) *Impoliteness: using language to cause offence*. Cambridge: Cambridge University Press.

Cunliffe, D. (2007) 'Minority languages and the internet: new threats, new opportunities' in Cormack, D. and N. Hourigan (eds) *Minority Language Media: concepts, critiques and case studies*. Clevedon: Multilingual Matters, pp. 133–50.

Cunliffe, D. and R. ap Dyfrig (2013) 'The Welsh language on YouTube: initial observations' in Jones, E.H.G. and E. Uribe-Jongbloed (eds) *Social Media and Minority Languages: convergence and the creative industries*. Bristol: Multilingual Matters, pp. 130–45.

Danet, B. and S.C. Herring (2007) *The Multilingual Internet: language, culture, and communication online*. Oxford: Oxford University Press.

Danet, B., L. Ruedenberg-Wright and Y. Rosenbaum-Tamari (1997) '"Hmmm ... where's that smoke coming from?" Writing, play and performance on Internet Relay Chat' *Journal of Computer-Mediated Communication* 2/4. DOI: 10.1111/j.1083-6101.1997.tb00195.x.

Dansieh, S.A. (2011) 'SMS texting and its potential impacts on students' written communication skills' *International Journal of English Linguistics* 1/2: 223–9.

Davies, B. and R. Harré (1990) 'Positioning: the discursive production of selves' *Journal for the Theory of Social Behaviour* 20/1: 43–63.

Davis, B.J. (2009) 'Status update: "Emily Bronte and her Playstation are overly friendly these days"'. Reposted with permission of Brian J. Davis on *Alienated* by Darren Wershler, 19 January. Available: http://www.alienated.net/poetics/status-update-focus-challenged/. Accessed 21 November 2013.

Davison, P. (2012) 'The language of internet memes' in Mandiberg, M. (ed.) *The Social Media Reader*. New York: New York University Press, pp. 120–34.

Debatin, B., J.P. Lovejoy, A. Horn and B.N. Hughes (2009) 'Facebook and online privacy: attitudes, behaviors, and unintended consequences' *Journal of Computer Mediated Communication* 15: 83–108.

De Jonge, S. and N. Kemp (2012) 'Text-message abbreviations and language skills in high school and university students' *Journal of Research in Reading* 35/1: 49–68.

del-Teso-Craviotto, M. (2006) 'Language and sexuality in Spanish and English dating chats' *Journal of Sociolinguistics* 10/4: 460–80.

Deumert, A. (2012) 'Txtpl@y: creativity in South African digital writing' in Allington, D. and B. Mayor (eds), *Communicating in English: Talk, text, technology*. London: Routledge, pp. 216–23.

—— (2014) 'The performance of a ludic self on social network(ing) sites' in Seargeant, P. and C. Tagg (eds) *The Language of Social Media: identity and community online*. Basingstoke: Palgrave Macmillan, pp. 23–45.

Deumert, A. and S.O. Masinyana (2008) 'Mobile language choices – the use of English and isiXhosa in text messages (SMS): evidence from a bilingual South African sample' *English World-Wide* 29/2: 117–47.

Dewey, C. (2013) 'From the U.K. to Vietnam, internet censorship on the rise globally' *The Washington Post* 6 August. Available: http://www.washingtonpost.com/blogs/worldviews/wp/2013/08/06/from-the-uk-to-vietnam-internet-censorship-on-the-rise-globally/. Accessed 21 November 2013.

Dey, R., Z. Jelveh and K.W. Ross (2012) 'Facebook users have become much more private: a large-scale study' *4th IEEE International Workshop on Security and Social Networking (SESOC)*, Lugano, Switzerland.

Doctorow, C. (2012) 'The curious case of internet privacy' *MIT Technology Review* 6 June. Available: http://www.technologyreview.com/news/428045/the-curious-case-of-internet-privacy/?nlid=nldly&nld=2012-06-06. Accessed: 4 January 2014.

Dołowy-Rybińska, N. (2013) 'Kashubian and modern media: the influence of new technologies' in Jones, E.H.G. and E. Uribe-Jongbloed (eds) *Social Media and Minority Languages: convergence and the creative industries*, Bristol: Multilingual Matters, pp. 119–29.

Donner, J. (2007) 'The rules of beeping: exchanging messages via intentional "missed calls" on mobile phones' *Journal of Computer-Mediated Communication* 13: 1–22.

Doring, N. (2002) '"1 bread, sausage, 5 bags of apples I.L.Y." – communicative functions of text messages (SMS)' *Zeitschrift für Medienpsychologie* 3.

Drasovean, A. (2012) 'Evaluative language in user comments online: an appraisal and corpus analysis of the website TED.com'. Unpublished MA dissertation, University of Birmingham.

Drasovean, A. and C. Tagg (in preparation) 'Evaluative language and its community-building role on TED.com: an appraisal and corpus analysis'.

Drouin, M.A. (2011) 'College students' text messaging, use of textese and literacy skills' *Journal of Computer Assisted Learning* 27: 67–75.

Drouin, M.A. and C. Davis (2009) 'R U Txting? Is the use of text speak hurting your literacy?' *Journal of Literacy Research* 41: 46–67.

Dubisar, A.M. and J. Palmeri (2010) 'Palin/Pathos/Peter Griffin: political video remix and composition pedagogy' *Computers and Composition* 27: 77–93.

Dudeney, G., N. Hockly and M. Pegrum (2013) *Digital Literacies*. Harlow: Pearson.

Durham, M. (2007) 'Language choice on a Swiss mailing list' in Danet, J. and S.C. Herring (eds) *The Multilingual Internet: language, culture, and communication online*. Oxford: Oxford University Press, pp. 319–39.

Durkin, K., G. Conti-Ramsden and A.J. Walker (2011) 'Txt lang: texting, textism use and literacy abilities in adolescents with and without specific language impairment' *Journal of Computer Assisted Learning* 27: 49–57.

Dyer, R., R. Green, M. Pitts and G. Millward (1995) 'What's the flaming problem? Or computer mediated communication: deindividuating or disinhibiting?' in Kirby, M., A. Dix and J. Finlay (eds) *Proceedings of the 1995 HCI Conference*. Cambridge: Cambridge University Press, pp. 289–302.

Eckersley, P., S. Schoen, K. Bankston and D. Slater (2006) 'Six tips to protect your search privacy' *Electronic Frontier Foundation* 14 September. Available: https://www.eff.org/wp/six-tips-protect-your-search-privacy. Accessed: 4 January 2014.

Eckert, P. (2006) 'Communities of practice' in Brown, K. (ed.) *Encyclopedia of Language and Linguistics*, London: Elsevier, pp. 683–5.

—— (2007) 'Messing with style' in Maybin, J. and J. Swann (eds) *The Art of English: everyday creativity*. Abingdon: Routledge, pp. 124–30.

Elia, A. (2007) 'An analysis of Wikipedia digital writing' *Proceedings of the 11th Conference of the European Chapter of the Association for*

Computational Linguistics, pp. 16–21. Available: http://clair.eecs.umich. edu/aan/paper.php?paper_id=W06-2804#pdf. Accessed: 29 June 2014.

Ellison, N., C. Steinfield and C. Lampe (2011) 'Connection strategies: social capital implications of Facebook-enabled communication practices' *New Media & Society* 13/6: 873–92.

Ellison, N.B., J. Vitak, C. Steinfield, R. Gray and C. Lampe (2011) 'Negotiating privacy concerns and social capital needs in a social media environment' in Tepte, S. and L. Reinecke (eds) *Privacy Online*. Berlin Heidelberg: Springer-Verlag, pp. 19–32.

Emigh, W. and S.C. Herring (2005) 'Collaborative authoring on the web: a genre analysis of two on-line encyclopedias' *HICSS-38*. Los Alamitos, IEEE Press.

Eshet, Y. (2004) 'Digital literacy: a conceptual framework for survival skills in the digital era' *Journal of Educational Multimedia and Hypermedia* 13/1: 93–106.

—— (2012) 'Thinking in the digital era: a revised model for digital literacy' *Issues in Informing Science and Information Technology* 9/2: 267–76.

Fairclough, N. (1992) *Discourse and Social Change*. Boston, MA: Addison Wesley.

Fairon, C. and S. Paumier (2006) 'A translated corpus of 30,000 French SMS' *LREC*. Geneva.

Fontaine, L. (2006) 'Where do we fit in? Linguistic inclusion and exclusion in a virtual community' in Buhrig, K. and J.D. ten Thije (eds) *Beyond Misunderstanding: the linguistic reconstruction of intercultural communication*. Amsterdam: John Benjamins, pp. 319–56.

Ford Rojas, J.-P. (2012) 'BBC radio presenter Richard Bacon calls in police over online abuse by obsessed Simon Mayo fan' *The Telegraph* 19 March. Available: http://www.telegraph.co.uk/culture/tvandradio/9151506/BBC-radio-presenter-Richard-Bacon-calls-in-police-over-online-abuse-by-obsessed-Simon-Mayo-fan.html. Accessed: 17 February 2014.

Frobenius, M. (2014) 'Audience design in monologues: how vloggers involve their viewers' *Journal of Pragmatics*. Article in press available: http://dx.doi.org/10.1016/j.pragma.2014.02.008. Accessed 6 June 2014.

Fung, L. and R. Carter (2007) 'New varieties, new creativities: ICQ and English-Cantonese e-discourse' *Language and Literature* 16/4: 345–66.

Furuholt, B. and E. Matotay (2011) 'The developmental contribution from mobile phones across the agricultural value chain in rural Africa' *Electronic Journal on Information Systems in Developing Countries* 48/7: 1–16.

Gains, J. (1999) 'Electronic mail – a new style of communication or just a new medium?: an investigation into the text features of e-mail' *English for Specific Purposes* 18: 81–100.

Gamo, T. (2010) 'Alas! Japan, land of social phobia' *JA News*. Available: http://en.janews.com.au/modules/articles/index.php?page=article&storyid=49. Accessed: October 2014.

Garcia, A.C. and J.B. Jacob (1999) 'The eyes of the beholder: understanding the turn-taking system in quasi-synchronous computer-mediated communication' *Research on Language and Social Interaction* 32/4: 337–67.

García, O. (2009) *Bilingual Education in the 21st Century*. Oxford: Wiley-Blackwell.

Gardner-Chloros, P. (2009) *Codeswitching*. Cambridge: Cambridge University Press.

Garratt, P. (2012) 'My life as a Twitter addict, and why it's more difficult to quit than drugs' *The Huffington Post* 28 February. Available: http://www. huffingtonpost.co.uk/patrick-garratt/twitter-addictions-more-difficult-to-quit-than-drugs_b_1305760.html. Accessed: 6 February 2014.

Gee, J.P. (1990) *Social Linguistics and Literacies: ideology in discourse* (3rd edn). London: Routledge.

—— (2004) *Situated Language and Learning: a critique of traditional schooling*. New York: Routledge.

—— (2005) 'Semiotic social spaces and affinity spaces: from the age of mythology to today's schools' in Barton, D. and K. Tusting (eds) *Beyond Communities of Practice: language, power and social context*. Cambridge: Cambridge University Press, pp. 214–32.

Geertsema, S., C. Hyman and C. van Deventer (2011) 'Short Message Service (SMS) language and written language skills: educators' perspectives' *South African Journal of Education* 31: 475–87.

Georgakopoulou, A. (1997) 'Self-presentation and interactional alliances in e-mail discourse: the style and code-switches of Greek messages' *International Journal of Applied Linguistics* 7/2: 141–64.

Ghanem, R. (2011) 'Arabizi is destroying the Arabic language' *Arab News* 19 April. Available: http://www.arabnews.com/node/374897. Accessed: 21 November 2013.

Gibbons, J.P. (1983) 'Attitudes towards languages and code-mixing in Hong Kong' *Journal of Multilingual and Multicultural Development* 4/2 and 3: 129–47.

Gibson, J.J. (1986) *The Ecological Approach to Visual Perception*. Hillsdale, NJ: Lawrence Erlbaum.

Giles, J. (2005) 'Internet encyclopaedias go head to head' *Nature* 438: 900–1.

Gill, M. (2010) 'Establishing authenticity in computer-mediated communication: the case of Nigerian letter fraud'. Talk given at the Georgetown Roundtable of Linguistics, 11 March.

Gillen, J. (2014) *Digital Literacies*. Abingdon: Routledge.

Gillen, J. and N. Hall (2009) 'The Edwardian postcard: a revolutionary moment in rapid multimodal communications'. Talk given at the British Educational Research Association Annual Conference. Manchester, 2–5 September.

—— (2010) 'Edwardian postcards: illuminating ordinary writing' in Barton, D. and U. Papen (eds) *The Anthropology of Writing: understanding textually-mediated words*. London: Continuum, pp. 169–89.

Gillen, J. and G. Merchant (2013) 'Contact calls: Twitter as a dialogic social and linguistic practice' *Language Sciences* 35: 47–58.

Gilster, P. (1997) *Digital Literacy*. New York: John Wiley and Sons.

Goffman, E. (1959) *The Presentation of Self in Everyday Life*. New York: Anchor Books.

—— (1975) 'Replies and responses' *Language and Society* 5: 257–313.

Goldman, S.R. (2010) 'Literacy in the digital world: comprehending and learning from multiple sources' in McKeown, M.G. and L. Kucan (eds) *Bringing Reading Researchers to Life*. New York: Guilford.

Goldsmith, K. (2011) *Uncreative Writing*. New York: Columbia University Press.

Goodman, S. (2007) 'Visual English' in Goodman, S., D. Graddol and T. Lillis (eds) *Redesigning English*. Abingdon: Routledge, pp. 113–60.

Goody, J. and I. Watt (1963) 'The consequences of literacy' *Comparative Studies in Society and History* 5/3: 304–45.

Graddol, D. and J. Swann (1989) *Gender Voices*. Oxford: Blackwell.

Graham, S.L. (2007) 'Disagreeing to agree: conflict, (im)politeness and identity in a computer-mediated community' *Journal of Pragmatics* 39: 742–59.

Granovetter, M.S. (1973) 'The strength of weak ties' *The American Journal of Sociology* 78/6: 1360–80.

Grinter, R.E. and M. Eldridge (2003) 'Wan2talk? Everyday text messaging' *ACM Conference on Human Factors in Computing System (CHI)*. New York: ACM Press, pp. 441–8.

Groom, N. and J. Littlemore (2010) *Doing Applied Linguistics: a guide for students*. Abingdon: Routledge.

Grossman, L. (2013) 'Google searches mined to uncover our true opinions' *New Scientist* 25 July. Available: http://www.newscientist.com/article/dn23934-google-searches-mined-to-uncover-our-true-opinions.html#.UsfVGdK2iSo. Accessed: 4 January 2014.

Gruger, W. (2012) 'PSY's "Gangnam Style" video hits 1 billion views, unprecedented milestone' *Billboard*. Available: http://www.billboard.com/biz/articles/news/1483733/psys-gangnam-style-video-hits-1-billion-views-unprecedented-milestone. Accessed: 21 February 2013.

Gumperz, J.J. (1982) *Discourse Strategies*. Cambridge: Cambridge University Press.

Haggan, M. (2007) 'Text messaging in Kuwait. Is the medium the message?' *Multilingua* 26: 427–49.

Halliday, M.A.K. (1983) *Spoken and Written Language* (2nd edn). Oxford: Oxford University Press.

—— (1985) *An Introduction to Functional Grammar*. London: Arnold.

Hanley, J.R. (2010) 'English is a difficult writing system for children to learn: evidence from children learning to read in Wales' in Hall, K., U. Goswami, C. Harrison, S. Ellis and J. Soler (eds) *Interdisciplinary Perspectives on Learning to Read: culture, cognition and pedagogy*. London and New York: Routledge, pp. 117–29.

Hanson-Smith, E. (2013) 'Online communities of Practice' in Chapelle, C.A. (ed.) *The Encyclopedia of Applied Linguistics*. Oxford: Wiley Blackwell, pp. 1–4.

Hård af Segerstad, Y. (2002) 'Use and adaptation of the written language to the conditions of computer-mediated communication'. Unpublished PhD thesis, University of Gothenburg.

Hardaker, C. (2010) 'Trolling in asynchronous computer-mediated communication: from user discussions to academic definitions' *Journal of Politeness Research* 6: 215–42.

—— (2013) '"Uh....not to be nitpicky, but...the past tense of drag is dragged, not drug." An overview of trolling strategies' *Journal of Language Aggression and Conflict* 1/1: 58–86.

Harré, R., and Langenhove, L.V. (eds) (1999) *Positioning Theory: moral contexts of intentional action*. Oxford: Blackwell.

Harré, R., and Moghaddam, F. (eds) (2003) *The Self and Others: positioning individuals and groups in personal, political and cultural contexts*. Westport, CT: Praeger.

Hassan, N. and A. Hashim (2009) 'Electronic English in Malaysia: features and language in use' *English Today* 25/4: 39–46.

Haugh, M. (2010) 'When is an email really offensive? Argumentativity and variability in evaluations of impoliteness' *Journal of Politeness Research* 6/1: 7–31.

Hayes, K. (2002) *Writing Machines*. Cambridge, MA and London: MIT Press.

Haythornthwaite, C. and L. Kendall (2010) 'Internet and community' *American Behavioural Scientist* 53/8: 1083–94.

Haythornthwaite, C., B. Wellman and L. Garton (1998) 'Work and community via computer-mediated communication' in Gackenbach, J. (ed.) *Psychology and the Internet: intrapersonal, interpersonal and transpersonal implications*. San Diego, CA: Academic Press, pp. 199–226.

Heath, S.B. (1983) *Ways with Words: language, life and work in communities*. Cambridge: Cambridge University Press.

Hebdige, D. (1984) *Subculture: the meaning of style*. New York: Methuen.

Heller, M. and C.W. Plaff (1996) 'Code-switching' in Goebl, H., P.H. Nelde, Z. Starý and W. Wöckl (eds) *Contact Linguistics*, vol. 1. Basingstoke: Mouton de Gruyter, pp. 594–609.

Henri, F. and B. Pudelko (2003) 'Understanding and analysing activity and learning in virtual communities' *Journal of Computer Assisted Learning* 19, 474–87.

Herley, C. (2012) 'Why do Nigerian scammers say they are from Nigeria?' *Microsoft Research*. Available: http://research.microsoft.com/pubs/167719/whyfromnigeria.pdf. Accessed: 23 January 2014.

Herring, S.C. (1993) 'Gender and democracy in computer-mediated communication' *Electronic Journal of Communication* 3: 1–17.

—— (1998) 'Virtual gender performances in Internet Relay Chat'. Talk presented at Texas A&M University, 25 September.

—— (1999) 'The rhetorical dynamics of gender harassment on-line' *The Information Society* 15: 151–67.

—— (2000) 'Gender differences in CMC: findings and implications' *CRSR Newsletter* 18/1.

—— (2002) 'Cyber violence: recognizing and resisting abuse in online environments' *Asian Women* 14: 187–212.

—— (2003) 'Gender and power in online communication' in Holmes, J. and M. Meyerhoff (eds) *The Handbook of Language and Gender*. Oxford: Blackwell, pp. 202–28.

—— (2004) 'Slouching toward the ordinary: current trends in computer-mediated communication' *New Media & Society* 6/1: 26–36.

—— (2007) 'A faceted classification scheme for computer-mediated discourse' *Language@Internet* 4. Available: http://www.languageatinternet.org/articles/2007/761. Accessed: 6 October 2014.

—— (2008a) 'Questioning the generational divide: technological exoticism and adult constructions of online youth identity' in Buckingham, D. (ed.) *Youth, Identity, and Digital Media*. Cambridge, MA: MIT Press, pp. 71–92.

—— (2008b) 'Virtual community' in Given, L.M. (ed.) *Encyclopedia of Qualitative Research Methods*. Thousand Oaks, CA: Sage.

—— (2012) 'Grammar in electronic communication' in Chapelle, C. (ed.) *Encyclopedia of Applied Linguistics*. Oxford: Wiley-Blackwell.

Herring, S.C. and J.C. Paolillo (2006) 'Gender and genre variation in weblogs' *Journal of Sociolinguistics* 10/4: 439–59.

Herring, S.C., D.A. Johnson and T. DiBenedetto (1995) '"This discussion is going too far!" Male resistance to female participation on the internet' in Hall, K. and M. Bucholtz (eds) *Gender Articulated: language and the socially constructed self*. New York: Routledge, pp. 67–96.

Herring, S.C., D. Stein and T. Virtanen (eds) (2013). *Handbook of Pragmatics of Computer-Mediated Communication*. Berlin: Mouton de Gruyter.

Herring, S.C., K. Job-Sluder, R. Scheckler and S. Barab (2002) 'Searching for safety online: managing "trolling" in a feminist forum' *The Information Society* 18: 371–84.

Herring, S.C., L.A. Scheidt, S. Bonus and E. Wright (2005) 'Weblogs as a bridging genre' *Information, Technology & People* 18/2: 142–71.

Hinnenkamp, V. (2008) 'Deutsch, doyc or doitsch? Chatters as languagers – the case of a German–Turkish chat room' *International Journal of Multilingualism* 5/3: 253–75.

Hockly, N. (2012) 'Digital literacies' *ELT Journal* 66/1: 108–12.

Huang, D. (2004) 'Code switching and language use in emails'. Unpublished PhD thesis. The University of Melbourne, Melbourne.

Hürriyet Daily News (2013) 'Fake social media accounts to be prevented: Turkish Deputy PM' *Hürriyet Daily News* 21 June. Available: http://www.hurriyetdailynews.com/fake-social-media-accounts-to-be-prevented-turkish-deputy-pm.aspx?pageID=238&nID=49189&NewsCatID=338. Accessed: 23 January 2014.

Huffaker, D.A. and S.L. Calvert (2005) 'Gender, identity and language use in teenage blogs' *Journal of Computer-Mediated Communication* 10/2. DOI: 10.1111/j.1083-6101.2005.tb00238.x.

Internet World Stats (2013) Available at: http://www.internetworldstats.com/stats.htm. Accessed: 11 October 2014.

Ito, M., S. Baumer, M. Bittanti, d. boyd and R. Cody (2010) *Hanging out, messing around and geeking out: kids living and learning with new media*. Cambridge, MA: MIT Press.

Izsák, R. (2013) 'Report of the Independent Expert on Minority Issues' Available: http://www.ohchr.org/Documents/HRBodies/HRCouncil/RegularSession/Session22/AHRC2249_English.PDF. Accessed: 18 February 2014.

Jacobson, S. (1966) *Unorthodox Spelling in American Trademarks*. Stockholm: Almqvist & Wiksell.

Jaffe, A. (2000) 'Introduction: non-standard orthography and non-standard speech' *Journal of Sociolinguistics* 4/4: 497–513.

Jenkins, H. (1992) *Textual poachers: television fans and participatory culture.* New York: Routledge.

—— (2006) *Convergence culture: where old and new media collide.* New York: New York University Press.

—— (2012) 'Quentin Tarantino's Star Wars? Grassroots creativity meets the media industry' in Mandiberg, M. (ed.) *The Social Reader.* New York: New York University Press, pp. 203–35.

Jennings, R. (2010) 'Google China news: censorship controversy causes closure?' *ComputerWorld.* Available: http://blogs.computerworld. com/15748/google_china_news_censorship_controversy_causes_closure. Accessed: 16 June 2014.

Johnson, I. (2013) 'Audience design and communication accommodation theory: use of Twitter by Welsh–English biliterates' in Jones, E.H.G. and E. Uribe-Jongbloed (eds) *Social Media and Minority Languages: convergence and the creative industries.* Bristol: Multilingual Matters, pp. 99–118.

Joinson, A. (1998) 'Causes and implications of disinhibited behaviour on the internet' in Gackenbach, J. (ed.) *Psychology and the Internet: intrapersonal, interpersonal and transpersonal implications.* San Diego, CA: Academic Press, pp. 43–58.

Jones, R.H. (2002) 'Mediated discourse and sexual risk: discourses of sexuality and AIDS in the People's Republic of China'. Unpublished PhD dissertation. Macquarie University, Sydney, Australia.

Jones, R.H. and C.A. Hafner (2012) *Understanding Digital Literacies: a practical introduction.* Abingdon: Routledge.

Jørgensen, J.N., M.S. Karrebaek, L.M. Madsen and J.S. Moller (2011) 'Polylanguaging in superdiversity' *Diversities* 13/2: 23–37.

Julien, H. and S. Barker (2008) 'How high-school students find and evaluate scientific information: a basis for information literacy skills development' *Library & Information Science Research* 31/1: 12–17.

Jurgenson, N. (2012) 'The IRL fetish' *The New Inquiry.* Available: http://thenewinquiry.com/essays/the-irl-fetish/. Accessed: 2 September 2013.

Kemp, N. (2011) 'Texting versus txtng: reading and writing text messages, and links with other linguistic skills' *Writing Systems Research* 2/1: 53–71.

Kemp, N. and C. Bushell (2011) 'Children's text messaging: abbreviations, input methods and links with literacy' *Journal of Computer Assisted Learning* 27: 18–27.

Khubchandani, L.M. (1997) *Revisualising Boundaries: a plurilingual ethos.* New Delhi: Sage.

Kiernan, P. (2012) 'Exploring identity negotiation in an online community' *JASFL Proceedings* 6.

Kiesler, S. and L. Sproull (1992) 'Group decision making and communication technology' *Organisational Behaviour and Human Decision Processes* 52: 96–123.

Knight, D. (2013) 'A corpus based approach to digital discourse'. Talk given at Language and New Media BAAL SIG workshop, University of Leicester, 22 November.

Knight, N.K. (2010) '"Still cool ... and American too!": an SFL analysis of deferred bonds in instant messaging humour' in N. Nørgaard (ed.) *Systemic Functional Linguistics in Use*. Available: http://static.sdu.dk/mediafiles//Files/Om_SDU/Institutter/ISK/Forskningspublikationer/OWPLC/Nr29/Naomi_Knight.pdf. Accessed: 6 October 2014.

Koutsogiannis, D. and B. Mitsikopoulou (2003) 'Greeklish and Greekness: trends and discourses of "glocalness"' *Journal of Computer Mediated Communication* 9/1. DOI: 10.1111/j.1083-6101.2003.tb00358.x.

Kramer-Dahl, A. (2003) 'Reading the "Singlish Debate": construction of a crisis of language standards and language teaching in Singapore' *Journal of Language, Identity, and Education* 2/3: 159–90.

Krasnova, H. S. Spiekermann, K. Koroleva and T. Hildebrand (2010) 'Online social networks: why we disclose' *Journal of Information Technology* 25: 109–25.

Kress, G. (2000) *Early Spelling: from convention to creativity*. Abingdon: Routledge.

Labov, W. (1966) *The Social Stratification of English in New York City*. Washington, DC: Center for Applied Linguistics.

—— (1972) *Sociolinguistic Patterns*. Philadelphia: University of Pennsylvania Press.

Lam, W.S.E. (2000) 'Literacy and the design of self: a case study of a teenager writing on the internet' *TESOL Quarterly* 34/4: 457–82.

Lange, P. (2007) 'Commenting on comments: investigating responses to antagonism on YouTube'. Talk given at the Society for Applied Anthropology Conference, Tampa, Florida. Available: http://sfaapodcasts.files.wordpress.com/2007/04/update-apr-17-lange-sfaa-paper-2007.pdf. Accessed: 19 February 2014.

Lankshear, C. and M. Knobel (2008) *Digital Literacies: concepts, policies and practices*. New York: Peter Lang.

Lave, J. and E. Wenger (1991) *Situated Learning: legitimate peripheral participation*. Cambridge: Cambridge University Press.

Lee, C. (2007a) 'Linguistic features of email and ICQ instant messaging in Hong Kong' in Danet, B. and S.C. Herring (eds) *The Multilingual Internet: language, culture, and communication online*. Oxford: Oxford University Press, pp. 184–208.

—— (2007b) 'Affordances and text-making practices in online instant messaging' *Written Communication* 24: 223–49.

—— (2014) 'Language choice and self-presentation in social media: the case of university students in Hong Kong' in Seargeant, P. and C. Tagg (eds) *The Language of Social Media: identity and community online*. Basingstoke: Palgrave Macmillan, pp. 91–111.

Lee, Y. (2012) 'South Korea: 160,000 kids between the ages of 5 and 9 are internet-addicted' *The Huffington Post* 28 November. Available: http://www.huffingtonpost.com/2012/11/28/south-korea-internet-addicted_n_2202371.html. Accessed: 6 February 2014.

Lemke, J. (2002). 'Language development and identity: multiple timescales in the social ecology of learning' in Kramsch, C. (ed.) *Language Socialization and Language Acquisition: ecological perspectives*. London: Continuum, pp. 68–87.

Lenihan, A. (2014) 'Investigating language policy in social media: translation practices on Facebook' in Seargeant, P. and C. Tagg (eds) *The Language of Social Media: identity and community online*. Baskingstoke: Palgrave Macmillan, pp. 208–27.

Leppänen, S. (2009) 'Playing with and policing language use and textuality in fan fiction' in Hotz-Davis, I., A. Kirchhofer and S. Leppänen (eds) *Internet Fictions*. Cambridge: Cambridge University Press, pp. 62–83.

Leppänen, S. and S. Peuronen (2012) 'Multilingualism on the internet' in Martin-Jones, M., A. Blackledge and A. Creese (eds) *The Routledge Handbook of Multilingualism*. London and New York: Routledge, pp. 384–402.

Leppänen, S., S. Kytölä, H. Jousmaki, S. Peuronen and E. Westinen (2014) 'Entextualization and resemiotization as resources for identification in social media' in Seargeant, P. and C. Tagg (eds) *The Language of Social Media: identity and community online*, Basingstoke: Palgrave Macmillan, pp. 112–36.

Lessig, L. (2004) *Free Culture: how big media uses technology and the law to lock down culture and control creativity*. London: The Penguin Press.

Leu, D.J. Jr., C.K. Kinzer, J. Coiro and D. Cammack (2004) 'Toward a theory of new literacies emerging from the Internet and other information and communication technologies' in Ruddell, R.B. and N. Unrau (eds) *Theoretical Models and Processes of Reading* (5th edn). Newark, DE: International Reading Association, pp. 1568–611.

Lexander, K.V. (2011) 'Texting and African language literacy' *New Media & Society* 13/3: 427–43.

Lillis, T. (2013) *The Sociolinguistics of Writing*. Edinburgh: Edinburgh University Press.

Ling, R. and H.A. Horst (2011) 'Mobile communication in the global south' *New Media & Society* 13/3: 363–74.

Ling, R. and B. Yttri (2002) 'Hyper-coordination via mobile phones in Norway' in Katz, J. and M. Aakhus (eds) *Perpetual Contact: mobile communication, private talk, public performance*. Cambridge: Cambridge University Press, pp. 139–69.

Litt, E. (2012) 'Knock, knock. Who's there? The imagined audience' *Journal of Broadcasting & Electronic Media* 56/3: 330–45.

Livingstone, S. (2008) 'Taking risky opportunities in youthful content creation: Teenagers' use of social networking sites for intimacy, privacy and self–expression' *New Media & Society* 10/3: 393–411.

Luzón, M.J. (2011) '"Interesting post, but I disagree": social presence and antisocial behaviour in academic weblogs' *Applied Linguistics* 32/5: 517–40.

—— (2013) 'Public communication of science in blogs: recontextualizing scientific discourse for a diversified audience' *Written Communication* 30/4: 428–57.

Lyons, M. (2007) *Ordinary Writings, Personal Narratives: writing practices in 19th and 20th century Europe*. Berne: Peter Lang.

MacKinnon, R. (2012) *Consent of the Networked: the worldwide struggle for internet freedom*. New York: Basic Books.

MacRae, D. (2013) 'Average UK texter sends two million words in their lifetime' *CBR* 6 August. Available: http://www.cbronline.com/news/mobile-and-tablets/average-uk-texter-sends-two-million-words-in-their-lifetime. Accessed: 21 November 2013.

Mac Uidhilin, N. (2013) 'Learning communities mediated through technology: pedagogic opportunities for minority languages' in Jones, E.H.G. and E. Uribe-Jongbloed (eds) *Social Media and Minority Languages: convergence and the creative industries.* Bristol: Multilingual Matters, pp. 146–58.

Madden, M. (2012) 'Privacy management on social media sites' *Pew Internet & American Life Project.* Available: http://pewinternet.org/Reports/2012/Privacy-management-on-social-media.aspx. Accessed: 13 August 2013.

Madianou, M. and D. Miller (2012) 'Polymedia: towards a new theory of digital media in interpersonal communication' *International Journal of Cultural Studies* 16/2: 169–87.

Malinowski, B. (1965) *Coral Gardens and their Magic.* Bloomington: Indiana University Press.

Mandiberg, M. (ed.) (2012) *The Social Media Reader.* New York: New York University Press.

Manguel, A. (1996) *The History of Reading.* New York: Viking.

Mapes, D. (2013) '"Bad" picture Monday: unflattering photos spur online movement' *Today* 8 April. Available: http://www.xojane.com/fun/pretty-girls-ugly-faces. Accessed: 10 February 2014.

Margulis, S.T. (2011) 'Three theories of privacy: an overview' in Tepte, S. and L. Reinecke (eds) *Privacy Online.* Berlin Heidelberg: Springer-Verlag, pp. 9–19.

Martin, J.R. and P.R.R. White (2005) *The Language of Evaluation: appraisal in English.* Basingstoke: Palgrave Macmillan.

Marwick, A. (2008) 'To catch a predator? The MySpace moral panic' *First Monday* 13/6. Available: http://firstmonday.org/article/view/2152/1966. Accessed: 6 October 2014.

Marwick, A. and d. boyd (2011) 'The drama! Teen conflict, gossip, and bullying in networked publics'. Talk given at *A Decade in Time: symposium on the dynamics of the internet and society,* Oxford Internet Institute, 22 September.

Marwick, A., D.M. Diaz and J. Palfrey (2010) 'Youth, privacy and reputation'. Available: http://cyber.law.harvard.edu/publications/2010/Youth_Privacy_Reputation_Lit_Review. Accessed: 12 August 2013.

Massengill Shaw, D., C. Carlson and M. Waxman (2007) 'An exploratory investigation into the relationship between text messaging and spelling' *New England Reading Association Journal* 43: 57–62.

Maybin, J. (2011) 'Intimate strangers' in Swann, J., R. Pope and R. Carter (eds) *Creativity in Language and Literature.* Basingstoke: Palgrave Macmillan, pp. 129–40.

Mayor, B. and D. Allington (2012) 'Talking in English' in Allington, D. and B. Mayor (eds) *Communicating in English: talk, text, technology.* Abingdon: Routledge, pp. 307–35.

Mbodj-Pouje, A. (2010) 'Keeping a notebook in rural Mali: a practice in the making' in Barton, D. and U. Papen (eds) *The Anthropology of Writing: understanding textually mediated worlds.* London: Continuum, pp. 126–44.

McCarthy, T. (2012) 'Google's new "tailored" privacy policy: how to circumvent the rules' the *Guardian* 29 February. Available: http://www.theguardian.com/technology/us-news-blog/2012/feb/29/google-privacy-policy-tips-and-tricks. Accessed: 4 January 2013.

McClure, E. (2001) 'The role of language in the construction of ethnic identity on the internet: the case of Assyrian activists in diaspora' in Moseley, C., N. Ostler and H. Ouzzate (eds) *Endangered Languages and the Media*. Bath: Foundation for Endangered Languages, pp. 68–75.

McHugh, J. (2013) '"Selfies" just as much for the insecure as show-offs' *Bunbury Mail* 10 February. Available: http://www.bunburymail.com.au/story/1407035/selfies-just-as-much-for-the-insecure-as-show-offs/. Accessed: 10 February 2014.

McIntosh, J. (2012) 'A history of subversive remix video before YouTube: thirty political video mashups made between World War II and 2005' *Transformative Works and Cultures* 9. Available: http://journal.transformativeworks.org/index.php/twc/article/view/371/299. Accessed: 8 August 2013.

McLaughlin, C. and J. Vitak (2011) 'Norm evolution and violation on Facebook' *New Media & Society* 14: 299–315.

mclennan, r. (2011) 'update' *Quill & Quire: Canada's Magazine of Book News and Reviews*. Available: http://www.quillandquire.com/reviews/review.cfm?review_id=7228. Accessed: 21 November 2013.

McLuhan, M. (1964) *Understanding Media: the extensions of man*. New York: Signet.

Meyerhoff, M. (2006) *Introducing Sociolinguistics*. London: Routledge.

Miller, D. and H. Horst (2012) 'The digital and the human' in Horst, H. and Miller, D. (eds) *Digital Anthropology*. London: Berg, pp. 3–35.

Miller, D. and J. Sinanan (2014) *Webcam*. Cambridge: Polity Press.

Milroy, L. (1987) *Language and Social Networks*. Oxford: Blackwell.

MLDF Media Forum (2010) 'Interview with Rosenthal Alves' *MLDF Media Forum 2010*. Available: http://www.youtube.com/watch?v=7JZp4pI5GBI. Accessed: 21 November 2013.

Moje, E. (2000) '"To be part of the story": the literacy practices of gangsta adolescents' *Teachers College Record* 102/3: 651–90.

Morel, E., C. Bucher, S. Pekarek Doehler and B. Siebenhaar (2012) 'SMS communication as plurilingual communication: hybrid language use as a challenge for classical code-switching categories' *Linguisticae Investigationes* 35/2: 260–88.

Moyer, M.G. and L. Martin Rojo (2007) 'Language, migration and citizenship: new challenges in the regulation of bilingualism' in Heller, M. (ed.) *Bilingualism: a social approach*. New York: Palgrave Macmillan, pp. 137–60.

Muysken, P. (2000) *Bilingual Speech: a typology of code-mixing*. Cambridge: Cambridge University Press.

Mwai, C. and D. Umutesi (2013) 'Rwanda: social media – is it killing human ties and interactions?' *The New Times* 8 August. Available: http://allafrica.com/stories/201308090341.html. Accessed: 6 February 2014.

Myers, G. (2010) *The Discourse of Blogs and Wikis*. London: Continuum.

Myers-Scotton, C. (1993) *Social Motivations for Code-Switching: evidence from Africa*. Oxford: Clarendon Press.

Neuman, J. (1996) 'Media developments and public policy' *Communications: the information society* 1/12: 24–7.

New London Group (1996) 'A pedagogy of multiliteracies: designing social futures' *Harvard Educational Review* 66/1: 60–92.

Newon, L. (2011) 'Multimodal creativity and identities of expertise in the digital ecology of a *World of Warcraft* guild' in Thurlow, C. and K. Mroczek (eds) *Digital Discourse: language in the new media*. Oxford: Oxford University Press, pp. 131–53.

Nishimura, Y. (2010) 'Impoliteness in Japanese BBS interactions: observations from message exchanges in two online communities' *Journal of Politeness Research* 6/1: 35–55.

Norton, B., Jones, S. and D. Ahimbisibwe (2013) 'Digital literacy, HIV/AIDS information and English language learners in Uganda' in Erling, E.J. and P. Seargeant (eds) *English and Development: policy, pedagogy and globalization*. Bristol: Multilingual Matters, pp. 182–203.

Ochs, E. (1992) 'Indexing gender' in Duranti, A. and C. Goodwin (eds) *Rethinking Context: language as an interactive phenomenon*. Cambridge: Cambridge University Press, pp. 335–58.

O'Mahoney, J. (2013) 'Twitter users can't spell' *The Telegraph* 29 May. Available: http://www.telegraph.co.uk/technology/twitter/10086819/Twitter-users-cant-spell.html. Accessed: 21 November 2013.

On the Media (2012) 'Why Nigerian email scams work' *On the Media*. Available: http://www.onthemedia.org/tags/scam/. Accessed: 23 January 2014.

O'Reilly, T. (2012) 'What is Web 2.0? design patterns and business models for the next generation of software' in Mandiberg, M. (ed.) *The Social Media Reader*. New York: New York University Press, pp. 32–52.

O'Sullivan, P.B. and A.J. Flanagin (2003) 'Reconceptualising "flaming" and other problematic messages' *New Media & Society* 5/1: 69–94.

Otsuji, E. and Pennycook, A.D. (2011) 'Social inclusion and metrolingual practices' *International Journal of Bilingual Education and Bilingualism* 14/4: 413–26.

Page, R. (2012a) *Stories and Social Media: identities and interaction*. Abingdon: Routledge.

—— (2012b) 'Developing evaluation in "The murder of Stephen Lawrence" Wikipedia article'. Talk given at the BAAL 2012, University of Southampton, 8 September.

—— (2013) 'Counter narratives and controversial crimes: a cross-cultural comparison of the Wikipedia article for the "Murder of Meredith Kercher"'. Talk given at the BAAL 2013, Herriot-Watt University, 5–7 September.

—— (2014) 'Hoaxes, hacking and humour: analysing impersonated identity on social network sites' in Seargeant, P. and C. Tagg (eds) *The Language of Social Media: identity and community on the internet*. Basingstoke: Palgrave Macmillan, pp. 46–64.

Pagliaro, L.A. (1983) 'The history and development of CAI: 1926–1981, an overview' *Alberta Journal of Educational Research* 29/1: 75–84.

Palfreyman, D. and M. Al Khalil (2007) '"A funky language for teenzz to use": representing Gulf Arabic in Instant Messaging' in Danet, B. and S.C.

Herring (eds) *The Multilingual Internet: language, culture, and communication online*. Oxford: Oxford University Press, pp. 43–63.

Panyametheekul, S. and S.C. Herring (2007) 'Gender and turn allocation in a Thai chat room' in Danet, B. and S.C. Herring (eds) *The Multilingual Internet: language, culture, and communication online*. Oxford: Oxford University Press, pp. 233–55.

Paolillo, J.C. (2007) 'How much multilingualism? Language diversity on the internet' in Danet, B. and S.C. Herring (eds) *The Multilingual Internet: language, culture, and communication online*. Oxford: Oxford University Press, pp. 408–30.

Papacharissi, Z. (ed.) (2011) *A Networked Self: identity, community, and culture on social network sites*. Abingdon: Routledge.

Pargman, D. and J. Palme (2009) 'ASCII imperialism' in Lampland, M. and S.L. Star (eds) *Standards and their Stories: how quantifying, classifying and formalizing practices shape everyday life*. New York: Cornell University Press, pp. 177–99.

Pariser, E. (2011) *The Filter Bubble: what the internet is hiding from you*. New York: Penguin Books.

Parks, M. (2011) 'Social network sites as virtual communities' in Papacharissi, Z. (ed.) *A Networked Self: identity, community, and culture on social network sites*. Abingdon: Routledge, pp. 105–23.

Pegrum, M. (2010) '"I Link, Therefore I Am": network literacy as a core digital literacy' *E-Learning and Digital Media* 7/4: 346–54.

—— (2011) 'Modified, multiplied, and (re-)mixed: social media and digital literacies' in Thomas, M. (ed.) *Digital Education: opportunities for social collaboration*. Basingstoke: Palgrave Macmillan, pp. 9–35.

Pellegrin, J.W., N. Chudowsky and R. Glaser (eds) (2001) *Knowing what Students Know: the science and design of educational assessment*. Washington, DC: National Academcy Press.

Perloff, M. (2010) *Unoriginal Genius: poetry by other means in the new century*. Chicago: University of Chicago Press.

Peuronen, S. (2011) '"Ride hard, live forever": Translocal identities in an online community of extreme sports Christians' in Thurlow, C. and K. Mroczek (eds) *Digital Discourse: language in the new media*. Oxford: Oxford University Press, pp. 154–76.

Philips, T. and D. Engle (2012) 'Facebook, the club: social networking on the dancefloor in Brazilian Amazon' the *Guardian* 19 January. Available: http://www.theguardian.com/technology/2012/jan/19/amazon-club-facebook. Accessed: 13 February 2014.

Pihlaja, S. (2011) 'Cops, popes, and garbage collectors: metaphor and antagonism in an atheist/Christian YouTube video thread' *Language@Internet* 8. Available: http://www.languageatinternet.org/articles/2011/Pihlaja. Accessed: 6 October 2014.

Plester, B. and C. Wood (2009) 'Exploring relationships between traditional and new media literacies: British preteen texters at school' *Journal of Computer-Mediated Communication* 14: 1108–29.

Plester, B., C. Wood and V. Bell (2008) 'Txt msg n school literacy: does texting and knowledge of text abbreviations adversely affect children's literacy attainment?' *Literacy* 42: 137–44.

Plester, B., M.-K. Lerkkanen, L.J. Linjama, H. Rasju-Puttonen and K. Littleton (2011) 'Finnish and UK English pre-teen children's text message language and its relationship with their literacy skills' *Journal of Computer Assisted Learning* 27/1: 27–48.

Plunkett, J. (2012) 'Decline of the phone call: Ofcom shows growing trend for text communication' the *Guardian* 18 July. Available: http://www. guardian.co.uk/technology/2012/jul/18/ofcom-report-phone-calls-decline. Accessed: 6 February 2014.

Poplack, S. (1980) 'Sometimes I'll start a sentence in English y termino en español: toward a typology of code switching' *Linguistics* 18: 581–618.

Pound, L. (1925) 'The kraze for "K"' *American Speech* 1/1: 43–4.

Powell, D. and M. Dixon (2011) 'Does SMS text messaging help or harm adults' knowledge of standard spelling?' *Journal of Computer Assisted Learning* 27: 58–66.

Praninskas, J. (1968) *Trade-Name Creation: processes and patterns*. The Hague: Mouton.

Pressley, M. and P. Aflerbach (1995) *Verbal Protocols of Reading: the nature of constructively responsive reading*. Hillsdale, NJ: Lawrence Erlbaum.

Price, E. (2012) 'Without social media, 18% of teens would stop communicating' *Mashable* 20 July. Available: http://mashable. com/2012/07/19/teens-stop-communicating/. Accessed: 6 February 2014.

Radia, P. and P. Stapleton (2009) 'Unconventional sources as a new convention: the shifting paradigm of undergraduate writing' *The Internet and Higher Education* 12, 3/4: 156–64.

Radstake, M. (2010) 'Relatie tussen het gebruik van nieuwe media en spellingvaardigheid bij vmbo-, havo- en vwo-leerlingen'. Master's thesis, Utrecht University.

Ramachandran, A., N. Feamster and S. Vempla (2007) Filtering spam with behavioural blacklisting. Paper presented at CCS 07. Available: http:// www.cc.gatech.edu/fac/feamster/papers/bb-ccs2007.pdf. Accessed: 11 October 2014.

RAND Reading Study Group (2002) 'Reading for understanding: toward an R&D program in reading comprehension'. Santa Monica, CA: RAND. Available: www.rand.org/pubs/monograph_reports/2005/MR1465.pdf. Accessed: 29 November 2013.

Ravid, G. (2007) 'Dominance and social structure in Wikipedia'. Talk given to the Friday Informatics Seminar, Department of Informatics, University of California, Irvine, 8 June.

Rheingold, H. (1993) *The Virtual Community: understanding on the electronic frontier*. Available: http://www.rheingold.com/vc/book/. Accessed: 14 January 2014.

Rodino, M. (1997) 'Breaking out of binaries: reconceptualizing gender and its relationship to language in computer-mediated communication' *Journal of Computer-Mediated Communication* 3/3. DOI: 10.1111/j.10836101.1997. tb00074.x.

Rosen, J. (2012) 'The people formally known as the audience' in Mandiberg, M. (ed.) *The Social Media Reader*. New York: New York University Press, pp. 13–16.

Rosen, L.D., J. Chang, L. Erwin, L.M. Carrier and N.A. Cheever (2010) 'The relationship between "textisms" and formal and informal writing among young adults' *Communication Research* 37/3: 420–40.

Rothenberg, T. (2013) 'Tennis player overcomes bullying and a hiatus' *The New York Times* 17 February. Available: http://www.nytimes. com/2013/02/18/sports/tennis/rebecca-marino-of-canada-overcomes-bullying-and-hiatus.html?_r=1&. Accessed: 17 February 2014.

Rowe, C. (2011) 'Whatchanade? Rapid language change in a private email sibling code' *Language@Internet* 8. Available: http://www.languageatin ternet.org/articles/2011/Rowe. Accessed: 6 October 2014.

Royal Geographical Society (with IBG) (2014) 'Digital divide in the UK' *Twentieth-Century Challenges*. Available: http://www.21st centurychallenges.org/60-seconds/what-is-the-digital-divide/. Accessed: 9 June 2014.

Sabella, R.A., J.W. Patchin and S. Hinduja (2013) 'Cyberbullying myths and realities' *Computers in Human Behavior* 29: 2703–11.

Saddlemire, C. (2013) 'A.V.A.T.A.R. (Anglos Valiantly Aiding Tragic Awe-inspiring Races)'. Posted on *Political Remix Video* 25 April. Available: http://www.politicalremixvideo.com/2013/04/25/tragic-%E2%80%A9awe-inspiring%E2%80%A9/. Accessed: 21 November 2013.

Sale, K. (1995) *Rebels Against the Future*. London: Addison Wesley.

Savicki, V., D. Lingenfelter and M. Kelley (1996) 'Gender language style and group composition in internet discussion groups' *Journal of Computer-Mediated Communication* 2/3. DOI: 10.1111/j.1083-6101.1996. tb00191.x.

Schaffer, D. (2012) 'The language of scam spams: linguistic features of "Nigerian fraud"' *ETC: A Review of General Semantics* 69/2.

Schroeder, J. (2013) 'Pretty girls ugly faces – how it felt to participate in the newest meme sweeping the internet' *Xojane* 11 February. Available: http:// www.xojane.com/fun/pretty-girls-ugly-faces. Accessed: 10 February 2014.

Schuler, D. (2003) 'Reports of the close relationship between democracy and the internet may have been exaggerated' in Jenkins, H. and D. Thorburn (eds) *Democracy and New Media*. Cambridge, MA: MIT Press, pp. 69–84.

Scollon, R. and S.B.K. Scollon (1981) *Narrative, Literacy and Face in Interethnic Communication*. Norwood, NJ: Albex. Main.

Scollon, R. and S.W. Scollon (2002) 'The problem of power' *The Axe Handle Academy*. Available: http://www.ankn.uaf.edu/curriculum/AxeHandleAca demy/axe/pop.htm. Accessed: 27 June 2014.

Scribner, S. and M. Cole (1981) *The Psychology of Literacy*. Cambridge, MA: Harvard University Press.

Script Encoding Initiative (2012) 'What is the script encoding initiative?' Available: http://linguistics.berkeley.edu/~dwanders/. Accessed: 18 February 2014.

Seargeant, P. and C. Tagg (2011) 'English on the internet and a post-varieties approach to language' *World Englishes* 30/4: 496–514.

—— (2014) 'Introduction: the language of social media' in Seargeant, P. and C. Tagg (eds) *The Language of Social Media: identity and community online*. Basingstoke: Palgrave Macmillan, pp. 1–20.

Seargeant, P., C. Tagg and W. Ngampramuan (2012) 'Language choice and addressivity strategies in Thai–English social network interactions' *Journal of Sociolinguistics* 16/4: 510–31.

Sebba, M. (2007) *Spelling and Society*. Cambridge: Cambridge University Press.

—— (2012) 'Researching and theorising multilingual texts' in Sebba, M., S. Mahootian and C. Jonsson (eds) *Language Mixing and Code-Switching in Writing: approaches to mixed-language written discourse*. London: Routledge, pp. 1–26.

Selfe, C.L. and P.R. Meyer (1991) 'Testing claims for on-line conferences' *Written Communication* 8/2: 163–92.

Sellen, A.J. and R.H.R. Harper (2003) *The Myth of the Paperless Office*. Cambridge, MA: MIT Press.

Shafie, L.A., N.A. Darus and N. Osman (2010) 'SMS language and college writing: the languages of the college texters' *International Journal of Emerging Technologies in Learning* 5: 26–31.

Shaghouri, T. (2003) 'Net addicts urged to quit chatting, take up sports' *Gulf News* 27 February. Available: http://gulfnews.com/news/gulf/uae/general/net-addicts-urged-to-quit-chatting-take-up-sports-1.348475. Accessed: 6 February 2014.

Shariff, S. (2005) 'Cyber-dilemmas in the new millennium: school obligations to provide student safety in a virtual school environment' *Journal of Education* 40/3: 457–77.

—— (2006) 'Cyber-dilemmas: gendered hierarchies, new technologies and cyber-safety in schools' *Atlantis* 31/1: 27–37.

Shortis, T. (2007a) 'Gr8 Txtpectations: the creativity of text spelling' *English Drama Media Journal* 8: 21–6.

—— (2007b) 'Revoicing Txt: spelling, vernacular orthography and "unregimented" writing' in Posteguillo, S., M.J. Esteve and M.L. Gea (eds) *The Texture of Internet: netlinguistics*. Cambridge: Cambridge Scholar Press, pp. 2–21.

Siebenhaar, B. (2006) 'Code choice and code-switching in Swiss-German Internet Relay Chat rooms' *Journal of Sociolinguistics* 10/4: 481–509.

Siegel, J., V. Dubrovsky, S. Kiesler and T.W. McGuire (1986) 'Group processes in computer-mediated communication' *Organizational Behaviour and Human Decision Processes* 37/2: 157–87.

Simon, S. (2012) 'Sexiest man alive gets "The Onion" taken seriously' *The Onion* 1 December. Available: http://www.npr.org/2012/12/01/166293306/the-onion-so-funny-it-makes-us-cry. Accessed: 21 November 2013.

Singh, J. (2012) 'Smartphone mania to impact social skills' *Light Reading* 14 December. Available: http://www.lightreading.in/lightreadingindia/news-analysis/155750/smartphone-mania-impact-social-skills. Accessed: 6 February 2014.

Skutnabb-Kangas, T. (2008) 'Language rights and bilingual education' in Cummins, J. and N. Hornberger (eds) *Encyclopedia of Language and Education* (2nd edn), vol. 5. *Bilingual education*. New York: Springer, pp. 117–31.

Smith, P. (1988) *Discerning the Subject*. Minneapolis: University of Minnesota Press.

Smith, P.K., J. Mahdavi, M. Carvalho, S. Fisher, S. Russell and N. Tippett (2008) 'Cyberbullying: its nature and impact in school pupils' *Journal of Child Psychology and Psychiatry* 49: 376–85.

Sneddon, R. (2000) 'Language and literacy: children's experience in multilingual environments' *International Journal of Bilingual Education and Bilingualism* 3: 265–82.

Solove, D.J. (2013) 'Five myths about privacy' *Washington Post Opinions* 13 June. Available: http://www.washingtonpost.com/opinions/five-myths-about-privacy/2013/06/13/098a5b5c-d370-11e2-b05f-3ea3f0e7bb5a_story_1.html. Accessed: 4 January 2013.

Spache, G.D. (1967) 'A reaction to computer-assisted instruction in initial reading: the Stanford project' *Reading Research Quarterly* 3/1: 101–9.

Spangler, T. (2013) 'Twitter's spam headache: more than 10 mil accounts might be bogus' *Variety* 13 October. Available: http://variety.com/2013/digital/news/twitters-spam-headache-more-than-10-mil-accounts-might-be-bogus-1200694134/. Accessed: 23 January 2014.

Spatafora, J.N. (2008) 'I'M learning 2 write? A study on how instant messaging shapes student writing'. Master's thesis, Queen's University.

Spooren, W. (2009) 'Bezorgde ouders? De relatie tussen chat en schrijfkwaliteit' in Spooren, W., M. Onrust and J. Sanders (eds) *Studies in Taalbeheersing 3*. Assen: Van Gorcum, pp. 331–42.

Sproull, L. and S. Kiesler (1986) 'Reducing social context cues: electronic mail in organizational communication' *Management Science* 32: 1492–512.

Squires, L. (2011) 'Voicing "sexy text": heteroglossia and erasure in TV news representations of Detroit's text message scandal' in Thurlow, C. and K. Mroczek (eds) *Digital Discourse: language in the new media*. Oxford: Oxford University Press, pp. 3–25.

Stenovec, T. (2013) 'Here are 5 ways to take control of your inbox and take back your life' *The Third Metric* 14 August. Available: http://www.huffingtonpost.com/2013/08/14/email-overload-control-inbox_n_3750393.html?ir=Technology&utm_campaign=081413&utm_medium=email&utm_source=Alert-technology&utm_content=FullStory. Accessed: 21 November 2013.

Stephens-Davidowitz, S. (2013) 'Unreported victims of an economic downturn'. Report published by the Harvard Department of Economics. Available: http://static.squarespace.com/static/51d894bee4b01caf88ccb4f3/t/51e22f38e4b0502fe211fab7/1373777720363/childabusepaper13.pdf. Accessed: 1 July 2014.

Street, B. (1984) *Literacy in Theory and Practice*. Cambridge: Cambridge University Press.

Stutzman, F., R. Capra and J. Thompson (2011) 'Factors mediating disclosure in social network sites' *Computers in Human Behavior* 27: 590–8.

Stvilia, B., Twidale, M., Gasser, L., Smith, L. (2005) Information Quality Discussions in Wikipedia. Technical Report ISRN UIUCLIS--2005/2+CSCW,2005.

Su, H.-Y. (2007) 'The multilingual and multiorthographic Taiwan-based internet: creative uses of writing systems on college-affiliated BBSs' in Danet, B. and S.C. Herring (eds) *The Multilingual Internet: language, culture, and communication online.* Oxford: Oxford University Press, pp. 64–86.

Suzuki, M. (2013) 'In Asia, ancient writing collides with the digital age' *AFP* 25 June. Available: http://www.google.com/hostednews/afp/article/ALeqM5hwCYkBmi_248-MMoIwV55Oh_HfHQ?docId=CNG.10b2d43 5477d3568cf04aba1732faba9.4b1. Accessed: 21 November 2013.

Swales, J. (1990) *Genre Analysis: English in academic and research settings.* Cambridge: Cambridge University Press.

Swann, J. (2006) 'The art of the everyday' in Maybin, J. and J. Swann (eds) *The Art of English: everyday creativity.* Abingdon: Routledge, pp. 3–53.

Tagg, C. (2009) 'A corpus analysis of SMS text messages'. Unpublished PhD thesis, University of Birmingham. Available: http://etheses.bham. ac.uk/253/1/Tagg09PhD.pdf. Accessed: 29 June 2014.

—— (2012) *The Discourse of Text Messaging.* London: Continuum.

—— (2013) 'Scraping the barrel with a shower of social misfits: everyday creativity in text messaging' *Applied Linguistics* 34/4: 480–500.

Tagg, C. and P. Seargeant (2012) 'Writing systems at play in Thai–English online interactions' *Writing Systems Research* 4/2: 195–213.

—— (2014) 'Audience design and language choice in the construction and maintenance of translocal communities on social network sites' in Seargeant, P. and C. Tagg (eds) *The Language of Social Media: identity and community on the internet.* Basingstoke: Palgrave Macmillan, pp. 161–85.

—— (forthcoming) 'Facebook and the discursive construction of the social network' in Georgakopoulou, A. and T. Spilioti (eds) *The Routledge Handbook of Language and Digital Communication.* Abingdon: Routledge.

Tagg, C., Baron, A. and Rayson, P. (2013) '"I didn't spel that wrong did i. Oops": analysis and standardisation of SMS spelling variation' *Lingvisticæ Investigationes* 35/2: 367–88.

Taiwo, R. (2009) 'Code-switching/mixing in Yoruba–English Nigerian SMS text messaging'. Talk given at the International Symposium on Bilingualism 7, Utrecht, 9 July.

Takahashi, T. (2014) 'Youth, social media and connectivity in Japan' in Seargeant, P. and C. Tagg (eds) *The Language of Social Media: identity and community on the internet.* Basingstoke: Palgrave Macmillan, pp. 186–207.

Taylor, A. and R. Harper (2003) 'The gift of the gab? a design oriented sociology of young people's use of mobiles' *Journal of Computer Supported Cooperative Work* 12/3: 267–96.

Tepper, M. (1996) 'Usenet communities and the cultural politics of information' in Porter, D. (ed.) *Internet Culture.* London: Routledge, pp. 39–54.

The Onion (2013) 'Internet users demand less interactivity: "we just want to visit websites and look at them", users say' *The Onion* 16 January. Available: http://www.theonion.com/articles/internet-users-demand-less-interactivity,30920/. Accessed: 21 November 2013.

The Unicode Consortium (2013). Available: www.unicode.org. Accessed: 15 August 2013.

Thurlow, C. (2005) 'Deconstructing adolescent communication' in Williams, A. and C. Thurlow (eds) *Talking Adolescence: perspectives on communication in the teenage years.* New York: Peter Lang, pp. 1–20.

—— (2006) 'From statistical panic to moral panic: the metadiscursive construction and popular exaggeration of new media language in the print media' *Journal of Computer-Mediated Communication* 11: 667–701.

Thurlow, C. and A. Brown (2003) 'Generation Txt? Exposing the sociolinguistics of young people's text-messaging' *Discourse Analysis Online* 1/1.

Thurlow, C. and A. Jaworski (2011) 'Banal globalisation? Embodied actions and mediated practices in tourists' online photo sharing' in Thurlow, C. and K. Mroczek (eds) *Digital Discourse: language in the new media.* Oxford: Oxford University Press, pp. 220–50.

Thurlow, C., L. Lengel and A. Tomic (2004) *Computer Mediated Communication: social interaction and the internet.* Thousand Oaks, CA: Sage.

Thurston, B. (2013) '#Unplug: Baratunde Thurston left the internet for 25 days, and you should, too' *Fast Company* 17 June. Available: http://www.fastcompany.com/3012521/unplug/baratunde-thurston-leaves-the-internet. Accessed: 21 November 2013.

Tokunga, R.S. (2010) 'Following you home from school: a critical review and synthesis of research on cyberbullying victimization' *Computers in Human Behavior* 26: 277–87.

Tsang, E. and E. Kao (2013) 'Internet warning as games fair hits Hong Kong' *South China Morning Post* 15 August. Available: http://www.scmp.com/news/hong-kong/article/1289333/internet-addiction-warning-games-fair-hits-town. Accessed: 6 February 2014.

Tseliga, T. (2007) '"It's all Greeklish to me!" Linguistic and sociocultural perspectives on Roman-alphabeted Greek in asynchronous computer-mediated communication' in Danet, B. and S.C. Herring (eds) *The Multilingual Internet: language, culture, and communication online.* Oxford: Oxford University Press, pp. 116–41.

Tsikerdekis, M. (2012) 'The choice of complete anonymity versus pseudonymity for aggression online' *Journal of Computer-Human Interaction* 2/8: 35–57.

Tsiplakou, S. (2009) 'Doing (bi)lingualism: language alternation as performative construction of online identities' *Pragmatics* 19/3: 361–91.

Turkle, S. (1995) *Life on the Screen: identity in the age of the internet.* New York: Simon and Schuster.

Unsworth, L. (2006) 'Towards a metalanguage for multiliteracies education: describing the meaning-making resources of language-image interaction' *English Teaching: practice and critique* 5/1: 55–76.

Vaisman, C. (2011) 'Performing girlhood through typographic play in Hebrew blogs' in Thurlow, C. and K. Mroczek (eds) *Digital Discourse: language in the new media.* Oxford: Oxford University Press, pp. 177–96.

Van Blerk, L.J. (2008) 'Identity work and community work through sociolinguistic rituals on Facebook'. Unpublished Honours Research Project, University of Cape Town.

Van Leeuwen, T. (2001) 'What is authenticity?' *Discourse Studies* 3: 392–7.

Varis, P. and X. Wang (2011) 'Superdiversity on the internet: a case from China' *Diversities* 13/2: 71–83.

Varnhagen, C.K., G.P. McFall, N. Pugh, L. Routledge, H. Sumida-MacDonald and T.E. Kwong (2010) 'lol: new language and spelling in Instant Messaging' *Reading and Writing* 23: 719–33.

Varis, P., X. Wang and C. Du (2011) 'Identity repertoires on the internet: opportunities and constraints' *Applied Linguistics Review* 2: 265–84.

Vásquez, C. (2014) '"Usually not one to complain but ...": constructing identities in user-generated online reviews' in Seargeant, P. and C. Tagg (eds) *The Language of Social Media: identity and community online.* Basingstoke: Palgrave Macmillan, pp. 65–90.

Velghe, F. (2011) 'Lessons in textspeak from Sexy Chick: supervernacular literacy in South African instant and text messaging' *Tilburg Papers in Culture Studies.*

Verheijen, L. (2013) 'The effects of text messaging and instant messaging on literacy' *English Studies* 94/5: 582–602.

Vertovec, S. (2007) 'Superdiversity and its implications' *Ethnic and Racial Studies* 30/6: 1024–54.

Viégas, F., M. Wattenberg and K. Dave (2004) 'Studying cooperation and conflict between authors with history flow visualisations' *CHI 2004.* Available: http://www.ifs.tuwien.ac.at/~silvia/wien/vu-infovis/articles/Viegas-CHI2004.pdf. Accessed: 8 August 2013.

Viégas, F., M. Wattenberg, J. Kriss and F. van Ham (2007) 'Talk before you type: coordination in Wikipedia' *40th Annual Hawai'i International Conference on System Services.*

Villa, D. (2005) 'Integrating technology into minority language preservation and teaching efforts: an inside job' *Language Learning and Technology* 6/2: 92–101.

Viswanathan, G. (1989) *Masks of Conquest.* New York: Columbia University Press.

Wagner, M. (2013) 'Luxembourgish on Facebook: language ideologies and writing strategies' in Jones, E.H.G. and E. Uribe-Jongbloed (eds) *Social Media and Minority Languages: convergence and the creative industries,* Bristol: Multilingual Matters, pp. 87–98.

Wallace, P. (1999) *The Psychology of the Internet.* Cambridge: Cambridge University Press.

Wang, X. (2010) '"I am not a qualified dialect rapper": genre innovation as authenticity' *Working Papers in Urban Language & Literacies* 64.

Warschauer, M. (1998) 'Technology and indigenous language revitalization: analyzing the experience of Hawai'i' *Canadian Modern Language Review* 55/1: 140–61.

Warschauer, M. and D. Grimes (2008) 'Audience, authorship, and artefact: the emergent semiotics of Web 2.0' *Annual Review of Applied Linguistics* 27: 1–23.

Warschauer, M., G.R. El Said and A. Zohry (2007) 'Language choice online: globalization and identity in Egypt' in Danet, B. and S.C. Herring (eds) *The Multilingual Internet: language, culture, and community online.* Oxford: Oxford University Press, pp. 303–18.

Waters, D. (2009) 'Spam overwhelms e-mail messages' *BBC News* 8 April. Available: http://news.bbc.co.uk/1/hi/technology/7988579.stm. Accessed: 23 January 2014.

Weber, R. (1986) 'Variation in spelling and the special case of colloquial contractions' *Visible Language* 20/4: 413–26.

Wei, L. (2011) 'Moment Analysis and translanguaging space: discursive construction of identities by multilingual Chinese youth in Britain' *Journal of Pragmatics* 43: 1222–35.

Weingarten, E. (2010) 'Goodbye, cruel words: English. It's dead to me' *The Washington Post* 19 September. Available: http://www.washingtonpost.com/wp-dyn/content/article/2010/09/13/AR2010091304476.html. Accessed: 6 October 2014.

Wells, H.G. (1928) *The Way the World is Going: guesses and forecasts of the years ahead*. London: Ernest Benn.

Wenger, E. (1998) *Communities of Practice: learning, meaning and identity*. Cambridge: Cambridge University Press.

Wesch, M. (2009) 'YouTube and you: experiences of self-awareness in the context collapse of recording webcam' *Explorations in Media Ecology* 8/2: pp. 19–34.

Whitaker, R. (2013) 'Proto-spam: Spanish prisoners and confidence games' *The Appendix* 23 October. Available: http://theappendix.net/issues/2013/10/proto-spam-spanish-prisoners-and-confidence-games. Accessed: 23 January 2014.

Wilkinson, D.M. and B.A. Huberman (2007) 'Assessing the value of cooperation in Wikipedia' *First Monday* 12/4. Available: http://firstmonday.org/article/view/1763/1643. Accessed 6 October 2014.

Willard, N. (2007) 'The authority and responsibility of school officials in responding to cyberbullying' *Journal of Adolescent Health* 41/6: S64–S65.

Williams, C. (1996) 'Secondary education: teaching in the bilingual situation' in Williams, C., G. Lewis and C. Baker (eds) *The Language Policy: taking stock*. Llangefni, UK: CAI, pp. 39–78.

Williams, R. (1974) *Television: Technology and Cultural Form*. London: Fontana.

Wilson, A. (2000) 'There's no escaping from third-space theory – borderland discourse and the in-between literacies of prison' in Barton, D., M. Hamilton and R. Ivanič (eds) *Situated Literacies*. London: Routledge, pp. 54–69.

Wilton, C. and M.A. Campbell (2011) 'An exploration of the reasons why adolescents engage in traditional and cyber bullying' *Journal of Educational Sciences & Psychology* 1/2: 101–9.

Winzker, K., F. Southwood and K. Huddlestone (2009) 'Investigating the impact of SMS speak on the written work of English first language and English second language high school learners' *Per Linguam* 25: 1–16.

Wisnieski, C. (2012) 'Facebook privacy notice chain letter is a hoax' *NakedSecurity: award-winning news, opinion, advice and research from Sophos*. Available: http://nakedsecurity.sophos.com/2012/06/05/facebook-privacy-notice-chain-letter-is-a-hoax/. Accessed 4 January 2014.

Wood, C., E. Jackson, L. Hart, B. Plester and L. Wilde (2011) 'The effect of text messaging on 9- and 10-year-old children's reading, spelling and phonological processing skills' *Journal of Computer Assisted Learning* 27: 28–36.

Wood, C., S. Meachem, S. Bowyer, E. Jackson, M. Luisa Tarczynski-Bowles and B. Plester (2011) 'A longitudinal study of children's text messaging and literacy development' *British Journal of Psychology* 102: 431–42.

Wray, R. (2002) 'First with the message' the *Guardian* 16 March. Available: http://www.theguardian.com/business/2002/mar/16/5. Accessed 26 November 2013.

Yardi, S., D. Romero, G. Schoenebeck and d. boyd (2010) 'Detecting spam in a Twitter network' *First Monday* 15/1. Available: http://firstmonday.org/article/view/2793/2431. Accessed 6 October 2014.

Yates, S.J. (1996) 'Oral and written aspects of computer conferencing' in Herring, S.C. (ed.) *Computer-Mediated Communication*. Amsterdam: John Benjamins, pp. 13–28.

Youssef, V. (1993) 'Children's linguistic choices: audience design and societal norms' *Language in Society* 22/2: 257–74.

Zak, D. (2013) '"Printing out the internet" exhibit is crowdsourced work of art' *The Washington Post* 26 July.

Zappavigna, M. (2011) 'Ambient affiliation: A linguistic perspective on Twitter' *New Media & Society* 13: 788–806.

—— (2012) *Discourse of Twitter and Social Media: how we use language to create affiliation on the web*. London: Continuum.

—— (2014) 'CoffeeTweets: bonding around the bean on Twitter' in Seargeant, P. and C. Tagg (eds) *The Language of Social Media: identity and community online*. Basingstoke: Palgrave Macmillan, pp. 139–59.

Zuckerberg, M. (2010) 'Facebook CEO Mark Zuckerberg: TechCrunch interview at the Crunchies'. Available: http://www.youtube.com/watch?v=LoWKGBloMsU. Accessed: 4 January 2014.

Index